First World War
and Army of Occupation
War Diary
France, Belgium and Germany

8 DIVISION
Divisional Troops
Northampton Yeomanry,
C Squadron,
Divisional Mounted Troops,
Divisional Cyclist Company
and 5 Brigade Royal Horse Artillery
1 January 1914 - 31 December 1916

WO95/1693

The Naval & Military Press Ltd
www.nmarchive.com
Published in association with The National Archives

Published by

The Naval & Military Press Ltd

Unit 10 Ridgewood Industrial Park,

Uckfield, East Sussex,

TN22 5QE England

Tel: +44 (0) 1825 749494

www.naval-military-press.com

www.nmarchive.com

This diary has been reprinted in facsimile from the original. Any imperfections are inevitably reproduced and the quality may fall short of modern type and cartographic standards.

© **Crown Copyright**
Images reproduced by permission of The National Archives, London, England, 2015.

Contents

Document type	Place/Title	Date From	Date To
Heading	8th Division Northants Yeo. Nov 1914-Mar 1915		
Heading	8th Division. 121/3971 Nortrampton Yeomanry Vol I 4.11-31.1214		
War Diary	Hursley	04/11/1914	04/11/1914
War Diary	Havre	10/11/1914	12/11/1914
War Diary	Estaires	14/11/1914	16/11/1914
War Diary	Lestrem	23/11/1914	31/12/1914
Heading	8th Division Northants Yeo. Jany To 4th March15		
Heading	8th Division Northants Yeo 1.1-4.3.15		
War Diary	Lestrem Parade Lestrem.	01/01/1915	18/01/1915
War Diary	Lestrem	19/01/1915	04/03/1915
War Diary	8th Division "C" Sqdn North'd Hussars Apl 1915-May 1916		
Heading	C Squadron Northumberland Hssrs April-Dec 1915		
Miscellaneous	To, Officer, I/e A.G.s. Office, The Base	13/03/1916	13/03/1916
Map			
War Diary	Merville. K.24.d.4.8 (Map.36a)	12/04/1915	12/04/1915
War Diary	Nollveall Monde G.27.d.6.6. (Map.36.)	04/04/1915	25/04/1915
War Diary	Au Grand Bois. L.10. C.6.3. (Map.36a)	27/04/1915	08/05/1915
War Diary	Croix (H.33.b.33. Map. 36) Blanche	09/05/1915	09/05/1915
War Diary	Au Grand Bois. L.10. C.6.3. (Map.36a)	10/05/1915	27/07/1915
War Diary	Au Grand Bois. L.10. C.6.3. (Map.36a)	02/08/1916	27/08/1916
War Diary	Rue De Courant. Le Doulieu. L.4. C.8.8 (Map. 36 A)	01/09/1915	17/12/1915
War Diary	Blaringhem 24 (Map. 5 A)	20/12/1915	23/12/1915
War Diary	Rue De Courant. Le Doulieu L. 4. C. 88. (Ma 36 A)	28/12/1915	30/12/1915
Heading	Confidential War Diary of B Squadron Northumberland Hussars From Jan 2nd 1915 To Febry 29th 1916		
War Diary	Rue De Courant, Le Doulieu L.4. C.8.8 (Map.36 A)	02/01/1916	29/02/1916
War Diary	Grand Rullecourt.	01/03/1916	19/03/1916
War Diary	Noyellette	20/03/1916	31/03/1916
War Diary	Ollincourt Chateau	01/04/1916	02/04/1916
War Diary	Agnicourt	04/04/1916	04/04/1916
War Diary	Agnicourt Sheet 62 D Square C T A 86	05/04/1916	30/04/1916
Heading	Confidential War Diary of C Squadron, Northumberland Hussars From May 1st To May 13 1916		
War Diary	Agnicourt Sheet 62 D Square B 7 A 8.6	01/05/1916	07/05/1916
War Diary	Agnicourt (Map 62) C.y.a.8.6	09/05/1916	13/05/1916
Heading	8th Division 8th Divl Mounted? Troops Feb-Apl 1916		
Heading	Confidential War Diary of 8th Divisional Mounted Troops From 1st Feb 1916 To 29th 1916		
War Diary	Rue De Courant Le Doulieu Map 36 A L.4. C. 8.8	01/02/1916	29/02/1916
Heading	Confidential War Diary of 8th Divisional Mounted Troops From 1st April 1916 To 30th April 1916		
War Diary	Olincourt	01/04/1916	04/04/1916
War Diary	Agnicourt Sheet 62 D. C. Y, A	08/04/1916	21/04/1916
War Diary	Agnicourt Sheet 62 D. C. Y, 8.6	22/04/1916	30/04/1916
Heading	8th Division 8th Divl Cyclist Coy. Nov 1914-May 1916		
Heading	8th Divisional Ajdist Coy Vol I 5.11-30.12.14		
Heading	Confidential War Diary of 8th Divisional Cyclist Coy	05/11/1914	30/12/1914

Heading	12th October To 31st December 1914		
War Diary	South lynch Near Winchester	12/10/1914	31/12/1914
War Diary	C. Lines	01/01/1914	02/01/1914
War Diary	A & "E" Lines	03/01/1914	04/01/1914
War Diary	C Lines	05/01/1914	06/01/1914
War Diary	B Lines	07/01/1914	08/01/1914
War Diary	A Lines	09/01/1914	11/01/1914
War Diary	Rouge Croix	12/01/1914	18/01/1914
War Diary	D. Lines	19/01/1914	19/01/1914
War Diary	Fosse. Pasdecalais	20/01/1914	20/01/1914
War Diary	Rouge Croix	21/01/1914	22/01/1914
War Diary	Fosse	23/01/1914	25/01/1914
War Diary	Rouge Croix	26/01/1914	31/01/1914
War Diary	Croix Barbee	01/02/1914	01/02/1914
War Diary	Rouge Croix	02/02/1914	02/02/1914
Heading	8th Division Cyclist Coy 1915		
Heading	8th Div Cyclist Coy 1-31 1.15		
War Diary	8th Divisional	31/12/1914	20/01/1915
War Diary	Fosse. Pasdecalais.	20/01/1915	20/01/1915
War Diary	Rouge Croix	21/01/1915	22/01/1915
War Diary	Fosse	23/01/1915	25/01/1915
War Diary	Rouge Croix	26/01/1915	31/01/1915
War Diary	Fosse	26/01/1915	27/01/1915
War Diary	Rouge Croix	28/01/1915	31/01/1915
Heading	8th Div Cyclist Coy 30.1-28.2.15		
War Diary	Rouge Croix	30/01/1915	31/01/1915
War Diary	Croix Barbee	01/02/1915	01/02/1915
War Diary	Rouge Croix	02/02/1915	02/02/1915
War Diary	Fosse	03/02/1915	03/02/1915
War Diary	Rouge Croix	04/02/1915	05/02/1915
War Diary	Croix Barbee	06/02/1915	17/02/1915
War Diary	Rue De Bacquerot	18/02/1915	19/02/1915
War Diary	Croix Barbee	20/02/1915	24/02/1915
War Diary	B. Lines. H. Q	25/02/1915	27/02/1915
War Diary	Lestrem	28/02/1915	28/02/1915
Heading	8th Div Cyclist Coy Vol IV 1-31 3.15		
Miscellaneous	8/ Divisional Cyclist Coy. March, 1915.		
War Diary	Lestrem	01/03/1915	31/03/1915
Miscellaneous	Operation Orders By Lt Col H Wickbam		
Miscellaneous			
Miscellaneous	Messages And Signals		
Miscellaneous	A Form. Messages And Signals.		
Heading	8th Division 8th Div Cyclist Coy		
Heading	8/ Divisional Cyclist Company April 1915		
Miscellaneous		01/04/1915	30/04/1915
Heading	8th Div Cyclist Coy 1-31.5.15		
War Diary	8/ Divisional Cyclist Company May 1915		
War Diary		01/05/1915	31/05/1915
Heading	8th Division 8th Divl: Cyclist Coy June 1915		
Heading	8/ Divisional Cyclist Coy. June. 1915		
War Diary		01/06/1915	30/06/1915
Heading	8th Division 8th Divl Cyclist Coy From 1st To 31st July 1915		
Miscellaneous		01/07/1915	31/07/1915
Heading	8th Division 8th Divl: Cyclist Coy Aug & Sept.15		
Heading	War Diary For August & September 1915		

Type	Location/Description	Start	End
War Diary		31/07/1915	08/08/1915
War Diary	R du Layes	09/08/1915	16/08/1915
War Diary	Grand Bois	17/08/1915	24/09/1915
War Diary	Rue Bataille	25/09/1915	26/09/1915
War Diary	Grand Bois	27/09/1915	01/10/1915
Heading	Confidential War Diary of 8th Divl Cyclist Coy From 1st Oct 15 To 31st Oct 15		
War Diary	Grand Bois	02/10/1915	31/10/1915
Heading	8th Divl Cyclist Co. Nov.1915		
War Diary	Grand Bois	01/11/1915	30/11/1915
Heading	8th Divl Cyclist Co December 1915		
War Diary	Grand Bois	01/12/1915	18/12/1915
War Diary	Le Croquet	19/12/1915	20/12/1915
War Diary	Niele	21/12/1915	21/12/1915
War Diary	On The March	21/12/1915	21/12/1915
War Diary	Capelle-Sur-La-Lys	22/12/1915	22/12/1915
War Diary	Le Croquet	23/12/1915	23/12/1915
War Diary	Grand Bois	24/12/1915	31/12/1915
Heading	8th Divl Cyclist Co Jan 1916		
War Diary	Grand Bois	02/01/1916	31/01/1916
Heading	Feb & March 1916		
Heading	8 Div Cyclist Coy Feb		
War Diary	Grand Bois	01/02/1916	08/02/1916
War Diary		23/02/1916	29/02/1916
Miscellaneous		09/02/1916	22/02/1916
Heading	Cyclist Coy		
War Diary		01/03/1916	31/03/1916
Heading	April & May 1916		
Miscellaneous	Confidential Officer i/c A Go Office Base	03/05/1916	03/05/1916
War Diary		01/04/1916	20/04/1916
War Diary	In The Field	21/04/1916	30/04/1916
Heading	Confidential Officer i/c A Gs Office Base Herewith War Diary March Of May 1916		
War Diary	In The Field	01/05/1916	31/05/1916
Heading	8th Division 5th Brigade R. H. A Nov 1914-Dec 1916		
Heading	8th Division 5th Brigade R. H. A 4.11-31.12.14		
Heading	War Diary 5th Brigade R.H.A Nov. 4th 1914-Dec 31st 1914		
War Diary	Hursley Park	04/11/1914	05/11/1914
War Diary	Havn	06/11/1914	11/11/1914
War Diary	Caudescure	14/11/1914	14/11/1914
War Diary	Levantie	15/11/1914	31/12/1914
Diagram etc	Appendix I		
Miscellaneous	Instructions For Action 8th Divisional Artillery.	16/12/1914	16/12/1914
Miscellaneous	A Form. Messages And Signals.		
Operation(al) Order(s)	8th Div. Operation Orders No. 5.	18/12/1914	18/12/1914
Miscellaneous	Instructions 8th Divisional Artillery For Action Night 18th-19th December, 1914.	18/12/1914	18/12/1914
Miscellaneous	Commanding 5th H.a. Bde Appendix IV		
Heading	8th, Division. 5th, Bde. R. H. A. January, 1915		
Miscellaneous	8th Division 5th Bde: R. H. A 28.12.14-31.1.15		
War Diary		28/12/1915	31/12/1915
War Diary		01/01/1915	31/01/1915
Heading	8th Division 5th Bde: R H A. 1-28.2.15		
War Diary		01/02/1915	28/02/1915
Heading	8th, Division. 5th, Bde, R. H. A. March, 1915.		

Heading	8th, Division	01/03/1915	01/03/1915
War Diary		01/03/1915	31/03/1915
Miscellaneous	Detailed Report Dealing With The Operation Of 10th To 14th March 1915 As Carried Art By 5th Brigade Report House Artillery	10/03/1915	14/03/1915
Miscellaneous		10/03/1915	12/03/1915
Miscellaneous	From O.C. L Battery R H A To Adjutant 5th Bde R H A	17/03/1915	17/03/1915
Miscellaneous			
Miscellaneous	1st Phase The Bombardment 30 Minutes		
Miscellaneous	2nd Phase. 30 Minutes Bombardment.		
Miscellaneous	3rd Phase After Trench Is Taken.		
Miscellaneous	Secret	09/03/1915	09/03/1915
Miscellaneous	Secret. Amended Time Table. (Timing 30 Minutes Earlier Than Previous Table).		
Miscellaneous	Second Phase. 8.5 a.m.		
Miscellaneous	Instructions For Actions 8th Division And Attached Artillery.	09/03/1915	09/03/1915
Miscellaneous	Further Instructions For Action 8th Division And Attached Artillery After The Capture Of Neuve Chapelle.		
Miscellaneous	Detailed Report Dealing With The Operation Of 10th 14th March 1915, As Carried Out By 5th Brigade, Royal Horse Artillery.	18/03/1915	18/03/1915
Miscellaneous	R H A Group		
Miscellaneous	Messages And Signals.		
Miscellaneous	A Form. Messages And Signals.		
Miscellaneous	Arrangement For Artillery Support 06 VII Division		
Miscellaneous	2 N. Objective 0 + 2 113 112 A. Q. U		
Miscellaneous			
Map	Neuve Chapelle.		
Map	Secret Right Section 8th Division		
Miscellaneous	A Form Messages And Signals.	11/03/1915	11/03/1915
Miscellaneous	A Form Messages And Signals.		
Miscellaneous	A Form Messages And Signals.	11/03/1915	11/03/1915
Miscellaneous	A Form Messages And Signals.		
Miscellaneous	A Form Messages And Signals.	12/03/1915	12/03/1915
Heading	8th Division. 5th, Bde. R.H.A April, 1915.		
Heading	8th Division 5th Bde RHA 1-30.4.15		
War Diary		01/04/1915	30/04/1915
Heading	8th, Division. 5th, Bde. R.H.A. May, 1915.		
Heading	8th, Division. 5th, Bde: R.H.A 1-31.5.15		
War Diary		01/05/1915	31/05/1915
Heading	8th, Division. 5th, Bde. R.H.A June, 1915.		
Heading	8th, Division. 5th, Bde. R.H.A. 1-30.6.15		
War Diary		01/06/1915	30/06/1915
Heading	8th, Division. 5th, Bde. R.H.A July, 1915.		
Heading	8th Division 5th Bde: RHA 1-31-7-15		
War Diary		01/07/1915	31/07/1915
Heading	8th, Division. 5th, Bde. R.H.A August, 1915.		
Heading	8th Division 5th Bde: R.H.A From 1-31. 8.15		
War Diary		01/08/1915	31/08/1915
Heading	8th, Division. 5th, Bde. R.H.A. September, 1915.		
Heading	8th Division 5th Brigade R.H.A Sep 1.15		
War Diary		01/09/1915	29/09/1915
War Diary	Z Battery Wire Cutting 21st-to 24th	30/09/1915	30/09/1915

Heading	8th, Division. 5th, Bde. R.H.A. October, 1915.		
Heading	8th Division 5th Bde. RHA Oct-15		
War Diary		01/10/1915	31/10/1915
Heading	8th, Division. 5th, Bde. R.H.A. November, 1915.		
Heading	8th Division 5th Bde R.H.A Nov		
War Diary		01/11/1915	30/11/1915
Heading	8th, Division. 5th, Bde. R.H.A. December, 1915.		
Heading	5th Bde R.H.A Dec		
War Diary		01/12/1915	31/12/1915
Heading	8th, Division. 5th, Bde, R.H.A. January, 1916.		
Heading	8th Div Bde R.H.A Jan		
War Diary		01/01/1915	31/01/1915
Heading	8th, Division. 5th, Bde, R.H.A February, 1916.		
War Diary		01/02/1915	28/02/1915
Heading	8th, Division. 5th, Bde, R.H.A. March, 1916.		
Heading	5th Bde R.H.A.		
War Diary		01/03/1915	29/03/1915
War Diary		16/03/1915	31/03/1915
War Diary		29/03/1915	31/03/1915
Heading	8th, Division. 5th, Bde, R.H.A April, 1916.		
War Diary		01/04/1915	30/04/1915
Heading	8th, Division 5th, Bde. R.H.A. May. 1916.		
War Diary		01/05/1915	31/05/1915
Heading	8th, Division 5th, Bde. R.H.A May, 1916.		
War Diary		01/06/1915	30/06/1915
Heading	8th Div. I. Corps. War Diary Headquarters. 5th Brigade, R. H. A July		
War Diary		01/07/1915	31/07/1915
Heading	8th, Division. 5th, Bde. R.H.A August, 1916.		
Heading	Confidential 8th Divisional Artillery. War Diary of 5th Brigade 180ra From 1-8-16 To 31-8-16 Volume 21 With Appendices Nos. None		
War Diary	Cuinchy	01/08/1916	04/08/1916
War Diary	Novelles	05/08/1916	13/08/1916
War Diary	Bethune	14/08/1916	27/08/1916
War Diary	Noeux Les Mines	28/08/1916	31/08/1916
Heading	8th, Division. 5th, Bde. R.H.A. September, 1916.		
Heading	Confidential. 8th Divisional Artillery. War Diary Of 5th Brigade Rha From 1-9-16 To 30.9.16 Volume X With Appendices Nos.		
War Diary	Noeux Les Mines	01/09/1916	15/09/1916
War Diary	Bethune	16/09/1916	30/09/1916
Heading	8th, Division. 5th, Bde. R.H.A October, 1916.		
Heading	Confidential 8th Divisional Artillery. War Of Diary 5th Brigade Rha From 1-10-16 To 31-10-16 Volume XXIV With Appendices Nos. Nil		
War Diary	Bethune	01/10/1916	02/10/1916
War Diary	Novelles	03/10/1916	03/10/1916
War Diary	Philosophe	04/10/1916	11/10/1916
War Diary	Novelles	12/10/1916	15/10/1916
War Diary	Cambrin	16/10/1916	21/10/1916
War Diary	Lapugnoy	22/10/1916	22/10/1916
War Diary	Bergueneuse	23/10/1916	23/10/1916
War Diary	Wamin	24/10/1916	24/10/1916
War Diary	Amplier	25/10/1916	25/10/1916
War Diary	Mirvaux	26/10/1916	26/10/1916

War Diary	Daours	27/10/1916	27/10/1916
War Diary	Citadell Camp	28/10/1916	28/10/1916
War Diary	Citadell	29/10/1916	31/10/1916
Heading	8th, Division 5th, Bde. R.H.A November, 1916.		
Heading	Confidential 8th. Divisional Artillery War Diary of 5 Brigade Rha From 1-11-16 To 30-11-16 Volume XXV With Appendices Nos.		
War Diary	Ginchy	01/11/1916	30/11/1916
Heading	8th, Division. 5th, Bde. R.H.A. December, 1916.		
Heading	Confidential. 8th, Divisional Artillery War Diary of 5 Brigade Rha From 1.12.16 To 31.12.16 Volume XXVI With Appendices Nos		
War Diary	Boisrault	01/12/1916	31/12/1916

8TH DIVISION

NORTHANTS YEO.
NOV 1914-MAR 1915

TO 6 CORPS

121/3971

8ᵗʰ division.

Northampton Yeomanry.

Vol I. 4.11. — 31.12.14.

Army Form C. 2118.

Northampton Yeomanry

WAR DIARY
or
INTELLIGENCE SUMMARY.
(Erase heading not required.)

Instructions regarding War Diaries and Intelligence Summaries are contained in F. S. Regs, Part II. and the Staff Manual respectively. Title pages will be prepared in manuscript.

Hour, Date, Place	Summary of Events and Information	Remarks and References to Appendices
HURSLEY Nov 4.	The Northamptonshire Yeomanry paraded at midnight & marched to SOUTHAMPTON arriving about 4 a.m. C Squadron has proceeded in forth to their respective Brigades. The Regiment embarked on the troop ship Thespis & crossed to HAVRE at midday Friday Nov 6th. The Regiment was under canvas at No 6 camp.	MN
HAVRE Nov 10.	Headquarters left HAVRE at 11.30 a.m. A Squadron at 5.30 p.m. & B Squadron at 10.30 p.m.	MN.
Nov 12	Headquarters & A Squadron detrained at MERVILLE early in the morning of this day. B Squadron detrained at BERGUETTE at 12.45 p.m. & marched to MERVILLE, the Headquarters Office & Division. The Regiment was billeted in farms on the outskirts of MERVILLE. Firing from the north could be heard.	MN.

Army Form C. 2118.

Northampton Yeomanry

WAR DIARY
or
INTELLIGENCE SUMMARY.
(Erase heading not required.)

Hour, Date, Place	Summary of Events and Information	Remarks and References to Appendices
ESTAIRES Nov 14	The Regiment marched to ESTAIRES 8 miles South of MERVILLE from billets on the road to SAILLY. The trenches of this portion of the front ran North & South at a distance of about 3 miles from the billets & had, previous to the arrival of the 8th Division, been held by the LAHORE Division. The Regiment was instructed by Major General Sir Henry Rawlinson, commanding the 4th Army Corps.	MM MM
Nov 16		MM
LESTREM Nov 23	The Regiment marched to LESTREM 2½ miles S.E. of ESTAIRES.T were billeted in the town and in farm houses West of the town.	MM
Nov 2 W	The Regiment lined the road West of LAGORGUE on the occasion of H.M. the King visiting his armies at the front. His Majesty was accompanied by	

Army Form C. 2118.

WAR DIARY
or
INTELLIGENCE SUMMARY.
(Erase heading not required.)

R.W.Houghton Lt.Colonel

Hour, Date, Place	Summary of Events and Information	Remarks and References to Appendices
LESTREM Feb 2 (cont)	Monsieur POINCARE, H.R.H. the Prince of Wales, General Joffre & Major General Sir Henry Rawlinson, M.P.	
Feb 7	B Squadron with the Colonel & a patrol verified a section of the trenches in A lines bordering the ESTAIRES & LA BASSÉE road leaving NEUVE CHAPELLE & about 3/4 in wide SSE of ROUGE CROIX. The Squadron rode to the headquarters of the Sherwood Foresters, 300yds N. of ROUGE CROIX. the No Officers returned with the horses to the billets & looked after them while the Squadron remained in the trenches. No left the fighting strength of the Squadron at 5 officers & 81 N.C.O.s & men. the Squadron left the headquarters of the Sherwood Foresters at 3.45 & reached the trenches at about 5.45 am the length of the trench allotted to the Squadron was 350 yds with the Sealforths on the left & the Sherwood	

Army Form C. 2118.

Northampton Yeomanry

WAR DIARY
or
INTELLIGENCE SUMMARY.
(Erase heading not required.)

Hour, Date, Place	Summary of Events and Information	Remarks and References to Appendices
LESTREM Dec 7 (cont)	Forrests on the right. The enemy's trenches were about 200yds away. The trenches held by Indian troops ran at right angles to the rear of the trench of the fire from the enemy against these trenches the Indian trenches to some extent enfiladed the trench held by the squadron. No attack was delivered by the enemy. The squadron was relieved at 7 p.m. on Thursday Dec 10 by A Squadron & the Worcestershire regiment. The weather had rained over all this time. The Squadron suffered considerably in their feet which were frozen & blistered & the sound. A Squadron occupied A line but only one trench occupied trenches identical with line held by B squadron. The squadron occupied the trenches for 4 days. Three men were wounded but severely.	NW.
Dec 10		

(3)

Army Form C. 2118.

WAR DIARY
INTELLIGENCE SUMMARY.
(Erase heading not required.)

G.O.Vaughan ? Squadron

Hour, Date, Place	Summary of Events and Information	Remarks and References to Appendices
LESTREM 6 10 (cont)	The men suffered in their feet in the severe wet which B Squadron had suffered.	MV
18ᵗʰ	Regiment proceeded along in support of reserve & reached 6 miles to S.E. ELLINGHEM back to road reserve. On their infantry already went by the 7ᵗʰ & 8ᵗʰ Division in column looking of the enemy's trenches. The attacks were suspended in this hill in front of the line trenches. After evening, then in hour even harder the trenches were retaken & the Germans with the use of hand bombs. The German advanced the line trenches along the communication trenches & reached one of the traverses for every three bombs originally into the line trenches hold & our own the Regiment was not called into & trenches ? about 8.45 am. MV	

WAR DIARY
or
INTELLIGENCE SUMMARY.

Army Form C. 2118.

E.P. Hertfordshire Jerusalem

Hour, Date, Place	Summary of Events and Information	Remarks and References to Appendices
LESTREM. Bze 26.	The Regiment was called out at 11.30 p.m. & marched to CROIX BARBÉE (about 4 miles distant) to act as local reserve, though information obtained through a deserter on a recent war expected. The information be incorrect. No actual attack took place.	M.N.
bze 28	Considerable artillery was employed by both sides along the Indian Lines South of LESTREM during the succeeding 2 days. The Germans were successful in pushing back our line to the Rue Oxford. Not signal worthy of "log" for 24 hours.	M.N.
bze 30 "	C Squadron were employed between Dusk & 10 p.m. in digging a communication trench close to A lines.	

WAR DIARY
INTELLIGENCE SUMMARY

Army Form C. 2118.

W.Houghton Greenwell

Hour, Date, Place	Summary of Events and Information	Remarks and References to Appendices
Leath Bon Dec 30 (cont)	The OD communication trench being Gullgwalk.	MN.
Dec 31.	A & B Squadrons were employed after dark in digging a new trench behind & lines for slightly higher ground. Some 25 SRS behind & lines for slightly higher ground. A driver in the Machine Gun team was shot through the leg while waiting at Rouen Crop for the regiment to return.	MN.

Index

SUBJECT.

8th Division

No.	Contents.	Date.
	Northants Yeo. Jany to 4th March 15	

8th Division

121/4612

Northampton Geo:

Vol II. 1.1. — 4.3.15.

Army Form C. 2118.

WAR DIARY
or
INTELLIGENCE SUMMARY.
(Erase heading not required.)

Instructions regarding War Diaries and Intelligence Summaries are contained in F. S. Regs., Part II. and the Staff Manual respectively. Title pages will be prepared in manuscript.

Hour, Date, Place	Summary of Events and Information	Remarks and References to Appendices
January 1st 1915 LESTREM	The Northamptonshire Yeomanry again marched to Rouge Croix, & dug	
Parade LESTREM 2-45 p.m.	as follows A Squadron behind A Line. B Squadron behind B Line.	
	C Squadron behind C Line. Tools from 24th Infy Brigade. Worked under	
	O.C. 16th Field Co R.E.	A7
January 3rd	A & C Squadron with party of O/Click to ROUGE CROIX to dig	
	behind C Line. Pte Sumner of E Squadron was killed. Work rendered	
	difficult owing to star shells in early part of evening. B Squadron dug	
	behind A Line. Pte Beasley shot thro' thigh.	A7
5th	A Squadron digging behind A Line. B & C Squadrons behind C Line. Corporal	
	Squires. R6. Two small wounded. Party of B. Squadron Officers eat for	
	draft as follows was made to O/C Cavalry Section 3rd Echelon. 2 Subalterns	
	4 Shoeing Smiths. 1 Saddler. 25 Privates.	A7
7th	A Squadron & 50 men from R. Sqt digging behind A Line. B. Sqt clearing	
	roadside Bench Beading to A Line. Bad digging owing to water to bare.	
	C. Sqt & 25 men B. Sqt digging redoubt behind D Line.	A7
8/6/18/15	Regiment digging with 75 men daily + 150 every alternate night to day	
	both cliffs behind A Line + high flank behind D Line.	A7

Army Form C. 2118.

WAR DIARY
or
INTELLIGENCE SUMMARY.
(Erase heading not required.)

Instructions regarding War Diaries and Intelligence Summaries are contained in F. S. Regs., Part II. and the Staff Manual respectively. Title pages will be prepared in manuscript.

Hour, Date, Place	Summary of Events and Information	Remarks and References to Appendices
January 19th 1915. LESTREM	Major Sir Charles Rosslyn rejoined with Messrs R. Courage Churchill, R.C. Elves & Mr Collier who were allotted to A, B, B, & C Sq's respectively.	(a)
" 20th	Major G. Middleton (A Sq't) returned. Digging operations as usual.	(a)
" 21st 1915.	Digging as usual.	(a)
" 22nd	Ditto.	(a)
" 23rd	"	(a)
" 24th	No digging party at night.	(a)
" 25th	B. Sq'n furnished digging party in morning. C. Sq'n were stopped from digging behind A Lines in consequence of heavy fire; & returned to their billets but normal conditions allowed B Sq'n to dig behind B Lines at 6pm, as also the Reg't stood Larmes until this hour.	(a)
" 26th	Digging as usual. A & C Sq's behind A Lines.	(a)
" 27th	" B. Sq't in morning, A Sq't (Cyclists at night.	(a)
" 28th	" by A, B & C Sq'ts & Cyclists at night, J'n Roxlands (AS't)	(a)
	A sapper & sergeant in the Cyclists wounded.	
" 29th	Digging as usual, B. Sq't & M.O. finding working party of 50 at night. R. Egerow brought draft of 11 men & 3 horses from Base.	(a)

Army Form C. 2118.

WAR DIARY
or
INTELLIGENCE SUMMARY.
(Erase heading not required.)

Instructions regarding War Diaries and Intelligence Summaries are contained in F. S. Regs., Part II. and the Staff Manual respectively. Title pages will be prepared in manuscript.

Hour, Date, Place	Summary of Events and Information	Remarks and References to Appendices
January 30th 1915. LESTREM.	A Sqn. digging behind A Line in morning. Pte Scott wounded in stomach.	(1)
31st	B+C Sqns digging in morning. Lieut R. Cazenove went into Hospital.	(1)
February 1st 1915.	A Sqn & Cyclists digging in morning.	(1)
2nd	B+C Sqns digging in morning. A Sqn at night behind D.Line.	(1)
3rd	B+C Sqns " " " Corporal Parker C.Sqn. wounded in knee.	(1)
4th	A Sqn " " - 15. B Sqn & Cyclists at night. Corporal Gutridge	(1)
5th	B. Sqn was wounded.	
	B, + C Sqns 15 men A. Sqn digging in morning. Sqn Parker B Sqn killed by	(1)
	Shrapnel whilst digging redoubt behind A Line.	(1)
6th	A Sqn + Cyclists digging behind A Line in the morning.	(1)
7th	B+C Sqns digging in the morning.	(1)
8th	A Sqn + Cyclists " " "	(1)
9th	B+C Sqns " " " Lieut Carrard to Hospital with appendicitis	(1)
10th to 14th	A Sqn + B.Sqns at ESTAIRES.	(1)
	Digging parties of 150 men each morning furnished by A Sqn + Cyclists + B+C Sqns. appendicitis.	(1)
15th to 20th	Digging as usual. Pte Evans of Middlesex Regt (Cyclist) killed 18th Feb.	(1)
21st	Lieut Sulivatt returned from Rouen with Draft of 67 men + 3 Horses.	(1)

Army Form C. 2118.

WAR DIARY
or
INTELLIGENCE SUMMARY.
(Erase heading not required.)

Instructions regarding War Diaries and Intelligence Summaries are contained in F. S. Regs., Part II. and the Staff Manual respectively. Title pages will be prepared in manuscript.

Hour, Date, Place	Summary of Events and Information	Remarks and References to Appendices
22nd February 1915 LESTREM	The Draft was allotted as follows:-	
	Headquarters & Machine Gun.	None.
	A Squadron.	7. 3.
	B. Squadron.	29 (1 rejoined) 10. X
	C "	17. 12.
		23. 13.
23rd "	A. Sqdn. to Balle Totains. No digging party required.	(1)
24th "	Regiment paraded at 9.30 in readiness for a Route March.	(1)
25th "	Training & Exercise	(1)
26th "	Cyclists digging at night behind B. Lines.	(1)
27th "	A, B, Sqdns & Cyclists digging at night behind B. Lines.	(1)
" "	A. B. & C. Sqdns. " " " Br. Chier Junction	(1)
28th "	Cyclists Gillett moved from FOSSE to LESTREM. Major H. R. Campbell	(1)
	& Rev. J. Bruce to office with 10.30 returns arrived from Base.	(1)
1st March 1915.	C. Sqdn. & Cyclists took over C. Lines trenches with 4th Batt. Cameron Highlanders	(1)
	under command of Col. Fraser for 3 days.	(1)
4th "	A. & B. Sqdn. relieved C. Sqdn. & Cyclists who had had no casualties except 2	(1)
	Cyclists wounded coming out of trenches.	(1)

(9, 29, 6) W 2794 100,000 8/14 H W V Forms/C. 2118/11.

8TH DIVISION

'C' SQDN NORTH'D HUSSARS
APL 1915 - MAY 1916

TO 13 CORPS

D.T.
8 Divn

SUBJECT.

No.	Contents.	Date.
	"C" Squadron Northumberland Hsrs April — Dec 1915 — May 1916	

To, Officer,
   i/c A.G.'s Office,
     The Base.

"C" Squadron,
Northd Hussars,
13-3-16.

Enclosed herewith please find War Diary of this Unit, from April, 12th 1915, which was the date on which the squadron was detached from the Regiment, to Feby. 29th 1916, which will now bring it up to date. I am sorry that I have not had this sent to you at the end of each month, but have omitted to do so, through an oversight. However, I will now do so in future, and hope that this will now put the matter in order.

H Sidney
Major,
Commanding "C" Squadron,
Northd Hussars.

Army Form C. 2118.

VOL. I.

WAR DIARY or INTELLIGENCE SUMMARY

(Erase heading not required.)

"C" Squadron. North'd Hussars.

April 1915.

Instructions regarding War Diaries and Intelligence Summaries are contained in F. S. Regs., Part II. and the Staff Manual respectively. Title Pages will be prepared in manuscript.

Place	Date	Hour	Summary of Events and Information	Remarks and references to Appendices
MERVILLE. K.24.d.4.8. (MAP.36A)	12-4-15	8.30 AM	Detached from Regiment & 1st Division to be Divisional Cavalry to 8th Division. Removed to billets at NOUVEAU MONDE G.27.a.6.6. (MAP.36.) S.Q.M.S. Crosan, J. having been sent to hospital, sick, is struck off the strength & Sergt. Larmour, J.S. appointed S.Q.M.S. in his stead.	
NOUVEAU MONDE.	14-4-15		3 O.R.s having been sent to hospital, sick, are struck off the strength.	
G.27.d.6.6.	15-4-15		Major Roland Haig D.S.O. appointed to Command 8th Div. Mtd. Troops.	
(MAP.36.)	21-4-15	8 AM	Supplied working party of 1 Officer & 50 O.R.s.	
	25-4-15	8.30 AM	Removed to billets at GRAND BOIS. L.10.c.6.3 (MAP.36A)	
AU GRAND BOIS. L.10.c.6.3. (MAP.36A)	27-4-15		1 Shoeing-smith rejoined Squadron from No.5 General Base Depot.	
	28-4-15		Draft of 14 men joined Squadron from No.5 General Base Depot.	

Army Form C. 2118.

VOL. II.

WAR DIARY "C" Squadron
or
INTELLIGENCE SUMMARY Joseph A. Hussars

(Erase heading not required.)

May, 1915.

Place	Date	Hour	Summary of Events and Information	Remarks and references to Appendices
AU GRAND BOIS	2-5-15	6.0 P.M.	Supplied a working party of 1 Officer & 22 O.R.s. 1 Shoeing-smith transferred to "A" Squadron.	
L.10.C.6.3. (MAP. 36 A)	5-5-15	6.0 P.M.	Supplied working party of 1 Officer & 40 O.R.s.	
	8-5-15	11.45 P.M.	Proceeded to CROIX BLANCHE H.33.8.2.3 (MAP 36) as per orders received, to "stand to" in reserve for AUBERS RIDGE attack.	
CROIX (H.33.8.33 MAP 36) BLANCHE	9-5-15	10.30 P.M.	Returned to billets at GRAND BOIS, but still under orders to "stand to."	
AU GRAND BOIS	10-5-15		Still under orders to "stand to."	
L.10.C.6.3. (MAP. 36 A)	14-5-15		2 Men attached to Squadron from Regt. Head-quarters. 1 Man transferred to Regt. Head-quarters. 5 Men taken on strength of Squadron from Regt. Head-quarters.	
	16-5-15		French soldier innkeeper Léon Stievenar of 42nd Batt. 12th Art. Coy, French Army, attached to Squadron.	
	18-5-15		1 Man having been sent to hospital, sick, is struck off the strength.	
	31-5-15	6.30 P.M.	1 Officer & 27 O.R.s paraded for working party.	

Hubro mj

Army Form C. 2118.

Vol. III

"C" Squadron, York'd Hussars.

June, 1915.

WAR DIARY or INTELLIGENCE SUMMARY

(Erase heading not required.)

Instructions regarding War Diaries and Intelligence Summaries are contained in F.S. Regs., Part II. and the Staff Manual respectively. Title Pages will be prepared in manuscript.

Place	Date	Hour	Summary of Events and Information	Remarks and references to Appendices
A tt GRAND BOIS	1-6-15		Major H. Sidney having been sent to hospital, sick, is struck off the strength. Capt. J.G.G. Rea takes over the command of the squadron.	
L.10.c.6.3 (MAP 36 A)	9-6-15		1 man, having been sent to hospital, is struck off the strength.	
	16-6-15	6.45 pm	Capt. J.G.G. Rea & 2nd Lt Hon. C.S.H. Ramsay & 50 O.Rs. paraded & proceeded to man front line trenches (F lines) in front of RUE TILLELOY (MAP 36:- N.13.B.8.) for a period of six days.	
	22-6-15		1 man wounded & having been sent to hospital, is struck off the strength. Trench party returned to billets. No. 4718 Pte Hudson H. having been granted a commission in the 3/8th Batt. D.L.I. is struck off the strength.	
	24-6-15		1 man having been sent to hospital, is struck off the strength.	
	29-6-15		8th Division joined III Corps, II Army. 2nd Lieut W.A. Leith, transferred to 2nd line Regt. in England.	

Khtm

Army Form C. 2118.

Vol. IV.

6. Squadron,
—Fothd. Aircard.

WAR DIARY
or
INTELLIGENCE SUMMARY

(Erase heading not required.)

July, 1915

Place	Date	Hour	Summary of Events and Information	Remarks and references to Appendices
Acq GRAND BOIS. L.10.C.6.3 (MAP.36ᴬ)	6-7-15	6.30 p.m.	Supplied working party of 1 Officer & 30 O.R.s.	
	7-7-15		Lieut. Hon. C.M. Ashley & 1 servant having joined squadron from No.5 General Base, are taken on strength.	
	12-7-15		4 N.C.O.s & 12 men commenced to parade daily to Brigade Bomb School for one month's instruction in a Course of Bombing at (MAP.36) H.31.a.6.8.	
	14-7-15		1 man having been sent to Hospital, sick, is struck off the strength.	
	17-7-15		Squadron commences to undergo a course of musketry on a 30 yards range.	
	18-7-15		1 man having been sent to Hospital, sick, is struck off the strength. 8ᵗʰ Division joined 1ˢᵗ Army.	
	21-7-15		Draft of 9 men joined the squadron from No.5 General Base Depot.	
	22-7-15		Motor Cyclist Addison, G.E. (Lce. Corpl.) transferred to Major R.E.s. 7ᵗʰ Div. as despatch rider.	
	26-7-15		Draft of 2 men arrived from No.5 General Base Depot.	
	27-7-15		No.16. Sergt. Greswith. J.J. having proceeded to England to take up Commission in 4th Hac. Bde. Q.I.A. (T.F.) is struck off the strength.	

A.Asham m

Army Form C. 2118.

VOL. V.

WAR DIARY or INTELLIGENCE SUMMARY

"C" Squadron, Suffolk Hussars.

August, 1915.

(Erase heading not required.)

Place	Date	Hour	Summary of Events and Information	Remarks and references to Appendices
Acq	2-8-16		1 Man, having been sent to hospital, sick, is struck off the strength.	
GRAND BOIS. L.10.c.6.3.	3-8-16		2nd Lieut R.L. Stokes & 2nd Lieut A.W. Milburn & 3 O.R.s having joined the squadron from No.5 General Base Depot, are taken on the strength.	
(MAP 36A.)	7-8-16		No.207 Corpl. Cubitland H. having proceeded to England to take up a commission in the 3rd Battd. R.F.A., is struck off the strength.	
	11-8-16		Draft of 3 men joined the squadron, from No.5 General Base Depot.	
	16-8-16		Draft of 1 man joined the squadron from No.5 General Base Depot.	
	20-8-16		1 Man, having been sent to hospital, sick, is struck off the strength.	
	27-8-16		Removed to billets in RUE DE COURANT (MAP 36A. L.4.C.8.8.) LE DOULIEU	
RUE DE COURANT LE DOULIEU L.4.C.8.8. (MAP 36A)	31-8-16		Interpreter Leon Brévière, having left the squadron, is struck off the strength.	

Army Form C. 2118.

WAR DIARY or INTELLIGENCE SUMMARY

(Erase heading not required.)

Vol. VI. "C" Squadron, 18th Hussars

September 1915

Place	Date	Hour	Summary of Events and Information	Remarks and references to Appendices
RUE de COURANT.	1-9-15		3 men, having been sent to base, pending discharge, are struck off the strength.	
LE DOULIEU. L.4.C.8.8. (MAP. 36A)	4-9-15	4.0 p.m.	Supplied working party of 20 men. Remainder of squadron commenced to build winter stabling for horses at L.4.d.2.2. (MAP. 36A)	
	6-9-15	4.0 p.m.	Supplied working party of 30 men.	
	11-9-15		Major H Sidney having rejoined squadron from No 5 Cavalry Base Depot, is taken on strength. 1 man transferred to "B" Squadron.	
	23-9-15		1 man joined squadron from "B" Squadron.	
	25-9-15	3.0 a.m.	Paraded & proceeded to RUE BATAILLE H.19.a.8.7. (MAP.36) to "stand to" in reserve, in support to infantry.	
	26-9-15	2.0 p.m.	Marched back to old billets at RUE de COURANT, LE DOULIEU. L.4.C.8.8. (MAP.36A)	
	28-9-15		2 Officers & 71 men attached to 24th Infantry Bde. at *FLEURBAIX for working party. They took Coreishe in consolidating the ground taken by the 23rd Infantry Bde. in the attack of the 25-9-15.	*H.21.a.2.2. (MAP.36).

A.W.Sidney Major

Army Form C. 2118.

VOL. VII.   "C" Squadron   October 1915.

WAR DIARY
or
INTELLIGENCE SUMMARY

(Erase heading not required.)

Instructions regarding War Diaries and Intelligence Summaries are contained in F. S. Regs., Part II. and the Staff Manual respectively. Title Pages will be prepared in manuscript.

Place	Date	Hour	Summary of Events and Information	Remarks and references to Appendices
Rue de Courant.	1-10-15		French Relief Outposts Rive de Fere of the 55th Att. de Champagne, is attached to squadron.	
Le Doulieu	6-10-15		Working party returned from FLEURBAIX	
L.4.C.8.8. (MAP 36.A.)	11-10-15	5.3 p.m.	Supplied working party of 1 Officer & 69 O.Rs.	
			2 men joined squadron from No.5 General Base Depot	
	12-10-15		1 man, having been sent to hospital, sick, is struck off the strength	
	14-10-15	4.0 a.m.	Supplied digging party of 1 Officer & 54 O.Rs.	
	15-10-15	4.0 a.m.	ditto.	
	16-10-15	6.30 a.m.	Supplied working party of 1 Officer & 68 O.Rs.	
	18-10-15	10 a.m. 4.30 p.m.	Supplied working party of 1 Officer & 34 O.Rs. 1 man wounded while on second working party, & having been sent to hospital, is struck off the strength	
	19-10-15		2 men having been sent to base for transfer to the A.S.C. (M.T.) are struck off the strength	
	21-10-15	6.15 a.m.	Supplied working party of 1 Officer & 48 O.Rs. 5 men, having been transferred to "A" Squadron, 7th Division to join Machine Gun Section are struck off the strength	Withdrawing

Army Form C. 2118.

WAR DIARY or INTELLIGENCE SUMMARY

Vol. VII. "C" Squadron, Fort d. Hussars.

October 1915

(Erase heading not required.)

Instructions regarding War Diaries and Intelligence Summaries are contained in F. S. Regs., Part II. and the Staff Manual respectively. Title Pages will be prepared in manuscript.

Place	Date	Hour	Summary of Events and Information	Remarks and references to Appendices
RUE de COURANT.	22-10-15	6.15am	Supplied working party of 1 Officer & 43 O.R.s	
LE DOULIEU.	23-10-15	7.15am	ditto.	
L.4.C.88. (MAP 36A)	24-10-15	7.15am	ditto.	
	25-10-15	7.15am	ditto.	
	26-10-15	7.15am	ditto.	
	27-10-15	7.15am	ditto.	
	28-10-15	7.15am	ditto.	
	31-10-15	7.15am	Supplied working party of 1 Officer & 70 O.R.s. Draft of 15 men arrived at Squadron from No.5 General Base Depot.	

WAR DIARY or INTELLIGENCE SUMMARY

Army Form C. 2118.

Vol. VIII. "C" Squadron, 6th D. Guards.

November 1915.

Place	Date	Hour	Summary of Events and Information	Remarks and references to Appendices
RUE de COURANT.	1-11-15	7.15 a.m.	Supplied working party of 1 Officer & 43 O.R.s.	
LE DOULIEU	2-11-15	7.15 a.m.	" " " " 1 Officer & 70 O.R.s.	
L.4.C.8.6. (MAP.36A.)	3-11-15	7.15 a.m.	" " " " 1 Officer & 43 O.R.s.	
		10.0 a.	Capt. J.Y.Y. Rea is a member of a Court of Enquiry, held at the Camp Commandant's Office, 8th Division Headquarters.	
	4-11-15	7.15 a.m.	Supplied working party of 1 Officer & 70 O.R.s.	
	5-11-15	7.15 a.m.	" " " " 1 Officer & 43 O.R.s.	
	6-11-15	7.15 a.m.	" " " " 1 Officer & 70 O.R.s.	
	7-11-15	7.15 a.m.	" " " " 1 Officer & 34 O.R.s.	
	8-11-15	7.15 a.m.	" " " " 1 Officer & 47 O.R.s.	
		8.30 a.m.	Six men attached to Divisional Sniping Corps & moved to billets in FLEURBAIX under Lieut. Saville of Cyclist Coy.	H.21.d.33. (MAP. 36)
	9-11-15	7.15 a.m.	Supplied working party of 1 Officer & 34 O.R.s.	Station moved
	10-11-15	7.15 a.m.	ditto.	
	11-11-15	7.15 a.m.	ditto.	

Army Form C. 2118.

VOL. VIII.

WAR DIARY
or
INTELLIGENCE SUMMARY. North Hussars.
(Erase heading not required.)

"E" Squadron

November 1915

Instructions regarding War Diaries and Intelligence Summaries are contained in F.S. Regs., Part II. and the Staff Manual respectively. Title Pages will be prepared in manuscript.

Place	Date	Hour	Summary of Events and Information	Remarks and references to Appendices
RUE DE COURANT.	12-11-15	7.15 a.m.	Supplied working party of 1 Officer & 34 O.R.s.	
LE DOULIEU.			1 man, having been sent to the base, pending discharge, is struck off the strength	
L.4.C.8.6. (MAP. 36ᴬ)	13-11-15	7.15 a.m.	Supplied working party of 1 Officer & 34 O.R.s.	
	14-11-15	7.15 a.m.	ditto	
	15-11-15	7.15 a.m.	ditto	
	16-11-15	7.15 a.m.	ditto	
	17-11-15	7.15 a.m.	ditto	
			No. 680. Pte. Money W. reported in War Office list as having been drowned in the sinking of Hospital Ship "Anglia" in the English Channel.	
	18-11-15	7.15 a.m.	Supplied working party of 1 Officer & 34 O.R.s.	
	19-11-15	7.15 a.m.	ditto	
	20-11-15	7.15 a.m.	ditto	
	21-11-15		Lieut. Hon. C.A. Ashley is a member of F.G.C.M. held at Sailly	
			1 man, having been sent to base, pending discharge, is struck off the strength	
			1 man " " transferred into 16ᵗʰ Squadron, R.F.C. " " " "	
	22-11-15	7.15 a.m.	Supplied working party of 1 Officer & 34 O.R.s.	
	23-11-15	7.15 a.m.	ditto	

Army Form C. 2118.

VOL. VIII.

WAR DIARY
or
INTELLIGENCE SUMMARY

"C" Squadron,
Hayfield Hussars

November 1915

(Erase heading not required.)

Instructions regarding War Diaries and Intelligence Summaries are contained in F. S. Regs., Part II. and the Staff Manual respectively. Title Pages will be prepared in manuscript.

Place	Date	Hour	Summary of Events and Information	Remarks and references to Appendices
RUE DE COZRANT	26-11-15		Commenced a Course of training in compliance with Divisional Orders	
LE DOUIEZ L.4.C.8.8. (MAP. 36ᴬ)	30-11-15		1 Man, having been transferred to R.F.C. is struck off strength. Lt. Hon. C.M. Astley appointed A.D.C. to G.O.C. 8ᵗʰ Division with his two servants is struck off the strength. Andrews	

Army Form C. 2118.

WAR DIARY
or
INTELLIGENCE SUMMARY

(Erase heading not required.)

"C" Squadron. North Somerset Yeomanry.

December 1915.

Vol. IX

Instructions regarding War Diaries and Intelligence Summaries are contained in F.S. Regs., Part II and the Staff Manual respectively. Title Pages will be prepared in manuscript.

Place	Date	Hour	Summary of Events and Information	Remarks and references to Appendices
Rue de COURANT.	3-12-15		1 man, being N.Y.R. sick, is struck off the strength.	
LE DOULIEU L.4.c.8.8. (MAP 36ᴬ)	13-12-15		1 man joined squadron from No.5 General Base Depôt.	
	17-12-15	8.30 a.m.	Moved to billets at BLARINGHEM (4) 41. (E) 24. (Map 5ᴬ), in First Army Training Area, to take part in manoeuvres with 8ᵗʰ Division.	
BLARINGHEM. (4) 41. (E) 24. (Map 5ᴬ)	20-12-15		First day of manoeuvres which finished at NIELLES (5) 38. (D) 15ˈ (Map 5ᴬ)	
	21-12-15		Second day " - COYECQUE (3) 36.5ˈ (C) 11.5ˈ (Map 5ᴬ)	
	22-12-15		Last day " - BLARINGHEM. (4) 41ˈ (E) 24ˈ (Map 5ᴬ)	
	23-12-15		Returned to billets in Rue de COURANT, LE DOULIEU. L.4.c.8.8. (MAP 36ᴬ)	
Rue de COURANT.	28-12-15		Draft of 8 men joined squadron from No.5 General Base Depôt.	
LE DOULIEU L.4.c.8.8. (MAP 36ᴬ)	30-12-15		Capt. F.G.G. Rea, is a member of F.G.C.M.	

W.H. Dung
Major

Confidential

War Diary

of

"C" Squadron Northumberland Hussars

from Jan 2nd April 12th 1915 to Feby 29th 1916.

Volumes $\frac{12 + 13}{1 \text{ to } XI}$ (inclusive)

Army Form C. 2118.

January, 1915

VOL. X. "C" Squadron, Northd. Hussars

WAR DIARY
or
INTELLIGENCE SUMMARY

(Erase heading not required.)

Place	Date	Hour	Summary of Events and Information	Remarks and references to Appendices
RUE de COURANT,	2-1-16		1 man, having been sent to hospital, is struck off the strength (sick.)	
LE DOULIEU.	5-1-16		1 man, having proceeded to No.5 General Base, pending discharge, is struck off the strength.	
L.4.C.8.8 (MAP. 36A)	11-1-16	8.0 a.m. 12.0 a.m.	Supplied two working parties at SAILLY BRICKFIELD G.16.b.7.8. to work in relief, each party consisting of 32 O.Rs. (MAP. 36.)	
	12-1-16		2nd Lt. R.L. Stobart is attached to Brigade Bomb School, near FLEURBAIX, for a 7 days course of instruction in Bomb-throwing. H.2.c.3.4. (MAP.36)	
	13-1-16	8.0 a.m. 12.0 a.m.	Supplied two working parties at SAILLY BRICKFIELD G.16.b.7.8. to work in relief, each party consisting of 32 O.Rs. (MAP. 36)	
	14-1-16		2 men, having been sent to base, pending discharge are struck off the strength.	
	15-1-16	8.0 a.m. 12.0 a.m.	Supplied two working parties, as on the 13th inst.	
	17-1-16	8.0 a.m. 12.0 a.m.	Ditto.	
	18-1-16		1 man, having joined squadron from No. 5 General Base, is taken on the strength.	
	19-1-16	8.0 a.m. 12.0 a.m.	Supplied two working parties, as on the 13th inst.	
	20-1-16		2nd Lt. R.L. Stobart is promoted Lieut. as from 12/11/15.	

A. Murray Major

Army Form C. 2118.

WAR DIARY
or
INTELLIGENCE SUMMARY

VOL X "C" Squadron, 1st Indian Cavalry

January 1916

(Erase heading not required.)

Instructions regarding War Diaries and Intelligence Summaries are contained in F. S. Regs., Part II. and the Staff Manual respectively. Title Pages will be prepared in manuscript.

Place	Date	Hour	Summary of Events and Information	Remarks and references to Appendices
RUE DE COURANT.	21-1-16	8 a.m. / 12 noon	Supplied two working parties, as on the 13th inst.	
LE DOULIEU.	22-1-16		All horses in the squadron are inoculated.	
L. 4. C. 8. 8. (MAP 36A)	23-1-16	8 a.m. / 12 noon	Supplied two working parties, as on the 13th inst.	
	26-1-16	6 a.m. / 12 noon	ditto	
	28-1-16	8 a.m. / 12 noon	ditto	
	31-1-16	8 a.m. / 12 noon	Supplied working parties as above, but number of men is reduced to 18.	

A M Daly
Major

Army Form C. 2118.

WAR DIARY
or
INTELLIGENCE SUMMARY

"C" Squadron, North Somerset
February 1916

Vol. XI

Instructions regarding War Diaries and Intelligence Summaries are contained in F. S. Regs., Part II. and the Staff Manual respectively. Title Pages will be prepared in manuscript.

(Erase heading not required.)

Place	Date	Hour	Summary of Events and Information	Remarks and references to Appendices
RUE de COURANT.	2-2-16	8.0 a.m. 12.0 a.m.	Supplied two working parties at SAILLY BRICKFIELD G.16.b.7.8., to work in relief, each consisting of 18 O.R.s. (MAP. 36)	
LE DOULIEU (MAP.36A)			Capt. J. J. Rea appointed Commander of "B" Squadron; and together with his two servants & two riding horses, is struck off the strength.	
L.4.C.8.8.	4-2-16	8.0 a.m. 12.0 a.m.	Supplied two working parties as on the 2nd inst. No. 207, S.Q.M.S. Larmer, J.T., who No. 161, Sergt Jaques, A.B. have re-engaged for the period of the war.	
	6-2-16	8.0 a.m. 12.0 a.m.	Supplied two working parties, as on the 2nd inst.	
	7-2-16		Draft of 5 men joined squadron from No. 5 General Base Depot.	
	8-2-16		1 man, having proceeded to the base, pending discharge, is struck off the strength.	
	9-2-16	8.0 a.m. 12.0 a.m.	Supplied two working parties, as on 2nd inst.	
	11-2-16	8.0 a.m. 12.0 a.m.	ditto. 1 man, having proceeded to base, pending discharge is struck off the strength. No. 674, Corpl Stephenson, J.W. has re-engaged for the period of the war.	
	14-2-16	8.0 a.m. 12.0 a.m.	Supplied two working parties, as on 2nd inst.	
	15-2-16		Major H Sidney is President and 2nd Lt Hon. C.F.H. Ramsay a member of a F.G.C.M. held at ESTAIRES L.29.b. (MAP.36A) 2nd Lieut. Smith, having joined the squadron from No.5 General Base Depot, are taken on the strength.	Arthur Smith

VOL. XI.

Army Form C. 2118.

WAR DIARY
or
INTELLIGENCE SUMMARY

"C" Squadron, 1st/1d Hussars.

February 1916.

(Erase heading not required.)

Instructions regarding War Diaries and Intelligence Summaries are contained in F.S. Regs., Part II. and the Staff Manual respectively. Title Pages will be prepared in manuscript.

Place	Date	Hour	Summary of Events and Information	Remarks and references to Appendices
RUE de COURANT. LE DOULIEZ (MAP.36A) L.4.c.8.8.	16-2-16	8.0 a.m. 12.0 a.m.	Supplied two working parties, no. on 2nd list. Tpr H. Sidney is a member of a G.C.M. held at SAILLY. G.16.c.8.4. (MAP.36.) No.753, Corpl. Walton. W.H. has been temporarily attached to Z Battery, R.H.A. for tank instruction.	
	18-2-16	8.0 a.m. 12.0 a.m.	Supplied two working parties, as on 2nd list.	
	19-2-16		1 Man, having proceeded to base, pending discharge, is struck off the strength.	
	20-2-16	8.0 a.m. 12.0 a.m.	Supplied two working parties, as on 2nd list.	
	22-2-16	7.45 a.m.	Supplied Special Party of 20 men for Police Duty at ESTAIRES. L.29.b. (MAP 36.)	
	24-2-16	11.45 p.m.	Message received from O.C. 8th Divl. Mtd Troops reporting Gas at N.65, but message cancelled 40 minutes later.	
	25-2-16	7.30 a.m. 8.45 a.m.	Supplied working party of 2 O.Rs. at Bae St. MAUR. G.18.d. (MAP.36) 14 O.Rs. SAILLY CHURCH. G.16.d.1.4. (MAP.36) Lieut R.L. Stobart is promoted Captain as from 2-2-16.	
	28-2-16	8.0 a.m. 12.0 a.m.	Supplied two working parties at S.E. side of SAILLY BRIDGE. G.16.c.8.6. (MAP.36.)	
	28-2-16		Major H. Sidney is attached temporarily to Headquarters, 8th Division, as A.P.M.	
	29-2-16	8.0 a.m. 12.0 a.m.	Supplied two working parties as on 26-2-16.	Stobart nd cpl

Army Form C. 2118

WAR DIARY
or
INTELLIGENCE SUMMARY

Page 1. Vol III. (Erase heading not required.)

Place	Date 1916 March	Hour	Summary of Events and Information	Remarks and references to Appendices
GRAND RULLECOURT	1	am.	1 Sergt & 4 men detached as additional police with 5th Div HQ. J.Sm	
	2	am.	Routine. Fatigue parties clearing snow from roads. J.Sm	
	3	"	Routine. Inspections. J.Sm	
	4	"	1 Officer & 23 men sent to 6th Corps for Road Control & police duties. J.Sm	
	5	"	Routine. J.Sm	
	6	"	Routine. J.Sm	
	7	"	Routine. J.Sm	
	8	"	Routine. J.Sm	
	9	"	Routine. J.Sm	
	10	"	Capt Morton-Hill D.A.A.D.S. to Machine Gun School Wisques for instruction in Hotchkiss Rifle. J.Sm	

Army Form C. 2118.

WAR DIARY
or
INTELLIGENCE SUMMARY.
(Erase heading not required.)

Page II Col III

Hour, Date, Place		Summary of Events and Information	Remarks and references to Appendices
GRAND RULLECOURT.	March 1916 11	Routine.	S.Jm
	12	Routine.	S.Jm
	13.	Routine.	S.Jm
	14	Routine. Reinforcements 12 O.R. from Base	S.Jm
	15	Marched to NOVELLETTE 1 Km. W of HABARQ. Billeted in huts taken over from French troops.	S.Jm
NOVELLETTE.	16	Routine. Cleaning up village &c	S.Jm
	17	Routine. do -	S.Jm
	18	2 Officers Patrols on reconnaissance but ARRAS front line	S.Jm
	19	Divine Service. Routine. Inspections.	S.Jm

Army Form C. 2118.

WAR DIARY
or
INTELLIGENCE SUMMARY.

Page 3. Vol III. (Erase heading not required.)

Hour, Date, Place		Summary of Events and Information	Remarks and references to Appendices
NOVELLETTE	1916		
	20	Officers patrols on Front Line. Course of instruction in Hotchkiss Rifle. S.Ym	
		1 Officer & O.R. Reinforcements & O.R. commenced.	
	21.	Officers patrols. Routine &c.	S.Ym
	22	Patrols. Foot Drill.	S.Ym
	23	Officers Patrols. Routine &c.	S.Ym
	24	Patrols. Routine &c	S.Ym
	25	Patrols. Routine Instruction in Hotchkiss map reading. Target Practice	S.Ym
	26	Routine. Inspections. Reinforcement 4 O.R.	S.Ym
	27	Squadron Drill. Removed Post in Front Line. Leaving for 4 I.B. Inf. Bde S of River SCARPE.	S.Ym

Army Form C. 2118.

WAR DIARY
or
INTELLIGENCE SUMMARY.
(Erase heading not required.)

Pagent Vol III

1916
March

Hour, Date, Place		Summary of Events and Information	Remarks and references to Appendices
NOYELLETTE.	28	Routine. Received orders to send 1 Troop to Indian Cavalry Corps for instruction, to commence on 1st April. Selected Troop. S/m	
	29.	Relief of observation post & visit to J sector by Sqn Leader + 2 O.R. O.I'm	
	30	Troop Drill. Routine. S/m	
	31.	Troop of 1 Offr. 37 O.R. 39 horses proceeded to MAVINS. to be attached to Innisklling Dragoons for a 1 month refresher course. S/m	

Army Form C. 2118.

WAR DIARY
or
INTELLIGENCE SUMMARY.
(Erase heading not required.)

Pages No. VII.

Instructions regarding War Diaries and Intelligence Summaries are contained in F.S. Regs., Part II. and the Staff Manual respectively. Title pages will be prepared in manuscript.

Hour, Date, Place		Summary of Events and Information	Remarks and references to Appendices
NOYELLETTE.	1916 March 28	Routine. Received orders to send 1 Troop to Indian Cavalry Corps for Instruction. To commence on 4th April. Selected troop.	
	29.	Relief of observation post & visit of I sector by Stakeman + 2 O.R.	B.Sm
	30	Troop Drill. Routine.	B.Sm
	31.	Troop of 1 Offr. 37 O.R. 39 horses proceeded to MAVINS. to be attached to Inniskilling Dragoons for a 1 month refresher course.	B.Sm

Army Form C. 2118.

Vol. XVII

WAR DIARY
or
INTELLIGENCE SUMMARY

(Erase heading not required.)

C Squadron
Northumberland Hussars

Instructions regarding War Diaries and Intelligence Summaries are contained in F. S. Regs., Part II. and the Staff Manual respectively. Title Pages will be prepared in manuscript.

Place	Date	Hour	Summary of Events and Information	Remarks and references to Appendices
OLLINCOURT CHATEAU	1/4/16		Received Orders from O.C. 8th Divisional Mounted Troops for the Squadron to remove to HENENCOURT (LENS II) on the 4th April 1916. No.652 Pte Bainbridge J.) Admitted to Hospital Struck Off the Strength 1/4/16. 1307 " Riddell R.) 1122 " Mentalides Pte)	R&S
	2.4.16.		No.652. Pte Bainbridge J.) Being discharged from Hospitals are taken on the Strength as from 2/4/16. 1307. " Riddell R.) No.499 Pte Crane J.G. having been Sent to the Base pending discharge, is Struck Off the Strength as from 2/4/16.	R&S
	4.4.16	7.46am	Squadron paraded to proceed to new Billets at AGNICOURT (Map 62.D.C. 7A.) Via. VILLERS.BOCAGE, MOLLIENS, MONTIGNY, BEHENCOURT. Arrived at new billets 10=30 A.M.	R&S
AGNICOURT			No.713 S.S. Allan J. granted Class I. Proficiency Pay as from 4/4/16. No.420 Sgt: Rutherford C. reverts to the ranks on joining the Squadron from 3rd Line Regt. 2nd Lieut. Hon C.J.M Ramsay to be Lieutenant as from 2/2/16. (War Office Authority No 10594 2/3/16).	R&S

Army Form C. 2118.

WAR DIARY
or
INTELLIGENCE SUMMARY

(Erase heading not required.)

"C" Squadron
19th Hussars

Vol. XIII

Instructions regarding War Diaries and Intelligence Summaries are contained in F. S. Regs, Part II. and the Staff Manual respectively. Title Pages will be prepared in manuscript.

Place	Date	Hour	Summary of Events and Information	Remarks and references to Appendices
AGNICOURT Sheet 62 D Square C 7a. 8.6	5/4/16		No 18114 Corpl Wilkins J.H. Having arrived at the Squadron from No. 1 General Base Depot & Pte. 32243 Pte. Rawling C.J. are taken on the strength as from 5/4/16.	RAJ
			No. 18114 Corpl Wilkins J.H. reverts to the ranks on joining the Squadron from 3rd in the Regt.	RAJ
	8/4/16		No. 851, Pte. Bell J. having returned from hospital, are taken on strength, as from 7/4/16. No. 1122, " Marsden V.	RAJ
	9/4/16		No. 1094, Pte. Donaldson B.C. having proceeded to England to take up Commission in 3/5th Batt North'd Fusiliers, is struck off the strength, as from 8/4/16.	RAJ
	10/4/16		Squadron horses are moved from open picketing into stables at AGNICOURT. These stables were previously disinfected, as there was a suspicion of mange. (Map 62 DC 7a)	RAJ
	11/4/16	10.a.m 7.45 p.m	Capt. R.J. Stobart is a member of a F.G.C.M. held at HENENCOURT. (LENS II) Received message:- "1 p.o.s. Royal Irish Rifles." (MAP ALBERT V. 27)	RAJ
	12/4/16		1 N.C.O. & 5 men are detached from the Squadron to re-join the 8th Divl Sniping Corps, for duty, at ALBERT No. 51, Sergt. Abercrombie J.J. having been sent to base pending discharge, are struck off the strength, as from 12/4/16. No. 618, Sgt. Bell J.	RAJ

WAR DIARY or INTELLIGENCE SUMMARY

Army Form C. 2118.

Vol. XI "C" Squadron North Hussars April 1916

Place	Date	Hour	Summary of Events and Information	Remarks and references to Appendices
AGINCOURT Sheet 62D Sqn C 7 & 8.6	14-4-16		No: 601, Pte. Wlathorne, having proceeded to England to take up a commission is 3/4th Batt. North'd Fusiliers, is struck off the strength, as from 14/4/16. Detailed 2 mounted men & 2 wh. cycles to act as orderlies to 8th Div: Signal Coy.	Rd/
	15-4-16		London Gazette, April 12th 1916. Temp.Lieut. Hon. C.F.M. RAMSAY, relinquishes his temporary rank of Lieut. owing to Lieut. F.C. BLAKE, joining the squadron on promotion. 2nd Lt. A.W. Milburn to be temporary Lieut. as from 14-1-16. Punishments: Ord F.G.C.M. held at HENEN COURT WOOD (F-SERT MAP) on 14/4/16. No. 656, Pte. Donaghy, J. } were tried on a charge of; "When on active service, " 1307, - Riddell, R. } Drunkenness" and sentenced to 90 days Field Punishment No.1.	Rd/
	16-4-16	6.0 p.m.	Received message; "Major FAURE will fly to-night." This relates to the flights made by a French Air Squadron & is issued as a warning for troops not to fire. Sixteen men & 3 N.C.O's. detailed for instruction in Road Traffic Control under A.P.M.	Rd/
	19-4-16		No:- 100, S.F.S. WATSON, & has re-engaged for the period of the war. All horse rugs are today collected & landed in to S.Q.M.S. Store.	Rd/
	20-4-16	10.0 a.m.	25 men of the Squadron have today witnessed a demonstration with a GERMAN "FLAMMENWERFER" at BRESLE. No. 233 Pte. Charlotte, L., having been sent to base, pending discharge, is struck off the strength, as from 19-4-16. 3 men & 4 Light Draught Horses have today reported to Camp Comdt. 8th Division to be detailed by him to assist the Natives in farm Work.	Rd/

Army Form C. 2118.

VOL. XIII.

WAR DIARY or INTELLIGENCE SUMMARY

"C" Squadron, Northd. Hussars.

April 1916.

(Erase heading not required.)

Place	Date	Hour	Summary of Events and Information	Remarks and references to Appendices
AGINCOURT. Sheet 62D Square 6 Ya & 6	21-4-16		No-12, S.S.M. GALLON, H. " 160, Sergt ROBSON, T.A. " 225, Pte. SWINHOE, J. } having been sent to base, pending discharge, are struck off the strength, as from 20-4-16. No 201, S.Q.M.S. LORIMER, J.F. promoted to be acting Squadron Sergt Major (Warrant Officer, Class II) with pay & allowances, as from 20/4/16. No. 497, Sergt. DICKINSON, J.E. promoted to be acting S.Q.M.S. with pay & allowances as from 20/4/16.	R.H.
	22-4-16		Major H. SIDNEY, having been temporarily attached to the 20th HUSSARS as Second in Command, is struck off the strength, as from 22/4/16.	R.H.
	23-4-16		No. 77, Sergt. BRANNEN, H, having been sent to base, pending discharge, is struck off the strength, as from 23-4-16.	R.H.
	24-4-16		No 674, Cpl Stephenson, J.W. & No 457, Cpl Forrest, L. are promoted acting Sergts, as from the 12-4-16 & 20-4-16 respectively	E.B.
	25-4-16		No. 548, L. Sergt Potts R.Y. is appointed Squadron Accountant as from 25/4/16.	E.B.
	26-4-16		Capt R.L. Pretent goes on leave from 26/4/16 & 6-5-16	E.B.
	27-4-16		Squadron parades mounted & drill order under Troop Leaders	E.B.

Army Form C. 2118.

Volume XIII

WAR DIARY
or
INTELLIGENCE SUMMARY

(Erase heading not required.)

6 Guards
Lewis Guns

Place	Date	Hour	Summary of Events and Information	Remarks and references to Appendices
ACHICOURT	28/4/16		5 Rating Plates come at the Squadron from 8th Div Train & are taken on the strength as from the 28-4-16	S.O.
Ghu. 62 D (Sqm C)	29/4/16		2nd Lieut Hon E.G.H. Ramsay is a member of a F.G.C.M. held at HENENCOURT (Div II)	S.O.
Sq 8 C	30/4/16		L/Cpl Jones leaves to day to proceed to MOLLIENS-AU-BOIS for a course of Instruction on Lewis Gun, & from 1-5-16 to 4-5-16 No 93 Sergt Banks having been sent to the course pending discharge, is struck off the strength as from the 30-4-16	S.O.

Confidential

War Diary

of

"C" Squadron, Northumberland Hussars,

from May, 1st to May, 15th 1916.

Volume XIV.

Army Form C. 2118.

WAR DIARY
or
INTELLIGENCE SUMMARY "C" Squadron Northumberland Hussars
(Erase heading not required.) May 1916

Instructions regarding War Diaries and Intelligence Summaries are contained in F. S. Regs., Part II. and the Staff Manual respectively. Title Pages will be prepared in manuscript.

Place	Date	Hour	Summary of Events and Information	Remarks and references to Appendices
AGNICOURT Sheet 62D Squ 6 To F.6	1-5-16		No 98 Sergt Bardle R having been sent to the base pending discharge is struck off the strength as from 30-4-16. Two Riders Horses having been sent to Major H. Leburg 20 Hussars are struck off the strength as from the 30-4-16. No 781 Pte Laester R and No 546 Pte Douglas L a having left the Squadron to join Major Sidney of 6 to temporarily attached to 20 Hussars are struck off the strength as from the 22-4-16 and 30-4-16 respectively. No 692 Pte Mitsche E. F. granted Class Z furlough to Eng UK from 27-2-16	RJS
	2-5-16		6 men and 1 NCO came the Squadron for the 8th Divl Sig by to act as Orderlies. No 700 Pte Dodds. E W having joined the Squadron from L 5 Reinfr Base Depot is taken on the strength as from 2-5-16	RJS
	3-5-16		No 1829 Pte Robertson R having the Squadron to rede Orderly to O.C. L 8th Div. No 985 Pte Mitcheson having been admitted into hospital is struck off the strength as from 2-5-16. 3 men leave the Squadron for the 8 Divl Sig by to act as orderlies.	RJS
	4-5-16		No 620 Pte Furnery J + No 1440 Pte Cookworth have today been resailed from the 8th Divl Sig by to to hospital. Two men are sent to replace them.	RJS
	5-5-16		Working Party of 1 NCO + 20 men paraded as usual No 28 Ore Relay tm to Bde 6 + MWs	RJS
	6-5-16		Lecture by Lieut Young on the law of the Respirator. No 1773 Pte Peart + No 912 Pte Stoney R.E. are admitted into hospital	RJS
	7-5-16		Bivoaues are constructed	RJS

Army Form C. 2118.

WAR DIARY or INTELLIGENCE SUMMARY

(Erase heading not required.)

Vol. XIV. "C" Squadron: Northumberland Hussars

May 1916.

Instructions regarding War Diaries and Intelligence Summaries are contained in F.S. Regs., Part II. and the Staff Manual respectively. Title Pages will be prepared in manuscript.

Place	Date	Hour	Summary of Events and Information	Remarks and references to Appendices
AGINCOURT (MAP 62 D) C.7.a.8.6.	8-5-16	7.30am	Supplied working party of 1 N.C.O. 20 men as previously.	RSS
	9-5-16		No. 1121, L/Cpl Jack, having been sent to hospital, is struck off strength. Received orders to proceed to BRIQUEMESNIL (as from 7-5-16) to join the XIII Corps, where the regiment of Northumberland Hussars is to be re-formed.	RSS
	10-5-16	8.45am	Squadron left AGINCOURT (map 62 D, C.7.a.8.6) & proceeded to BRIQUEMESNIL (AMIENS 17 w) & is attached now to 18th Division, XIII Corps.	RSS
	11-5-16		8 men, having been isolated for 9 days with suspected Cerebro spinal meningitis, are examined & result of examination being negative, these men are ordered to rejoin squadron.	RSS
	12-5-16		Day spent in building bivouacs for men. Stores exercised in morning.	RSS
	13-5-16		"A" & "B" Squadrons arrive at BRIQUEMESNIL. (B/ AMIENS 17) and Major D Burrell, takes temporary command of the regiment. The regiment now being reformed, War Diary will from this date be rendered regimentally.	RSS

R L Stobart Capt.

8TH DIVISION

8TH DIVL MOUNTED TROOPS
FEB - APL 1916

CONFIDENTIAL.

War Diary

of

8th Divisional Mounted Troops

from 1st Feb. 1916 to 29th Feb 1916

(Volume 1)

Army Form C. 2118.

WAR DIARY
or
INTELLIGENCE SUMMARY

(Erase heading not required.) 8th DIVISIONAL MOUNTED TROOPS

Place	Date	Hour	Summary of Events and Information	Remarks and references to Appendices
RUE DE COURANT LE DOULIEU MAP 36a L.4.C.S.8.	1-2-16		Eyelet Coy. supply 15 N.C.O.s & men for working party at SAILLY BRICKFIELDS. Civ. Uniforms Claim 3 kits.	RPH
	2-2-16		NORTH'D HUSSARS "C" SQD. provide working party. Civ. Uniforms Claim 2 kits & one Mackintosh. Draft of 2 men arrived for Div. Cyclist Coy.	RPH
	3-2-16		Cyclist Coy supply working party. Civ. Uniforms claim 4 kits & 2 not known.	RPH
			CAPT. G. G. REA, "C" SQD. NORTHUMBERLAND HUSSARS leaves to take command of "B" SQD.	
	4-2-16		N.H. provide working party. Civ. Uniform - light bed for sweeping also very rough wind, constructed 1 new front in right & left section	RPH
	5-2-16		Cyclist Coy provide working party. Civ. Uniform claim 2 kits	RPH
	6-2-16		Draft of 5 men arrive for NORTH'D HUSSARS. Civ. Uniform claim 1 kit and constructed new front in left half.	RPH
	7-2-16		N.H. provide working party. Civ. Uniform claim 1 kit.	RPH
	8-2-16		Cyclist Coy. provide working party. Civ. Uniform - weather conditions unfavourable for sweeping no addl. front.	RPH
	9-2-16		N.H. provide working party. Civ. Uniform - Lately finished no shots fired. LIEUT. H.N. SWANN left the Cyclist Coy for duty on 3rd. CORPS STAFF.	RPH

WAR DIARY

8th DIVISIONAL MOUNTED TROOPS

INTELLIGENCE SUMMARY

Army Form C. 2118.

(Erase heading not required.)

Place	Date	Hour	Summary of Events and Information	Remarks and references to Appendices
RUE DE COURANT LE DOULIEU (map 36a L.4.C.8.8.)	10.2.16	3.15 pm	Cyclist Coy. supplied 15 NCOs t men for working party at SAILLY BRICKFIELDS. Civil. Snipers - Nil. Nil German.	RAA
	11.2.16		N H supplied working party as above. Civ. Snipers - nothing observed no shots fired.	RAA
	12.2.16		Cyclist Coy. supplied working party. Civ. Snipers - nothing observed no shots fired.	RAA
	13.2.16		Civil. Snipers - nothing observed no shots fired.	RAA
	14.2.16		N.H. supplied working party. Civ. Snipers - Steam(?) Rct(?) one result not known	RAA
	15.2.16		Cyclist Coy supply working party. Civ. Snipers - Nothing observed. no shots fired.	RAA
	16.2.16		N H supply working party. Civ. Snipers - claim 1 Rct, and observe large enemy working party in front of F.3. That informed Artillery observation officer who immediately opened fire on them with good effect.	RAA
	17.2.16		Cyclist Coy supplied working party. Civ. Snipers - nothing observed no shots fired.	RAA
	18.2.16		N.H. supplied working party. Civ. Snipers - Claim 1 Rct.	RAA
	19.2.16		Cyclist Coy - supplied working party. Civ. Snipers - Nothing observed no shots fired. Night hay constructed 3 forts in New Line.	RAA

WAR DIARY or INTELLIGENCE SUMMARY

Army Form C. 2118.

(Erase heading not required.) **8th Divisional Mounted Troops**

Place	Date	Hour	Summary of Events and Information	Remarks and references to Appendices
RUE DE COURANT LE DOULIEU (Map 36a L.4.C.8.8.)	20.2.16		N.H. supply working party. Div. Cyclists – Claim 2 kits & one not known. Right half constructed 3 tents in new line.	AA
	21.2.16		Div. Cyclists – Claim 2 kits and 3 recruits not known. Cyclist Coy. supply 1 N.C.O. & 20 men to work at Sailly Church and depot. Cyclist Coy supply 1 N.C.O. & 20 men to work at Bac. St. Maur & 1 N.C.O. & 10 men to work at Sailly Church and depot.	AA
	22.2.16		N.H. provide 20 N.C.Os & men for special duty in Estaires. Div. Cyclists – Nothing finished, no shots fired. Right half constructed three tents in new line.	AA
	23.2.16		Cyclist Coy supply working parties at Bac. St. Maur. Div. Cyclists – Claim 12 kits.	AA
	24.2.16	11.45 am 12.00	N.H. supply working party of two reliefs each of 25 N.C.O. & men at Sailly Bridge. Div. Cyclists – nothing abnormal, no shots fired. Received warning of Gas at N.65. Warning cancelled.	AA
	25.2.16		Cyclist Coy supply working party at Sailly Bridge. N.H. supply working parties at Bac. St. Maur & Sailly Church and depot. Capt. Savile (4th Cyclists) joining 2nd Battn. Middlesex Regt. Lieut. W.E.C. Pentaly takes over command of Cyclist Coy from this day. Div. Cyclists – nothing abnormal, no shots fired. 2/Lt Lawrence spotted German 5.9 Battery opposite Post F.1. He immediately pointed it out to the Artillery observation officer of D Battery who opened fire on it.	AA

2449 Wt. W14957/M90 750,000 1/16 J.B.C. & A. Forms/C.2118/12.

Army Form C. 2118.

WAR DIARY
or
INTELLIGENCE SUMMARY

(Erase heading not required.) 8th DIVISIONAL MOUNTED TROOPS

Place	Date	Hour	Summary of Events and Information	Remarks and references to Appendices
RUE DE COURANT. LE DOULIEU	26-2-16		N.H. softly working party at SAILLY BRIDGE. Divl. Cyclists - claim one hut.	AA
MAP 36a L.4.C.&R.	27-2-16		LIEUT. E.C.F. BLAKE taken on strength of 8"Sqdn. NORTHD HUSSARS. 2/LIEUT DRUMMELL " " " 3 O.R. " " " 5 O.R. taken on strength of Divl. Cyclist Coy. Divl. Cyclists - nothing observed no shots fired.	AA
	28-2-16		Cyclist Coy. softly working party at SAILLY BRIDGE. Divl. Cyclists - Nothing observed, no shots fired. MAJOR H. SIDNEY. D.C. 8"Sqdn. NORTHD HUSSARS. takes over duties of A.P.M. to 8th Division. LIEUT W.E.C. PICKTHALL O.C. Divl. Cyclist Coy. takes over charge of 3rd CORPS SNIPING SCHOOL. LIEUT H.E. MURPHY takes command of Divl. Cyclist Coy.	AA
	29-2-16		N.H. softly working party at SAILLY BRIDGE. Divl. Cyclists - claim 3 rats and 1 uncertain. Draft of 2 O.R. received for Divl. Cyclist Coy.	AA

CONFIDENTIAL

Vol II

War Diary

of

8th Divisional Mounted Troops.

from 1st April 1916 to 30th April 1916

WAR DIARY or INTELLIGENCE SUMMARY

Army Form C. 2118.

8th DIVISIONAL MOUNTED TROOPS

Place	Date	Hour	Summary of Events and Information	Remarks and references to Appendices
OLINCOURT	1-4-16		N.H. and Cyclist Coy, Northd. Hussars & Head Quarters in various places	RH
	7-4-16	8am	Divl. Mtd. Trps. moved independently from OLINCOURT. The Northd. Hussars proceeded to billets at AGNICOURT via VILLERS BOCAGE, MOLLIENS, MONTIGNY, BEHENCOURT. (Sheet 62D, E.7.a) The 8th Divl. Cyclist Coy. proceeded to billets at HENENCOURT moving by VILLERS BOCAGE – MOLLIENS – MONTIGNY – BEHENCOURT – DAIZIEUX. (Sheet 62D, D.3.C.)	M
AGNICOURT Sheet 62D. C.7.A.	8-4-16		Divl. Cyclist Coy. provide fatigue party of 2 N.C.Os. & 33 men to work permanently at Ammunition Dumhead PIESELLES Station	M
	10-4-16		Divl. Cyclist Coy. provide working party of 1 Officer and 30 men to work at No. 6. R.E. Park at MERICOURT/STATION daily. (Sheet 62D, J.4.cent.)	M
	12-4-16		Divl. Snipers moved to ALBERT to commence duty. (Sheet 62D, E.4.) 2nd Lt. A.W. MILBURN to be temp. i/c from 14-1-16.	RA
	17-4-16		2.O.R. reinforcements arrived for the Divl. Cyclist. Coy.	RM
	18-4-16		Divl. Snipers – Building and improving Snipers posts Left area.	RM
	19-4-16		Divl. Snipers – Building & improving Snipers posts Right area	RH
	20-4-16		Divl. Snipers – Building and improving Snipers posts Right area.	RH
	21-4-16		Divl. Snipers – Building and improving posts Right area. 2nd Lieut. M.W. de BELABRE joined the Divl. Snipers to assist in instruction	RH

WAR DIARY or INTELLIGENCE SUMMARY

Army Form C. 2118.

(Erase heading not required.) 8th DIVISIONAL. MTD. TRPS.

Place	Date	Hour	Summary of Events and Information	Remarks and references to Appendices
AGNICOURT sheet 62D. L.4.a.8.6	22-4-16		MAJOR H. SIDNEY, O.C., 2nd Sqdn. NORTH'D. HUSSARS. DIV'L SNIPERS — Report weather unfavourable for observation. No shots fired.	RM
	23-4-16		Div'l Snipers — Claim 1 hit and 3 uncertain results.	RM
	24-4-16		34 N.C.O. and men arrived at Div'l. M.T. tps. H.Q. AGNICOURT from Div'l Cyclist Coy for instruction in Sniping. Div'l Snipers — Claim 1 hit and 1 uncertain.	RM
	25-4-16		Div'l Snipers — Observed that work had been done on German t[r]ench M.17.5.6. sheet ALBERT.	RM
	26-4-16		Div'l Snipers — Claim 2 hits and one uncertain. Div'l Cyclist fatigue party at FLESSELLES intelligence by 25 Inf. Bde.	RM
	27-4-16		Div'l. Snipers — Claim 2 hits. Observed work in progress on Enemy 3rd line trench.	RM
	28-4-16		Div'l. Snipers — 2 uncertain results.	RM
	29-4-16		Div'l Snipers — Claim 1 hit.	RM
	30-4-16		34 other ranks of the Div'l. Snipers have School of Instruction at AGNICOURT to Commence duty at ALBERT.	RM

8TH DIVISION

8TH DIVL CYCLIST COY.
NOV 1914 – MAY 1916

Starts Oct 1914

121/3976

8th Divisional Cyclist Coy.

Vol I. 5.11 — 30.12.14

war 1916

Confidential

War Diary

of

8th Divisional Cyclist Coy:
from date of embarkation. Nov. 5th '14

November 5th

Leave HURSLEY Park Camp 3 a.m. to march to SOUTHAMPTON. Embark 10 a.m. in THESPIS.

6th Arrive HAVRE 6.30 a.m. Disembark 4.30 p.m. and march to No 6 Camp without transport.

November

7th — Transport arrives No 6 Camp. Exchanged 2 horses Nos 1 & 4 for 2 heavy draught.   HP

8th — Handed in 2 horses No 2 & 3 as unfit & received 2 heavy draught in exchange.   HP

9th — Entrained at HAVRE   HP

10th — Detrained at HAZEBROUCK & marched after dark to billets near MERVILLE   HP

11th —

12th — Changed some of billets to others in same neighbourhood to enable Yeomanry horses to be stabled   HP

November.

13th Moved to SAILLY sur LYS and went into billets.
Horse No 10 taken sick on road.
  HP

14th

15th

16th Horse No 10 dies of influenza.
  HP

17th

18th

19th

20th

21st Lt SAVILE & 12 others of No 1 Platoon
" PICKTHALL " " " 2 "
& " EVETTS " " " " "
proceed to HdQrs of 23rd, 24th & 25th Inf: Bgdes respectively on detached duty — principally for patrolling roads & telephone wires & search for snipers in rear of trenches.
  HP

November

22nd

23rd

24th

25th Moved to L'ESTREM & billeted in main street near Chateau. Remainder of Nos 1, 2 & 3 platoons proceeded to 23rd, 24th & 25th Bgdes. respectively.

26th

27th Horse No 11 heavy draught, drawn from Mobile Vet. Section at LA GORGE

28th

29th

30th

December

1st

2nd   Lined road MERVILLE — LA GORGUE road on occasion of visit of H.M. the King, the French President &c &c. 2.30 p.m.

3rd   Lt. LAWRENCE returned to duty with 2/R.B on account of knee not being strong enough for bicycling. Lt. BOSVILLE 3/Shropshire L.I. joined for duty in his place.

4th

5th   Moved billets to chateau on right bank of R. LAWE, ½ mile S.E. of LESTREM near FOSSE village.

6th   Practice alarm, assembled PONT RIQUEUL.

7th

8th & 9th

10th   50 men dug in 3rd line trenches near RIEZ BAILLEUL.

December.

11th

12th 50 men dig trenches as on 10th inst.

13th

14th 50 men dig trenches as before. Nos 1, 2, & 3 Platoons rejoin from duty with infantry brigades, and are billeted round chateau

15th

16th

17th

18th

19th Last night (18th–19th) Coy: was held in brigade (25th) reserve at La FLINQUE during attacks delivered by 8th Div: Returned to billets 7 a.m.

20th Remained in billets under orders to turn out at moments notice.

December

21ˢᵗ   Ditto.

22ⁿᵈ

23ʳᵈ   Lt GRIFFIN & Nº 4 Platoon
      — BOSVILLE & " 5 "   } are
      2Lt WILLOUGHBY " 6 "
sent to 23ʳᵈ, 24ᵗʰ & 25ᵗʰ Bgde Hᵈ Qʳˢ
on detachment.

24ᵗʰ

25ᵗʰ

26ᵗʰ   11 p.m. proceeded to CROIX BARBEE
in Divisional Reserve.

27ᵗʰ   Returned to billets near FOSSE
at 7 am

28ᵗʰ

29ᵗʰ   5 first reinforcements from A. Cycle Corps joined.

30ᵗʰ   2Lt WILLOUGHBY admitted to hospital.
20 men under R.E. repair trenches
in B lines. 7 to 11 pm.

12TH OCTOBER TO 31ST DECEMBER 1914.

8th Division Cyclist Coy.

Army Form C. 2118.

WAR DIARY
or
INTELLIGENCE SUMMARY.
(Erase heading not required.)

Instructions regarding War Diaries and Intelligence Summaries are contained in F.S. Regs., Part II. and the Staff Manual respectively. Title pages will be prepared in manuscript.

Hour, Date, Place	Summary of Events and Information	Remarks and references to Appendices
12th October 1914 SOUTH LYNCH near WINCHESTER	Capt R.M HEATH DSO 2/Middx Reg, Lieut J.B. EVETTS 2/Sea Rifles, 20 other ranks 2/Middx Reg * assembled from 8th Division 4 " " 2/W.York Reg. infantry camps in HURSLEY Park 15 " " 2/Sea. Rifles and camped next to HQ Northampton Imperial Yeomanry at S. LYNCH	* including Cy Sergt Maj J. PARIS. Cy. Qr.Mr.Sergt A.F.G. PARCELL
13th October	Lieut W.E.G. PICKTHALL 2/W.York Reg 18 other ranks 2/Devon Reg. 14 " " 2/W. York Reg } joined the company 1 " " 2/Sea Rifles 13 " " 2/Middx Reg	
14th October	Lieut A.B.W.SAVILE 2/Middx Reg 3 other ranks " " 17 " " 1/Sherwood Foresters } joined the company 105 Bicycles drawn from CHANDLERS FORD Station.	
15th 16th 17th	nil	

Army Form C. 2118.

WAR DIARY
or
INTELLIGENCE SUMMARY.
(Erase heading not required.)

Instructions regarding War Diaries and Intelligence Summaries are contained in F.S. Regs., Part II. and the Staff Manual respectively. Title pages will be prepared in manuscript.

Hour, Date, Place	Summary of Events and Information	Remarks and references to Appendices
18th October 1917	Nil	
19th	Nil	
20th	Nil	
21st	Nil	
22nd	Nil	
23rd	Nil	
24th	Nil	
25th	Nil	
26th	Nil	
27th	100 bicycles drawn from Ordnance Store for extra establishment	

(73989) W.4141-463. 400,000. 9/14. H.&J.Ltd. Forms/C. 2118/10.

Army Form C. 2118.

WAR DIARY
or
INTELLIGENCE SUMMARY.
(Erase heading not required.)

Instructions regarding War Diaries and Intelligence Summaries are contained in F.S. Regs., Part II. and the Staff Manual respectively. Title pages will be prepared in manuscript.

Hour, Date, Place	Summary of Events and Information	Remarks and references to Appendices
28th October 1914	Capt J.A.A. Griffith 30/16 Os and Men 2nd Lincoln Regt. Lieut Lawrence & 20/16 Os & men 2nd Rifle Bde. Lieut J.A. Willoughby 9.1.4/16 Os 0 men 2nd Northampton Regt. 9.16.1.6.0 and men 1st Worcester Regt joined company on increase of establishment.	
29th October 6.45 a.m.	The Company paraded for Divisional Route March.	
30th October	Nil	
31st October	Nil	
1st November	Nil	
2nd "	Capt. H.E.M. Portis R.R.C. joined Company as 2nd in command. Lieut G.S. Barrow, Corps of Interpreters joined this day.	

Army Form C. 2118.

WAR DIARY
or
INTELLIGENCE SUMMARY.
(Erase heading not required.)

Instructions regarding War Diaries and Intelligence Summaries are contained in F.S. Regs., Part II. and the Staff Manual respectively. Title pages will be prepared in manuscript.

Hour, Date, Place	Summary of Events and Information	Remarks and references to Appendices
2nd November 1915	Nil	
3rd November 12 noon	Orders were received for General Mobilization. Company to parade (see details) at 2 a.m. on 5th and march to Southampton.	

Army Form C. 2118.

WAR DIARY
or
INTELLIGENCE SUMMARY.
(Erase heading not required.)

Instructions regarding War Diaries and Intelligence Summaries are contained in F.S. Regs., Part II. and the Staff Manual respectively. Title pages will be prepared in manuscript.

Hour, Date, Place	Summary of Events and Information	Remarks and references to Appendices
5th November 1914	Leave HURSLEY PARK CAMP 8 a.m. to march to SOUTHAMPTON. Embark 10 a.m. on THESPIS.	
6th November	Arrive HAVRE 6.30 am Disembark 4.30 pm and march to No 6 camp without transport	
7th November	Transport arrives No 6 camp. Exchanged 2 horses 110/94 for 2 heavy draught.	
8th November	Handed in 2 horses No 2 & 3 riding and received 2 heavy draught in exchange.	
9th November	Entrained at HAVRE	
10th November	Detrained at HAZEBROUCK and marched after dark to billets near MERVILLE.	
11th November	Nil	
12th November	Changed our billets. Bothen in same neighbourhood to make room any horses to be stabled.	

(73989) W4141—463. 400,000. 9/14. H.&J.Ltd. Forms/C. 2118/10.

Army Form C. 2118.

WAR DIARY
or
INTELLIGENCE SUMMARY.
(Erase heading not required.)

Hour, Date, Place	Summary of Events and Information	Remarks and references to Appendices
13th November	Moved to SAILLY sur LYS and went into Billets	
14th November	Horse No 10 taking sick on road.	
15th November	Nil	
16th November	Horse No 10 died of influenza	
17th November	Nil	
18th November	Nil	
19th November	Nil	
20th November	Nil	
21st November	LIEUT. Saville + 12 others of No1 Platoon proceeded to dispose of 23rd, 24th, + 25th Inf. Bde. respectively on finished duty principally for patrolling roads + telephone wires and search for snipers in rear of trenches. Picthalla - 2 EVETTS 9 - 3	

WAR DIARY
or
INTELLIGENCE SUMMARY.

(Erase heading not required.)

Army Form C. 2118.

Instructions regarding War Diaries and Intelligence Summaries are contained in F.S. Regs., Part II and the Staff Manual respectively. Title pages will be prepared in manuscript.

Hour, Date, Place	Summary of Events and Information	Remarks and references to Appendices
22nd November	Nil	
23rd November	Nil	
24th November	N.S.	
25th November	Moves to LESTREM area billets in man street and CHATEAU. Remainder of Nos 1, 2, 3 platoons forwarded to 23rd, 24th & 25th Bns respectively.	
26th November	Nil	
27th November	Home No 11 heavy draughts drawn from No. Bn to this shut. at LA GORGUE.	
28th November	Nil	
29th November	Nil	
30th November	Nil	

Army Form C. 2118.

WAR DIARY
or
INTELLIGENCE SUMMARY.
(Erase heading not required.)

Instructions regarding War Diaries and Intelligence Summaries are contained in F. S. Regs., Part II. and the Staff Manual respectively. Title pages will be prepared in manuscript.

Hour, Date, Place	Summary of Events and Information	Remarks and references to Appendices
1st December	Nil	
2nd December	Royal MERVILLE – LA GORGUE road on occasion of visit of H.M. the King, the French President 2.0 & 2.30 p.m.	
3rd December	Lt. Laurence returned to duty with 9/R.B. on account of knee not being strong enough for bicycling. Lt. Boswell of Shropshire L.I. joined for duty in his place.	
4th December	Nil	
5th December	Moved billets to chateau on right bank of R. LAWE, ½ mile SE of LESTREM near FOSSE village. Practice alarm, assembled PONT REQUEUL	
6th December	Nil	
7th December	Nil	
8th December	Nil	

Army Form C. 2118.

WAR DIARY
or
INTELLIGENCE SUMMARY.
(Erase heading not required.)

Instructions regarding War Diaries and Intelligence Summaries are contained in F.S. Regs., Part II. and the Staff Manual respectively. Title pages will be prepared in manuscript.

Hour, Date, Place	Summary of Events and Information	Remarks and references to Appendices
9th December	Nil	
10th December	50 men dug in 2nd line trenches near RIEZ. BAILLEUL.	
11th December	Nil.	
12th December	50 men dig trenches as on 10th inst.	
13th December	Nil	
14th December	50 men dig trenches as before. Nos 1, 2 & 3 Platoons return from duty with Infantry Brigades, and are billeted round Chateau.	
15th December	Nil	
16th December	Nil	
17th December	Nil	
18th December	Nil	

Army Form C. 2118.

WAR DIARY
or
INTELLIGENCE SUMMARY.
(Erase heading not required.)

Instructions regarding War Diaries and Intelligence Summaries are contained in F.S. Regs., Part II. and the Staff Manual respectively. Title pages will be prepared in manuscript.

Hour, Date, Place	Summary of Events and Information	Remarks and references to Appendices
19th December	Last night (18th/19th) Coy. was held in Brigade (25th) reserve at La FLINQUE during attacks delivered by 8th Division. Returned to billets 7.a.m.	
20th December	Remained in billets under orders to turn out at moments notice.	
21st December	ditto	
22nd December	Nil	
23rd December	Lt GRIFFIN & No 4 Platoon } were sent to 23rd, 24th & 25th BOSVILLE & No 5 } Bgde H'd Qrs in attachment Lt WILLOUGHBY & No 6	
24th December	Nil	
25th December	Nil	
26th December	11 p.m. proceeded to CROIX BARBEE in Divisional Reserve	
27th December	Returned to billets near FOSSE at 7 a.m.	

(73989) W4141—463. 400,000. 9/14. H.&J.Ltd. Forms/C. 2118/10.

Army Form C. 2118.

WAR DIARY
or
INTELLIGENCE SUMMARY.
(Erase heading not required.)

Instructions regarding War Diaries and Intelligence Summaries are contained in F.S. Regs., Part II. and the Staff Manual respectively. Title pages will be prepared in manuscript.

Hour, Date, Place	Summary of Events and Information	Remarks and references to Appendices
28th December	Nil	
29th December	5 first reinforcements from A. Cycle Corps joined.	
30th December	Lt WILLOUGHBY admitted to hospital. 20 men under R.E. repair trenches in B. Lines.	
31st December	50 men under R.E. employed trench work in C. Lines.	

Army Form C. 2118.

WAR DIARY
or
INTELLIGENCE SUMMARY.
(Erase heading not required.)

Instructions regarding War Diaries and Intelligence Summaries are contained in F.S. Regs., Part II. and the Staff Manual respectively. Title pages will be prepared in manuscript.

Hour, Date, Place	Summary of Events and Information	Remarks and references to Appendices
1st January 1915. "C" Lines 11 — 11 p.m	70 men under R.E. employed in trench work.	
2nd January	Nil	
3rd " 'A' 'B' 'C' Lines	70 men under R.E. employed in trench work.	
4th January	Nil	
5th " "C" Lines 11 — 10 p.m	Slight outbreak of Skin Disease in No. 3. Platoon isolated as far as possible. 50 men repair trenches	
6th January	Nil	

Army Form C. 2118.

WAR DIARY
or
INTELLIGENCE SUMMARY.
(Erase heading not required.)

Instructions regarding War Diaries and Intelligence Summaries are contained in F. S. Regs., Part II and the Staff Manual respectively. Title pages will be prepared in manuscript.

Hour, Date, Place	Summary of Events and Information	Remarks and references to Appendices
7th January 1915. "B" Lines 9.30pm–5am.	Lieut Evetts proceeds on leave (7th – 13th). Lieut Pickthall & 40 men dig fire trench under R E	
8th January	Lieut Barrows proceeds on leave (8th – 15th)	
9th January 4 fines 5am. "a" 4pm – 9.30pm	Lieut Searle & 50 men dig trench. 20 men under N.C.O. R E dig trench	
10th January	Nil	
11th "	Nil	
12th " ROUGE CROIX 1.30 a.m.	Lieut Searle and 40 men dig under R E	

Army Form C. 2118.

WAR DIARY
or
INTELLIGENCE SUMMARY.
(Erase heading not required.)

Instructions regarding War Diaries and Intelligence Summaries are contained in F.S. Regs., Part II. and the Staff Manual respectively. Title pages will be prepared in manuscript.

Hour, Date, Place	Summary of Events and Information	Remarks and references to Appendices
13th January 1915 Rouge Croix 5.30am	Lieut Sickthall and 40 men dig under R.E. Eselis returns from leave.	
14th January	Lieut Davils proceeds on leave till 21st.	
15th Rouge Croix	Lieut Evetts & 40 men dig trenches Lieut Barrow returns from leave	
16th January	Nil	
17th Rouge Croix	Lieut Sickthall & 65 men dig trenches Pte Thresher (Devons) wounded (arm)	

WAR DIARY

or

INTELLIGENCE SUMMARY.

(Erase heading not required.)

Army Form C. 2118.

Instructions regarding War Diaries and Intelligence Summaries are contained in F.S. Regs., Part II and the Staff Manual respectively. Title pages will be prepared in manuscript.

Hour, Date, Place	Summary of Events and Information	Remarks and references to Appendices
16th January 1916.	A very heavy fall of snow, with much colder weather followed by à thaw about midday. The roads & country side which had been dried up by high wind, are again reduced to slush. A very dark night	
19th January. D. Knus 5.30 p.m.	Snow still on the ground but warmer weather and a thaw. Lieut Evetts & 65 men paraded for digging and completion of redoubt. ~~Plan of redoubt on next letter~~ The redoubt has a high command and is conspicuous & has no cover from front. Burst of high explosive shell dropping right into the centre. The work ends sharply completed but nearly all the earth put into the traverses has to be carried up by hand as it is too far to throw from the bottom of the ditch. A fairly light night with a little rain. Swarm Roads flooded.	

Army Form C. 2118.

WAR DIARY
or
INTELLIGENCE SUMMARY. J2

(Erase heading not required.)

Instructions regarding War Diaries and Intelligence Summaries are contained in F. S. Regs., Part II and the Staff Manual respectively. Title pages will be prepared in manuscript.

Hour, Date, Place	Summary of Events and Information	Remarks and references to Appendices
1915. January 20th. FOSSE. PAS DE CALAIS.	Thaw continues. Practically all snow disappeared. CAPTAIN. H.C.M. PORTER went on leave to ENGLAND. 21st - 27th Jan both dates inclusive. LIEUT. H.B.N. SAVILE returned from leave.	J.F.E. Lieut.
January 21st. ROUGE CROIX. 5.30 p.m. — 11.15 p.m.	LIEUT. N.E.C. PICTHALL & 65 men paraded for digging under the direction of the R.E. The Redoubt behind D. LINES was almost finished, but work was hindered by heavy rain. The roads on the way down to the trenches were flooded in places, & very difficult to cycle on.	Sketch of Redoubt in Note Book. Jan.y 19th/15 J.F.E. Lieut.
January 22nd.	Nil	J.F.S. Lieut
January 23rd. FOSSE.	The continuation of the Redoubt behind D LINES was cancelled for to-day, owing to heavy weather. Bye-roads still under water in many places	J.F.E. Lieut

(73989) W4141—463. 400,000. 9/14. H.&J.Ltd. Forms/C. 2118/10.

WAR DIARY
or
INTELLIGENCE SUMMARY.

Army Form C. 2118.

Hour, Date, Place	Summary of Events and Information	Remarks and references to Appendices
January 24th FOSSE.	177 NCO's men are now permanently transferred to the ARMY CYCLE CORPS from date, December 12th, 1914.	J.T.E. Lieut
January 25th FOSSE. 8.45 am. 9 am. 10 am.	Fairly heavy rifle & machine gun fire in the direction of NEUVE CHAPELLE, from about 11 pm until 9 am of 24th/25th until 9 am this morning. On a much heavier out-burst being heard at 8.45 am O.C. CYCLE Coy was ordered to move off at a moment's notice, as a precaution. Fire slackened considerably. Received following message. "O.C. Div. Cyclists. 25th. First corps reports that hostile attack on their lines appears imminent - AAA. Be ready to turn out at a moment's notice AAA. Acknowledge AAA. O.C. Dn. Mounted Troops."	

Army Form C. 2118.

WAR DIARY
or
INTELLIGENCE SUMMARY.
(Erase heading not required.)

Hour, Date, Place	Summary of Events and Information	Remarks and references to Appendices
2.15 p.m.	Following message received. Div. Cyclists 25th. Please detail working party of 65 men to be at Rouge Croix at 5.30 p.m. today AAA Div. Mounted Troops.	
Rouge Croix. 4.30 p.m.	Lieut. H.B.W. Savile + 65 men paraded for digging under direction of R.E. & carried on the making of the Redoubt behind A Lines.	J.F.Edwent. J.F.Edwent
Fosse. 6.55 p.m.	Message received to "Resume normal conditions".	
January 26th.	Nil	
January 27th.	Capt. R.M. Heath, D.S.O. went on leave to England 28th Jany & 3rd March both dates inclusive. Capt. H.C.M. Porter returned from leave, & took over command of the Company from this day.	J.F.Edwent J.F.Edwent
January 28th		

(73989) W4941—463. 400,000. 9/14. H.&J. Ltd. Forms/C. 2118/10.

Army Form C. 2118.

WAR DIARY
or
INTELLIGENCE SUMMARY.

(Erase heading not required.)

Instructions regarding War Diaries and Intelligence Summaries are contained in F.S. Regs., Part II. and the Staff Manual respectively. Title pages will be prepared in manuscript.

Hour, Date, Place	Summary of Events and Information	Remarks and references to Appendices
January 28th Rouge Croix 10 pm – 5.45 am.	Lieut. J.F. Evetts with 65 men paraded for digging with the R.E. A Redoubt behind B LINES was almost completed. Sergt. F. Kinchin (1342) was slightly wounded. Right breast. Notad mitted to hospital. Bright moonlight night. Sharp frost, all roads in excellent condition for cycling.	J.F. Evetts Lieut
January 30th 29th Rouge Croix 5 pm – 10:30 pm	Cpl. Evans and 7 men paraded for digging under the R.E. A Redoubt behind B LINES was constructed. Sharp frost, all roads in good condition	J.F. Evetts Lieut

Army Form C. 2118.

WAR DIARY
or
INTELLIGENCE SUMMARY.

(Erase heading not required.)

Hour, Date, Place	Summary of Events and Information	Remarks and references to Appendices
January 30 & ROUGE CROIX 4.20 pm - 11 pm	CAPT H.C.M. PORTER + 50 men parades for supper made an return of the R.E. A reconnaissance ride to the Regnt returned. 13 lines were almost completed	9 to front
January 31st	Nil	9 to rear

8th Ind Cyclist Coy

WAR DIARY
or
INTELLIGENCE SUMMARY

Army Form C. 2118.

(Erase heading not required.)

Instructions regarding War Diaries and Intelligence Summaries are contained in F.S. Regs., Part II. and the Staff Manual respectively. Title pages will be prepared in manuscript.

Hour, Date, Place	Summary of Events and Information	Remarks and references to Appendices
January 30th ROUGE CROIX 4.20 pm – 11 pm	Capt. H.C.M. PORTER & 50 men paraded for digging under direction of the R.E. "A" reverse side to the Redoubt-trench B line was almost completed.	J.F.E. Lieut
January 31st	Nil	J.F.E. Lieut
February 1st CROIX BARBÉE 8.30 am – 2.10 pm	Lieut. H.B.N. SAVILE & 65 men paraded for digging under the direction of the R.E. A Redoubt-trench A line was met. The road was very heavy after the thaw & was for cycling.	J.F.E. Lieut
February 2nd ROUGE CROIX 5.30 pm – 10.30 pm	Lieut. N.F.C. PICTHALL and men paraded for digging under the direction of the R.E. A Redoubt-trench D line & H.Q. were constructed. Very heavy rain, & dark night.	J.F.E. Lieut

Index

Cyclists

SUBJECT.

No.	Contents.	Date.
	8th Division Cyclist Coy 1915.	

12/4327

8th Dio. l Goldlid Coy.

Vol III. 1-31.1.15

Nil

8th Divisional
December het Coy.   11

31st 50 men under RE employed trench work in C. lines.

January 1915

1st 70 men under RE employed trench work 4 – 11 pm C lines.

2nd

3rd Ditto in A & C lines

4th

5th Slight outbreak of skin disease in No 3 Platoon; platoon isolated as far as possible.
50 men ~~dig~~ repair trenches in C lines 4 to 10 pm.

6th

7th Lt EVETTS proceeds on leave.
" Pickthall & 70 men dig fire trench in B lines – 9.30 pm – 5 am

8th 2 Lt Barrow goes on leave till 15th

Jan 9th Lt Savile & 50 men dig A Lines 8 am
20 men under L CO & RE dig in C Lines
7-9.30 pm

10th

11th

12th Lt Savile & 70 men dig under RE at
Rouge Croix 1.30 am (D Lines)

13th Lt Pickthall & 70 men dig Rouge Croix 5.30 am

Lt Evetts returns from leave
Jan 14. Lt Savile proceeds on leave till 21st

Jan 15 Lt Evetts & 70 men dig Rouge Croix 5.30 am
2 Lt Barton returns from leave

Jan 16

Jan 17 Lt Pickthall & 65 men dig Rouge Croix 5.30
Pte Thresher (Devons) wounded (arm)

January 18th

A very heavy fall of snow, with much colder weather in the early morning, followed by a thaw about midday.

The roads & country side, which had been dried up by high winds, are again reduced to slush.

A very dark night.

J. F. E. St.

January 19th

Snow still on the ground, but warmer weather & a thaw.

LIEUT EVETTS & 65 men paraded at 5.30 p.m. for digging, & completion of the "redoubt" behind "D" LINES. A plan of the redoubt is given below

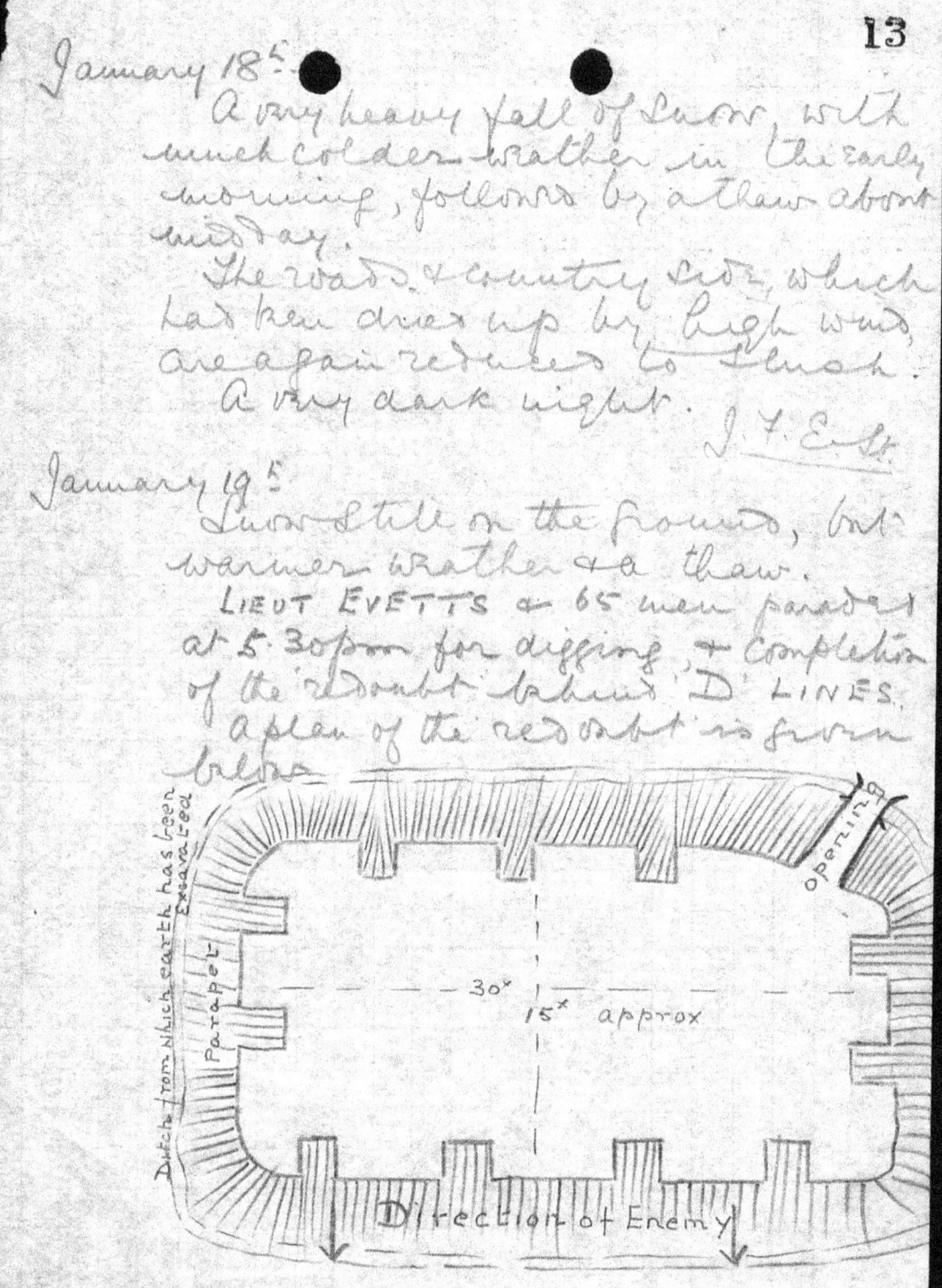

The redoubt has a high command & is conspicuous, & has no cover from 'back burst' of high explosive shell dropping right into the centre.

Section through parapet.

Revetment of Hillesden Canvas.   +4'6"   Direction of enemy.
±0
Anchor.   Ditch from which earth has been taken

The work was nearly completed, but nearly all the earth put into the traverses has to be carried up by hand as it is too far to throw from the bottom of the ditch.

A fairly light night, with a little rain, & warm. Roads flooded

J.F.E.St

January 20th.
Still thawing. Practically all the snow has disappeared.
CAPTAIN H.C.M. PORTER went on leave 21st - 27th Jan both dates inc
LIEUT. H.B.N. SAVILE returned from leave
↓ Continued in file ↓

8th Divisional Cyclist Coy

WAR DIARY
or
INTELLIGENCE SUMMARY.
(Erase heading not required.)

Army Form C. 2118.

Hour, Date, Place	Summary of Events and Information	Remarks and references to Appendices
1915. January 20th. FOSSE. PAS DE CALAIS.	Thaw continues. Practically all frost disappeared. CAPTAIN H.N. PORTER went on leave to ENGLAND 21st – 27th Jan both dates inclusive. LIEUT. H.B.N. SAVILE returned from leave.	J.F.E. Lieut
January 21st. ROUGE CROIX. 5.30 p.m. – 11.15 p.m.	LIEUT. N.E.C. PICTHALL & 65 men paraded for digging under the direction of the R.E. The Redoubt traced out, work was hindered by heavy rain. D. LINES was almost finished. The roads on the way down to the trenches were flooded in places & very difficult to cycle on.	Sketch of Redoubt in Note Book Jan.t 19t/15 J.F.E. Lieut J.F.E Lieut
January 22nd.	Nil	
January 23rd. FOSSE.	The continuation of the Redoubt & hind D LINES was cancelled for today, owing to frosty weather. Bye-roads still under water in many places	J.F.E. Lieut

Army Form C. 2118.

WAR DIARY
or
INTELLIGENCE SUMMARY.
(Erase heading not required.)

Instructions regarding War Diaries and Intelligence Summaries are contained in F.S. Regs., Part II. and the Staff Manual respectively. Title pages will be prepared in manuscript.

Hour, Date, Place	Summary of Events and Information	Remarks and references to Appendices
January 24th FOSSE.	177 NCO's men are now permanently transferred to the ARMY CYCLE CORPS from date December 12th 1914.	J.F.E. Lieut
January 25th FOSSE. 8.45 am. 9 am. 10 am.	Fairly heavy rifle & machine gun fire in the direction of NEUVE CHAPELLE, at about 11 pm lasting in night of 24th/25th until 9 am this morning. On a Staff learning information at 8.45 am O.C. CYCLE COY issues orders to move off at a moments notice, as a precaution. Fire Sleepers accordingly. Received following message. O.C. DIV CYCLISTS. 25th. First corps reports that hostile attack on their lines appears imminent AAA. Be ready to turn out at a moments notice AAA Acknowledge AAA. O.C. DIV. MOUNTED TROOPS.	

Army Form C. 2118.

WAR DIARY
or
INTELLIGENCE SUMMARY.
(Erase heading not required.)

Instructions regarding War Diaries and Intelligence Summaries are contained in F.S. Regs., Part II and the Staff Manual respectively. Title pages will be prepared in manuscript.

Hour, Date, Place	Summary of Events and Information	Remarks and references to Appendices
2.15 pm.	Following message received. Div. Cyclists. 25th. Please detail working party of 6's men to tr at Rouge Croix at 5.30 pm today AAA Div. Mounted Troops.	
Rouge Croix. 4.30 pm.	Lieut. H.B.W. Savile & 6 men paraded for digging under direction of R.E.'s. Carried on the working of the Redoubt behind A LINES.	J.F. Edent.
Fosse. 6.55 pm.	Message received to 'Resume normal conditions'.	J.F. Edent
January 26th	Nil	
January 27th	Capt. R.M. Heath. D.S.O. went on leave to England 28th Jany & 3rd March both dates inclusive. Capt. H.C.M. Porter returned from leave & took over command of the Company from this day	J.F. Edent

(7.3989) W4141–463. 400,000. 9/14. H.&J. Ltd. Forms/C. 2118/10.

WAR DIARY
or
INTELLIGENCE SUMMARY.

Army Form C. 2118.

Hour, Date, Place	Summary of Events and Information	Remarks and references to Appendices
January 28th ROUGE CROIX 10 pm – 5.45 am	Lieut. J.F. EVETTS with 65 men paraded for digging under the R.E. A Redoubt behind 'B' LINES was almost completed. Sergt. F. KINCHIN (1342) was slightly wounded Right breast. Not admitted to hospital. Bright moonlight night. Sharp frost. All roads in excellent condition for cycling.	J.E. Lieut
January 29th ROUGE CROIX 5 pm – 10.30 pm	Cpl. EVANS and 7 men paraded for digging under the R.E. A Redoubt behind 'B' LINES was Constructed. Sharp frost, all roads in good condition	J.E. Lieut

Army Form C. 2118.

WAR DIARY
or
INTELLIGENCE SUMMARY.

(Erase heading not required.)

Instructions regarding War Diaries and Intelligence Summaries are contained in F.S. Regs., Part II. and the Staff Manual respectively. Title pages will be prepared in manuscript.

Hour, Date, Place	Summary of Events and Information	Remarks and references to Appendices
January 30th ROUGE CROIX 4.20 pm - 11 pm	Capt H.C.M. PORTER + 50 men paraded for Digging under direction of the R.E. A reserve trench to the Regimental trenches B Lines was almost completed	9.7. Recent
January 31st	Nil	9.7.3 Recent

Running copy
Henry Graham
J Brand
Running 31/1

for Capt & Co.

12/
4636

Sta Dis l Gebid Coy

Vol 144 — 30.1 — 28.2.15

8th Prov'l Cyclist Coy.

WAR DIARY or INTELLIGENCE SUMMARY.

Army Form C. 2118.

(Erase heading not required.)

Hour, Date, Place	Summary of Events and Information	Remarks and references to Appendices
January 30th ROUGE CROIX 4.20 pm – 11 pm	Capt. H.C.M. PORTER & 50 men paraded for digging under direction of the R.E. A reverse slit to the Redoubt behind B LINES was almost completed.	J.F.E. Lieut
January 31st	Nil	J.F.E. Lieut
February 1st CROIX BARBEE 8.30am – 2.10 pm	Lieut. H.B.N. SAVILE and 65 men paraded for digging under the direction of the R.E. A Redoubt behind A LINES was made. The road here run heavy after the thaw & bad for cycling.	J.F.E. Lieut
February 2nd ROUGE CROIX 5.30 pm – 10.30 pm	Lieut. M.F.C. PICTHALL and 50 men paraded for digging under the direction of the R.E. A Redoubt behind D LINES H.Q. was constructed. Very heavy rain, & a dark night.	J.F.E. Lieut

8th Divisional Cyclist Coy

WAR DIARY
or
INTELLIGENCE SUMMARY.
(Erase heading not required.)

Army Form C. 2118.

Hour, Date, Place	Summary of Events and Information	Remarks and references to Appendices
February 3rd FORSE.	Captain R.M. Heath. D.S.O. returned from leave in England, took over command of the Company. Lieut. N.E.C. Picthall went on leave February 4th–10th, both dates inclusive.	J.F.E. Lieut
February 4th ROUGE CROIX 7.45pm – 2.15am	Lieut. J.F. Evetts and 65 men paraded for digging work in direction of the R.E. Q' Resort. Inland B. Lines. H.Q. was completed. The road was very heavy. A bright & moonlight night after 10 pm.	J.F.E. Lieut
February 5th	Nil	J.F.E. Lieut
February 6th CROIX BARBÉE 7.45am – 2 pm	Captain H.C.M. Porter & 60 men paraded for digging work in direction of the R.E. A Resort. near Croix Barbée was noted.	J.F.E. Lieut
February 7th –	Horse No 5 C.C. Bay mare, heavy draught, was sent down at M.V.H. La Gorgue, suffering from laminitis.	J.F.E. Lieut

2nd Gurkha Coy

Army Form C. 2118.

WAR DIARY
or
INTELLIGENCE SUMMARY.
(Erase heading not required.)

Instructions regarding War Diaries and Intelligence Summaries are contained in F.S. Regs., Part II. and the Staff Manual respectively. Title pages will be prepared in manuscript.

Hour, Date, Place	Summary of Events and Information	Remarks and references to Appendices
February 8th 7.45am – 1.15pm CROIX BARBÉE	LIEUT. H.B.N. SAVILE and 60 men Parats from aggyng near the direction of W.R.E. A Redoubt near CROIX BARBÉE was constructed, & loopholes amenshales to Clearstures of fire. A house was pulled in to a state of defence.	J.R. Lieut
February 9th	Nil	J.R. Lieut
February 10th CROIX BARBÉE 7.45am – 1pm	LIEUT. J.F. EVETTS and 60 men Paraits for digging near the R.E. A Redoubt behind B LINES was constructed. LIEUT. N.E.C. RETTMA LL returned from leave in ENGLAND.	J.F. Evetts
February 11th	LIEUT. J.G.B. BOSVILLE went on leave to ENGLAND February 11th – 19th but later in civvies. Horse No 12 – brown chestnut – drawn from Mobile-Vet Sec: LA GORGUE in place of No C.C.5.	J.F. Evetts

1st Oxford Cyclist Coy

WAR DIARY
or
INTELLIGENCE SUMMARY.
(Erase heading not required.)

Army Form C. 2118.

Instructions regarding War Diaries and Intelligence Summaries are contained in F.S. Regs., Part II. and the Staff Manual respectively. Title pages will be prepared in manuscript.

Hour, Date, Place	Summary of Events and Information	Remarks and references to Appendices
February 12th:- CROIX BARBÉE 7.45 am - 12.30 pm	LIEUT. W.F.C. PICTHALL + 60 men paraded for digging under the direction of the R.E. Work on the Redoubts behind B LINES was continued. The roads were in bad condition owing to snow and weather.	J.F.E. Kent
February 13th:-	Nil	J.F.E. Kent
February 14th:- CROIX BARBÉE 7.45 am - 12.30 pm	LIEUT. H.B.N. SAVILE + 60 men paraded for digging under the direction of the R.E. Work on the Redoubts behind B LINES was continued. Very heavy rain + high winds -	J.F.E. Kent
February 15th:-	Nil	J.F.E. Kent

Official Cyclist Coy

WAR DIARY or INTELLIGENCE SUMMARY.

(Erase heading not required.)

Army Form C. 2118.

Instructions regarding War Diaries and Intelligence Summaries are contained in F.S. Regs., Part II. and the Staff Manual respectively. Title pages will be prepared in manuscript.

Hour, Date, Place	Summary of Events and Information	Remarks and references to Appendices
February 16th CROIX BARBÉE 7.45am – 12.30am	LIEUT. J.F. EVETTS & 60 men Paraded for digging with the R.E. Work on the redoubt behind B LINES was continued. A fine, bright morning, but the road where still very soft & heavy for cycling.	J.F. Edent
February 17th	LIEUT. J.G.B. BOSVILLE returned from leave	J.F.E. Lieut
February 18th RUE DE BACQUEROT 6.30pm – 2 am	LIEUT. N.E.C. PICTHALL & 60 men Paraded & new completed a new redoubt behind the junction of C and D lines. No. 1446 PTE. A. EVANS was killed at 10.30 pm. Type of work constructed :— Profile. Plan of Revetment. Borrow Pit.	J.F. Edent

Army Form C. 2118.

Stafford Gabot Coy

WAR DIARY or INTELLIGENCE SUMMARY.

(Erase heading not required.)

Instructions regarding War Diaries and Intelligence Summaries are contained in F.S. Regs., Part II. and the Staff Manual respectively. Title pages will be prepared in manuscript.

Hour, Date, Place	Summary of Events and Information	Remarks and references to Appendices
February 19th	Nil	J.F.E. Lieut
February 20th CROIX BARBÉE 12.30 pm - 4 pm	LIEUT. H.B.N. SAVILE + 50 men parades for digging under the direction of the R.E. Work behind B LINES was continued	J.F. Edwin
February 21st	Nil	J.F. Edwin
February 22nd CROIX BARBÉE 9 am - 12.45 pm	LIEUT. N.E.C. PICTHALL + 50 men parades to assist with the direction of the R.E. Work on A' post near CROIX BARBÉE was continued	J.F. Edwin
February 23rd	Nil	J.F. Edwin
February 24th	Nil	J.F. Edwin
February 25th B. LINES. H.Q. 1.40 pm - 6.30 pm 5.30 pm - 10 pm	CAPTAIN H.C.M. PORTER + 20 men reported at B LINES H.Q. for work under the R.E. The Redoubt near the H.Q. was completed. LIEUT. H.B.N. SAVILE + 30 men constructed a new Support trench in rear of C LINES —	J.F. Edwin

8th Bn Cyclist Coy.

WAR DIARY
INTELLIGENCE SUMMARY.

Army Form C. 2118.

Hour, Date, Place	Summary of Events and Information	Remarks and references to Appendices
February 26th BLINES H.Q. 6.15 pm – 11.30 pm	LIEUT. W.E.C. PICTHALL + 50 men paraded for digging within the R.E. Work was carried on in support trench. Casualties – Nil	J. Felner
February 27th	Nil	J. Felner
February 28th LESTREM 12 noon	H.Q. + Nos 1, 2, + 3 Platoons moved to new billets in LESTREM village.	J. Felner

Rudolph Strutt Capt
Comg. 8/Devil Cycle Coy.

1-3-15

Stn Ocio e Geluh Crz:

Vol IV 1 - 31.3.15

Army Form C. 2118.

WAR DIARY

or

INTELLIGENCE SUMMARY.

(*Erase heading not required.*)

Instructions regarding War Diaries and Intelligence Summaries are contained in F.S. Regs., Part II. and the Staff Manual respectively. Title pages will be prepared in manuscript.

Hour, Date, Place	Summary of Events and Information	Remarks and references to Appendices
	8/Divisional Cyclist Coy.	
	March, 1915.	

WAR DIARY or INTELLIGENCE SUMMARY

Army Form C. 2118.

9th Divisional Cyclist Company

Hour, Date, Place	Summary of Events and Information	Remarks and references to Appendices
LESTREM 11 a.m. 1st March 7 p.m. 1st March	No. 4 Platoon (two sections) reported from 23rd Infy Bgde. The Coy. 103 strong, relieved A Coy 2/Middx Regt. in the left portion of the Coy section of C division trenches at 7 p.m., the remainder of the left section being relieved by "C" Squadron of Northamptonshire Yeomanry. Lieut. BUSVILLE with 20 others joined the Coy. at C division 7 p.m. Distribution as follows:— Capt HEATH Lieut SAVILE 50 other ranks 8/CC 1 machine gun 4/Cameron } in left sub-section with Telephone Lieut PUCKTHALL 24 others 8/CC } in left centre sub-section Sergt DOTTS 24 others 8/CC 7 „ NY } in right centre sub-section Major BUCKNALL N.Y. Lieut WHITNABY 45 others 1 machine gun 4/Cameron } in right sub-section	(Omission from 27th Feb. Lieut EVETTS, Scottish Rifles, admitted to hospital with injured knee).

WAR DIARY
or
INTELLIGENCE SUMMARY.
(Erase heading not required.)

Army Form C. 2118.

Instructions regarding War Diaries and Intelligence Summaries are contained in F.S. Regs., Part II and the Staff Manual respectively. Title pages will be prepared in manuscript.

Hour, Date, Place	Summary of Events and Information	Remarks and references to Appendices
1st March (cont.)	2/Lt HORTON N.Y.? in detached post. 15 others. 2/Lt BOSVILE with 45 others B/CC in ration carries and brought forward HdQrs. C Coys. Very little firing during the night. The right hand portion of D Coys occupied by Sherwood Foresters. The centre & right sections of C Coys occupied by 4/Cameron. The O.R. & C Coys being the Co. of 4/Cameron.	
2nd March 11 a.m.	All quiet except occasional	Butt
6.30 p.m.	Remanded No 4 Platoon repaired at an loopholes. Lieut PIERTHALL gazed thro' a porthole by bullet.	Butt
8.0 p.m.	relieved him by Lieut. BOSVILE. No 6 Platoon from 25 Bty on reground H.Qrs at LESTREM	Butt
3rd March	Sniping as yesterday.	Butt

Army Form C. 2118.

WAR DIARY
or
INTELLIGENCE SUMMARY.
(Erase heading not required.)

Instructions regarding War Diaries and Intelligence Summaries are contained in F.S. Regs., Part II and the Staff Manual respectively. Title pages will be prepared in manuscript.

Hour, Date, Place	Summary of Events and Information	Remarks and references to Appendices
4th March 3.30 p.m.	Sniping as before. Telephone operator wounded in forearm when passing trenches.	
8.30 p.m.	Left section C. divn. relieved by A & B Squadrons N.Y. 1 man B/cc wounded on way out about 300 yds. short of Rue BACQUEROT. Returned to billets in LESTREM.	R.n.H.
5th March	NB 2nd part of the French work.	R n H
6th March	N.Y.	R n H
7th March 4.30 p.m.	Captain PORTER, Lieuts. PICKTHALL & SWANN with 112 other ranks proceeded to C divn H⁹ Qrs, where they were joined by 11 others from platoon with 24th Inf. Bgde. to occupy with C. Squadron N.Y. the left section of C. divn — the turn C. Squadron under Major MILLER N.Y. being on left of section & the B/cc on right.	R n H

(73989) W4141–463. 400,000. 9/14. H.&J.Ltd. Forms/C. 2118/10.

Army Form C. 2118.

WAR DIARY
or
INTELLIGENCE SUMMARY.
(Erase heading not required.)

Hour, Date, Place	Summary of Events and Information	Remarks and references to Appendices
8th March 12 noon.	Received orders to proceed with remainder of Coy. to H'Qrs. D lines the evening at 7 p.m. with a view to reoccupying the right centre section of D lines; that the 123 men under Capt PORTER in C lines being transferred to right centre section D lines.	
6 p.m.	Capt HEATH, & Lieut SAVILE with 33 others left LESTREM for D lines.	
10.30 p.m.	Relieved SHERWOOD FORESTERS in right centre section D lines.	[signature]
9th March. 12.30 a.m.	Lt. PICKTHALL's detached post joined the company from C lines. Coy. was distributed as follows:— Nos. 1, 2, and 3 platoons facing SE on SW side of road leading through trenches to MOULIN DE PIETRE; nos. 4, 5, and 6 platoons being responsible for road barrier and trenches to NE side of road. The right section D lines held by one coy. 4th CAMERONS, the left centre section held by NORTHANTS YEOMANRY	

WAR DIARY
or
INTELLIGENCE SUMMARY.

(Erase heading not required.)

Army Form C. 2118.

Instructions regarding War Diaries and Intelligence Summaries are contained in F.S. Regs., Part II. and the Staff Manual respectively. Title pages will be prepared in manuscript.

Hour, Date, Place		Summary of Events and Information	Remarks and references to Appendices
9th March.	7 p.m.	Intermittent sniping during the day. Operation order, marked (A), by Lt. Col. WICKHAM received.	See Appendix CSB
10th March.	7.30 a.m. 8 a.m. 3.8 p.m.	Our artillery bombardment commenced. Our artillery bombardment ceased. Message T.33. despatched, to which an answer was later received that "the artillery would attend to it. That trench however was never shelled. Consequently the enemy was able to withdraw later with their machine gun from (the advance) trench opposite, with their moral unimpaired, though they must have suffered certain casualties from their our rifle fire. About 300 prisoners were seen being marched away, to the rear of the right of C lines. Casualties to midnight — 1 man wounded.	See Appendix
11th March.		All quiet except for bombardment by our guns. Orders were received today not to fire to our front during the day.	CSB CSB

Army Form C. 2118.

WAR DIARY
or
INTELLIGENCE SUMMARY.
(Erase heading not required.)

Instructions regarding War Diaries and Intelligence Summaries are contained in F. S. Regs., Part II. and the Staff Manual respectively. Title pages will be prepared in manuscript.

Hour, Date, Place	Summary of Events and Information	Remarks and references to Appendices
12th March. 2.2 a.m.	Message (B) received.	See Appendix.
2.15 a.m.	Message (C) received.	See Appendix.
4.45 a.m.	Message (D) received.	See Appendix.
5.15 a.m.	The Coy. under Capt. PORTER, (less 4 men per platoon under Capt. HEATH) moved along the trenches to C lines.	
6.50 a.m.	Capt. PORTER returned with men of the Coy. saying that C lines were blocked with men of WILTSHIRE Regiment, driven from the trenches which they had previously captured from the enemy, and with men of the CAMERONS; consequently there was no room for more troops there. All men of Coy. returned to former stations in Right Centre, D Line.	
10.20 a.m.	1 Coy. of WARWICKS arrived with orders to hold the road through trenches with half the coy. on each side of the road. But as the right centre D lines was held by the cyclists and left centre had been evacuated by the NORTHANTS YEOMANRY, Capt. HEATH sent our coy. to the left centre section. About this time verbal orders were received from Staff Captain, 22nd Infy. Bde., that the Right Centre Section, D lines, was now under the orders of the 22nd Infy. Bde. (VII Div.), and that all troops in D lines were to be 150 yards clear or east side of the road during our bombardment which was to commence at 12 noon.	

Army Form C. 2118.

WAR DIARY
or
INTELLIGENCE SUMMARY.

(Erase heading not required.)

Instructions regarding War Diaries and Intelligence Summaries are contained in F.S. Regs., Part II. and the Staff Manual respectively. Title pages will be prepared in manuscript.

Hour, Date, Place	Summary of Events and Information	Remarks and references to Appendices
12th March. 11.45 a.m.	Accordingly, CYCLISTS from N.E. side of road were brought over to 150 yards clear of S.W. side of road, and Nos. 2 and 3 platoons closed further to the right so as to leave the necessary space clear.	
11.50 a.m.	Our bombardment commenced.	
12.30 p.m.	Our bombardment on front trenches of enemy ceased. Infantry of VII Div. were seen to our right front advancing N.E., and cleared the enemy's trenches on our right front.	
1.15 p.m.	Between 200-300 enemy from trenches on my right front came out and surrendered. (They were fired at by the machine gun from the enemy's advanced trench opposite [N.B. This was the trench and machine gun which I had asked the artillery to fire on yesterday.] One man came over from this advanced trench and surrendered to us. Enemy then evacuated this advanced trench in front of Right of Right Centre, D Coy.	
1.30 p.m.	About 200 men of the WARWICKSHIRE regiment crowded into our trenches.	
2.30-4.30	Our trenches were heavily bombarded by the enemy's guns, causing a loss of 5 killed and 18 wounded.	
6.15 p.m.	150 GRENADIER GUARDS and 100 details of other units,	

WAR DIARY
or
INTELLIGENCE SUMMARY

(Erase heading not required.)

Army Form C. 2118.

Hour, Date, Place	Summary of Events and Information	Remarks and references to Appendices
March 12th	Working parties, bomb throwers, engineers etc. came into our trenches. The GRENADIERS lay down in the open behind our fire trench and bivouacked there.	
6.30 p.m.	Message received from Right section D lines, that the CAMERONS were shortly to leave D lines.	
7.30 p.m.	As telephone communication was still interrupted, Capt. HEATH handed over command of the section to Capt. PORTER and proceeded to H.Q. D lines for orders, and thence to H.Q. of O.C., C and D lines, but could get no information except that the WARWICKS would shortly leave D lines. Thence he went to H.Q. 22nd Infy. Bde., explained to the Brigadier commanding 22nd Infy. Bde. the situation in the Right centre D lines, and informed him that the CAMERONS had gone away, gathering that they had gone so without any instructions from him. After communicating with H.Q. VII Div, the Brigadier commanding 22nd Infy. Bde. decided to replace the CAMERONS in Right centre section D lines with VII Div MOUNTED TROOPS.	
March 13th 2 a.m.	Capt. HEATH returned to the barrier on the road through the trenches with Staff Capt., 22nd Infy. Bde., where was the O.C. WARWICKS, and arranged with him that the CYCLISTS should not be sent forward to the newly captured German trench, as he had ordered during Capt. HEATH's absence.	
4 a.m.	Guided VII Div. MTD. TROOPS into Right section D lines.	

Army Form C. 2118.

WAR DIARY
or
INTELLIGENCE SUMMARY.
(Erase heading not required.)

Instructions regarding War Diaries and Intelligence Summaries are contained in F.S. Regs., Part II. and the Staff Manual respectively. Title pages will be prepared in manuscript.

Hour, Date, Place	Summary of Events and Information	Remarks and references to Appendices
March 13th		
4.45 a.m.	Capt. HEATH rejoined the Right Centre, D lines, and resumed command.	
5.45	50 GRENADIER GUARDS came into trenches and took over 60 yards on extreme left of right half of section.	
6.15	1 Coy. WARWICKS under Lt. ROBERTS came into trenches, 3 platoons going up to new firetrench, one platoon going into our support trench.	
7.45	Bde. Major, 22nd Infy. Bde, visited trenches and ordered the VIIth Div. Mounted Troops to leave Right sector, as the CAMERONS had returned. They went out through right centre section.	
8 a.m.		
10.15.	Details of R.E. working parties, bomb-throwers etc. came into trenches.	
11.	1 Coy. WARWICKS came into trenches from rear and went up to front by new communication trench dug during the night between R. centre section and captured German trench in front. O.C. Coy. said he had orders to attack recent house in front of our trenches with as many men as he could collect.	
12 noon.	Major Lloyd with his coy. WARWICKS arrived in R. centre section D lines from rear, and remained there, as he had left touch with his C.O. and had no orders.	
12.30 p.m.	Heavy bombardment by enemy commenced	
4.30	Bombardment ceased, though occasional shells continued	

WAR DIARY
or
INTELLIGENCE SUMMARY.
(Erase heading not required.)

Army Form C. 2118.

Hour, Date, Place	Summary of Events and Information	Remarks and references to Appendices
March 13th	to come into trenches till dark. Our casualties during their second day's bomb advancement were:— Killed 2, Wounded 18, Missing 1	The missing man was later found to have been admitted to Hospital, suffering from frostbite.
6.45 p.m.	Message (E) received, to say we should be relieved at 7 o'clock by the ROYAL WELSH FUSILIERS	See Appendix
7.30 p.m.	Brigadier commanding 22nd Infy. Bde. visited the barrier on road through trenches	[signature]
10 p.m.	CYCLISTS relieved by about 125 R.W.F. Coy. then returned to billets at LESTREM.	[signature]
March 14th	Nil	[signature]
March 15th	Nil	[signature]
March 16th	Nil	

WAR DIARY
or
INTELLIGENCE SUMMARY.

(Erase heading not required.)

Army Form C. 2118.

Hour, Date, Place	Summary of Events and Information	Remarks and references to Appendices
March 17th	nil	G.B.
March 18th	Orders were received to proceed to the trenches in as great strength as possible. 5 Officers and 103 Other ranks paraded at 5 p.m. The Coy. was stationed in support works, N.E. of NEUVE CHAPELLE, S. of RUE TILLELOY, distributed as follows. At point 20 7 Capt PORTER, Lt SWANN and 50 men. At point 6 Lt SAVILE and 2 platoons. Capt. HEATH, in command of the 25th Infy Bde Reserve, remained at the Bde Reserve H.Q., N. of RUE TILLELOY with 2 Coys Lincoln Regt.	G.B.
March 19th 7 p.m.	The Coy. was employed in burying dead and improving their trenches. Lt SAVILE and 50 men reported at R.IR.RIF.H.Q. as support for minor enterprise. Returned 12.20 a.m.	G.B.
March 20th 11.25 a.m.	The Coy. was similarly employed in burial and trench improvements. Message received ordering CYCLISTS to return to their billets	G.B.
12.40 p.m.	machine from present position at 8.30 p.m.	
3.15 p.m.	25th Infy Bde. Res. H.Q. shelled	
4.0 p.m.	ditto. ditto.	
8.30 p.m.	Casualties :- nil. Coy. returned to billets at LESTREM.	

Army Form C. 2118.

WAR DIARY
or
INTELLIGENCE SUMMARY.
(Erase heading not required.)

Instructions regarding War Diaries and Intelligence Summaries are contained in F. S. Regs., Part II. and the Staff Manual respectively. Title pages will be prepared in manuscript.

Hour, Date, Place	Summary of Events and Information	Remarks and references to Appendices
March 21st	nil.	SB
March 22nd	nil.	SB
March 23rd	nil.	SB
March 24th 10 a.m.	The Coy. moved from its billets at LESTREM to billets in LA GORGUE	SB
March 25th 2.30 p.m.	The Coy. moved from LA GORGUE to billets N. of LAVENTIE and N.W. of the Railway (square G.34(b)Ref. map LILLE, 36)	SB
March 26th	nil.	SB
March 27th	nil.	SB
March 28th	Lt. A.E. NORMAN, 3rd Batt: EAST SURREY Regt., 2nd Lt. H.E. MURPHY, 3rd Batt: ROYAL FUSILIERS, and 50 other ranks joined the company from England. Lt. NORMAN was posted to No. 3 Platoon, 2nd Lt. MURPHY to No. 6 Platoon.	SB
March 29th 9 a.m.	Lt. SAVILE with no. 1 Platoon, Lt. PICKTHALL with no. 2 Platoon	

Army Form C. 2118.

WAR DIARY
or
INTELLIGENCE SUMMARY.

(Erase heading not required.)

Instructions regarding War Diaries and Intelligence Summaries are contained in F.S. Regs., Part II. and the Staff Manual respectively. Title pages will be prepared in manuscript.

Hour, Date, Place	Summary of Events and Information	Remarks and references to Appendices
March 29th	reported at the Head quarters of the 23rd and 25th INFY. BDES., respectively and were attached thenceforward to those Brigades for duty.	
2.30 p.m.	Lt. NORMAN and 25 men paraded to represent the BRITISH EXPEDITIONARY FORCE at the funeral at SAILLY-SUR-LA-LYS of two men of the 143rd FRENCH (Territorial) Regiment, killed the previous day by the explosion of a bomb dropped from a German aeroplane.	
March 30th	Nil.	
March 31st	Nil.	

Rendered to Staff Capt. Com 2:8/ Divl Cyclists
2-4-15

(A) rec'd 7pm 9th

Operation Orders
by Lt. Col. H. Wickham
Commanding C & D Lines
Ref map 1:20000 & 1:5000

1. The village of NEUVE CHAPELLE will be attacked & aflame by assault columns. After which a further advance will be made to gain the line AUBERS — LE PLOUICH — LA CLIQUETERIE FARM — LIGNE LE GRAND

The attack on the village of Neuve Chapelle will be carried out in two stages by the 8th Div.

First Objective: Enemy's front & support trenches opposite B Lines.

Second Objective E & E Cops

of NEUVE-CHAPELLE village on the right & MOATED GRANGE on the left.
The Indians will co-operate on the right flank of the 8th Div.

2. Troops in C & D lines will keep up a heavy rifle fire & M.G. fire on enemy trenches in their front from the moment the artillery bombardment begins (7.30 am)
The infantry attack will commence at 8.5 am after which time men will be strictly cautioned against firing towards the line of advance on their supply.

3. In the event of an advance being ordered 4 orderlies have be with telephone operators as ready despatch

Sgnd. E. Lowther
Capt & Adjt

Notes.

1. During the advance the Infantry will indicate their positions as they get forward by the use of Verey's lights.

2. Bombing parties will mark their position in captured trenches by blue signalling flags. The Grenadiers of the Indian Corps are using pink flags for the same purpose.

3. Great care must be exercised by officers to see that their men do not join in with the Infantry attack.

JG Lowther
Capt & Adj

MESSAGES AND SIGNALS.

Prefix	Code	m.	Words	Charge	This message is on a/c of :	Recd. at	m.
Office of Origin and Service Instructions.			Sent	(B)		Date	
			At	m.	Service.	From	
			To				
			By		(Signature of "Franking Officer.")	By	

TO O C BATTALION, O C CAMERON
O C A SQUADRON B, C,

| Sender's Number | Day of Month | In reply to Number | **AAA** |

The Bombardment will begin at 7.80 AM and the attack at 8 am unless postponed on account of this mist AAA D lines should be cleared by 7 am not 6.30 am.

C.M. A squadron to
Cdr. B Squadron

Received
pr Burton Capt
8.2. and
12/3/15

From S.H. R.
Place
Time

The above may be forwarded as now corrected. (Z)

Censor. Signature of Addressee or person authorised to telegraph in his name
*This line should be erased if not required.

3662 M. & Co. Ltd. Wt. W929/549—100,000. 6/14. Forms C2121/10.

"A" Form.

MESSAGES AND SIGNALS.

No. of Message _____

Prefix **SM** Code ____ m. Words Charge This message is on a/c of: Recd. at ____ m.
Office of O___ and Service Instructions. Sent Date ____
 At ____ m. Service. From ____
 To (Signature of "Franking Officer.") By ____
 By

TO | O C CYCLIST D. LINES | A B and C SQUADRONS
   | A COY. CAMERONS |

Sender's Number | Day of Month | In reply to Number | **AAA**
C L 78 | 12 | |

Reference G 570 the clearing
of D Lines should be carried
out very secretly AAA
2. 2nd Bde of ○ Divn
will keep watch over trenches
temporarily vacated AAA

A.G. m.
   S.
ask Insp..

Received 2.30 am
M Denton Capt

From Q H Q S
Place
Time 2.15 AM

The above may be forwarded as now corrected. (2)

Censor. Signature of Addressor or person authorised to telegraph in his name
*This line should be erased if not required.

"A" Form.

MESSAGES AND SIGNALS.

Prefix SM Code CLRA Words 55 Charge
Office of Origin and Service Instructions.
Sent
At
By
(Signature of "Franking Officer.")

Recd. at ___ m.
Date 12.3.15
From HQ
By H. Newton

O C RIGH CENTRE
O C A squadron O C B squadron
O C C squadron

Sender's Number CDL21
Day of Month 12th
In reply to Number
AAA

Further orders from 8th Div
say bombardment commences
7.30 AM instead of 4 AM AAA
permission has been given
to clear lines before
daylight in order to insure
secrecy AAA Very few men
may be left to maintain
fire to 7 AM AAA

C. M. D & B R Newton
Capt
Rcd 4.45 am

From O C C and D LINES
Place
Time 3.59

"A" Form. Army Form C. 2121.

MESSAGES AND SIGNALS.

To: Eighth Divisional Cyclists

Sender's Number	Day of Month	In reply to Number	AAA
BM 452	Thirteenth		

You will be relieved tonight about 7 pm by the R Welsh Fus please arrange for an officer to point out Trenches and meet officer from above regiment.

Rec'd 6.45 pm

From 2/ W/ Bde
Place
Time 4.55 pm

Signature of Addressee: Elgar Thurlow
Capt
BM

121/5256

8th Division.

8th Div'l Cyclist Coy.

Vol II 1 — 30.4.15.

Army Form C. 2118.

WAR DIARY

INTELLIGENCE SUMMARY.

(Erase heading not required.)

Instructions regarding War Diaries and Intelligence Summaries are contained in F.S. Regs., Part II and the Staff Manual respectively. Title pages will be prepared in manuscript.

8/Divisional Cyclist Company.

April. 1915.

Hour, Date, Place	Summary of Events and Information	Remarks and references to Appendices

Army Form C. 2118.

WAR DIARY
or
INTELLIGENCE SUMMARY. CSB

(Erase heading not required.)

Instructions regarding War Diaries and Intelligence Summaries are contained in F.S. Regs., Part II. and the Staff Manual respectively. Title pages will be prepared in manuscript.

Hour, Date, Place	Summary of Events and Information	Remarks and references to Appendices
April 1st. 7.15 p.m — 1.30 a.m	Lt. H.N. SWANN and 50 men paraded at RUE PETILLON under the direction of the R.E. This party was used for carrying material up to the trenches and for repairing communication trenches.	CSB
April 2nd.	Nil.	CSB
April 3rd.	Nil.	CSB
April 4th 1.30 p.m.	Lt. H.B.W. SAVILE and no.1 platoon rejoined the Coy.	CSB
April 5th	Nil.	CSB
April 6th 6.55 p.m — 12.30 a.m	Two working parties, under Lt. SAVILE and 2nd Lt. MURPHY, each of 25 N.C.O.s and men paraded and under the direction of the R.E. They were employed in the right and left sectn, right Bde, respectively, in carrying up materials. They returned at 12.30 a.m. and 1 a.m. respectively. Casualty :- one man wounded	CSB
April 7th	Nil.	CSB

Army Form C. 2118.

WAR DIARY
or
INTELLIGENCE SUMMARY.

(Erase heading not required.)

Instructions regarding War Diaries and Intelligence Summaries are contained in F.S. Regs., Part II. and the Staff Manual respectively. Title pages will be prepared in manuscript.

Hour, Date, Place	Summary of Events and Information	Remarks and references to Appendices
April 8th	Nil.	SSB
April 9th	Nil.	SSB
April 10th	Nil.	SSB
April 11th	On this and subsequent days a permanent working party was found by the Coy. for the construction of works at S.W. end of the RUE PETILLON (N.8.b., N.9.a., N.8.c.), the party consisting of Nos. 4 and 6 Platoons under Capt. PORTER, and the platoon commanders, and work being carried on in daylight from 9.30 a.m. to 4 p.m. Lt. MURPHY and no. 6 Platoon undertook the construction of work no.1 b., situated at the point N.8.b.7.6. in the N.W. angle formed by the RUE PETILLON and the road into which it runs. A rough plan of the work is appended.	SSB

Road to ROUGE DE BOUT and SAILLY sur LA LYS

⊕ = Water-Butt
▨ = Dug-out
▭ = Latrine

RUE PETILLON

Army Form C. 2118.

WAR DIARY
or
INTELLIGENCE SUMMARY. (B)
(Erase heading not required.)

Instructions regarding War Diaries and Intelligence Summaries are contained in F.S. Regs., Part II. and the Staff Manual respectively. Title pages will be prepared in manuscript.

Hour, Date, Place	Summary of Events and Information	Remarks and references to Appendices
April 11th	Lt. SWANN and no. 4 Platoon undertook the completion of work I.C., situated at Map. S N.9.a.3.7. when construction was taken over by the party, the work consisted of the fire position and 4 bombproof shelters. The party was to erect a back parapet, strengthen the bombproof shelters and improve the work generally. A rough plan is attached:— ↑ Communication trench, the mouth of which is about 80 yards from the RUE PETILLON. Direction of Enemy → ▨ = Bombproof shelters ⛔ = Trees	

Army Form C. 2118.

WAR DIARY
or
INTELLIGENCE SUMMARY.
(Erase heading not required.)

Instructions regarding War Diaries and Intelligence Summaries are contained in F.S. Regs., Part II. and the Staff Manual respectively. Title pages will be prepared in manuscript.

Hour, Date, Place	Summary of Events and Information	Remarks and references to Appendices
12th April 9.30 a.m – 4 p.m. 3-15 p.m	Working party as above. Casualty:- 1 man wounded. Lt. SAVILLE and no 1 Platoon rejoined the 23rd INFY BDE. H.Q.	SB
13th April. 9.30 a.m – 4 p.m.	Working party as above. Casualty:- 1 man wounded.	SB
14th April. 9.30 a.m – 4 p.m.	Working party as above. The Company moved to new billets, at LE NOUVEAU MONDE on the ESTAIRES—SAILLY main road.	SB
15th April. 9.30 a.m – 4 p.m.	Working party as above.	SB
16th April. 9.30 a.m – 4 p.m.	Working party as above. Casualty:- 1 man wounded.	SB
17th April. 9.30 – 4 p.m.	Working party as above. Captain H.C.M. PORTER, having been detailed for duty as Bde. Machine Gun Officer, 24th INFY. BDE., was struck off the strength of the Coy.	SB
18th April.	Working party as above. Lt. MURPHY and no. 6 Platoon, having finished the work lt., undertook the improvement and completion of work 1a, situated at N.8.a.5.3., on the S.E. side of RUE TILLELOY. Of this work the part previously constructed consisted of the fire-positions, these not having been built up to a	

Army Form C. 2118.

WAR DIARY
or
INTELLIGENCE SUMMARY. GB

(Erase heading not required.)

Instructions regarding War Diaries and Intelligence Summaries are contained in F. S. Regs., Part II. and the Staff Manual respectively. Title pages will be prepared in manuscript.

Hour, Date, Place	Summary of Events and Information	Remarks and references to Appendices
18th April	sufficient height, and 5 large dugouts inadequately protected. The party had therefore to improve and built up the fire positions, to strengthen the Bomb proof shelters to erect obstacles, and to make numerous improvements in detail. A rough sketch of the work is appended. ▨ = Bomb proof shelter ⊕ = water butt ▭ = latrine ↯ = hedge [sketch map showing RUE TILLELOY, position with M.G., shelters, direction of enemy] Casualties :- 1 man wounded	GB

Army Form C. 2118.

WAR DIARY
or
INTELLIGENCE SUMMARY. SB

(Erase heading not required.)

Instructions regarding War Diaries and Intelligence Summaries are contained in F.S. Regs., Part II. and the Staff Manual respectively. Title pages will be prepared in manuscript.

Hour, Date, Place	Summary of Events and Information	Remarks and references to Appendices
18th April (continued)	No. 5 platoon rejoined the Coy, from the 24th Inf. Bde; Lt. BOSVILE, however, remained with the Brigade till such time as he could be relieved of his duties as bomb instructor.	SB
19th April	Working party as before.	SB
20th April	Working party as before. 2nd Lieut E.S. MOLYNEUX joined the Coy. for duty.	SB
21st April	Working party as before. Lt. J.G.B. BOSVILE was admitted to hospital	SB
22nd April. 8.15 a.m.	Lt. NORMAN and a working party of 90 N.C.O's and men were engaged, under the 15th Coy, R.E., in improving the SAILLY-ROUGE DEBOUT road. 12 N.C.O's and men were passed out from a course of instruction in bombthrowing as qualified, and returned to duty.	
7.15 p.m.	Lt. MURPHY and a working party of 50 N.C.O's and men were employed in carrying up materials to the Right Bde. trenches S.E. of the RUE PETILLON, under the direction of the 1st HOME COUNTIES R.E. The permanent working parties were (this day) continued.	SB
23rd April	The permanent working party found by No 6 Platoon was employed as usual.	SB

WAR DIARY
or
INTELLIGENCE SUMMARY.

Army Form C. 2118.

(Erase heading not required.)

Hour, Date, Place	Summary of Events and Information	Remarks and references to Appendices
24th April.	Working parties as usual. Nos 1 and 2 Platoons reported to Coy. from the 23rd and 25th Inf. Bdes. respectively.	GB
25th April.	The permanent working parties found since April 11th were discontinued and returned to duty.	GB
26th April.	The Coy. changed billets, moving to barns on the two roads running N. and S. through square L.9.c. (W. of DOULIEU)	GB
27th April	Nil	GB
28th April 8.0 p.m. — 11.30 p.m.	A working party, consisting of Nos. 5 and 6 Platoons under 2/Lt MOLYNEUX and Lt MURPHY respectively, paraded under the 2nd Field Coy. R.E. at RUE DU BOIS cross-roads and were employed in digging support-trenches	GB
29th April.	Nil.	GB
30th April.	Lt NORMAN and 25 other ranks of No. 3 Platoon were attached for temporary duty to the A.P.M., 2ND ARMY, at HAZEBROUCK.	GB

Rudolph Heath Capt
Comn 8/Divl Cycle Coy

8ten Div. l'Golist Corp.

Bd. VII 1 – 31.5.15.

Army Form C. 2118.

WAR DIARY
or
INTELLIGENCE SUMMARY.
(Erase heading not required.)

Instructions regarding War Diaries and Intelligence Summaries are contained in F.S. Regs., Part II. and the Staff Manual respectively. Title pages will be prepared in manuscript.

Hour, Date, Place	Summary of Events and Information	Remarks and references to Appendices
	8/Divisional Cyclist Company May, 1915.	

Army Form C. 2118.

WAR DIARY
or
INTELLIGENCE SUMMARY. GSB
(Erase heading not required.)

Instructions regarding War Diaries and Intelligence Summaries are contained in F.S. Regs., Part II. and the Staff Manual respectively. Title pages will be prepared in manuscript.

Hour, Date, Place	Summary of Events and Information	Remarks and references to Appendices
May 1st	A tactical scheme was carried out in conjunction with the NORTHUMBERLAND HUSSARS, C. Squadron.	GSB
May 2nd	Nil.	GSB
May 3rd	Lt. NORMAN and No. 3 Platoon rejoined the Company. Lt DAVIES and 33 other ranks were employed as a working party, billetted in disused trenches	GSB
May 4th	Nil.	GSB
May 5th	Nil.	GSB
May 6th	Lt. PICKTHALL, Lt. NORMAN and nos. 2, 3, and 6 platoons were employed as a working party, under the 15th Field Coy, R.E., in digging communication trenches S.E. of RUE PETILLON, in front of no. 1 H.Q. Casualty :— 1 man wounded.	GSB
May 7th	Lt SWANN and no 4 Platoon were attached to the 23rd Inf. Bde. for duty Lt NORMAN " no. 3 Platoon " " " 24th " " " Lt MURPHY " no. 6 Platoon " " " 25th " " " Lt MURPHY " " " GSB	
7:30 p.m	The Operation Orders received earlier were deferred for another 24 hours	GSB

Army Form C. 2118.

WAR DIARY
or
INTELLIGENCE SUMMARY.
(Erase heading not required.)

Instructions regarding War Diaries and Intelligence Summaries are contained in F.S. Regs., Part II. and the Staff Manual respectively. Title pages will be prepared in manuscript.

Hour, Date, Place		Summary of Events and Information	Remarks and references to Appendices
May 8th	11.30 p.m.	The Coy. (less 3 platoons, attached to Brigade) paraded and left for CROIX BLANCHE, in connection with projected operations.	SSB
May 9th	1.30 a.m.	The Coy. arrived at CROIX BLANCHE	
	5 a.m.	Shelter trenches were dug 100 yards N. of the crossroads	
	8 p.m.	Orders were received to return to billets. The Coy. then returned to its billets S.W. of DOULIEU.	
		Casualties:– (all in detached platoons)	
		1 Officer (Lt NORMAN) wounded:– (since died of wounds).	
		2 men wounded	
May 10th	9.15 a.m.	Lt. MURPHY and no 6 Platoon rejoined the Coy. from 25th Inf. Bde. 1 man wounded in action this day.	SSB
May 11th		Lt. NORMAN died of wounds in MERVILLE Hospital	SSB
May 12th		No 3 Platoon rejoined the Coy. from 26th Inf. Bde. Lt J.G.B. BOYLE invalided to England, was struck off the strength of the Coy.	SSB
May 13th		nil	SSB
May 14th		nil	SSB

Army Form C. 2118.

WAR DIARY
or
INTELLIGENCE SUMMARY. SB

(Erase heading not required.)

Instructions regarding War Diaries and Intelligence Summaries are contained in F.S. Regs., Part II. and the Staff Manual respectively. Title pages will be prepared in manuscript.

Hour, Date, Place	Summary of Events and Information	Remarks and references to Appendices
May 15th	A tactical exercise was carried out in conjunction with the NORTHUMBERLAND HUSSARS ("C" Squadron)	SB
May 16th	The Coy. changed its billets, moving to the road W. and N. of the road junction L.10.d.	SB
May 17th	nil.	SB
May 18th	nil	SB
May 19th	nil.	SB
May 20th	2nd Lt. E.D.S. CASWELL, 6th Batt. RIFLE BDE., reported for duty and was taken on the strength from this day. 2nd Lt. E.D.S. CASWELL took over command of No. 3 Platoon.	SB
May 21st	nil	SB
May 22nd	2nd Lt. CASWELL and 30 men was employed as a working party on RUE TILELOY under the 15th FIELD Coy RE., in carrying materials etc.	SB
May 23rd	Lt. H.M. SWANN and No. 3 platoon rejoined the Coy. from 23rd Inf. Bde.	SB

WAR DIARY or INTELLIGENCE SUMMARY.

Army Form C. 2118.

(Erase heading not required.)

Instructions regarding War Diaries and Intelligence Summaries are contained in F.S. Regs., Part II. and the Staff Manual respectively. Title pages will be prepared in manuscript.

Hour, Date, Place	Summary of Events and Information	Remarks and references to Appendices
May 24th	Nil.	SSB
May 25th	A tactical exercise was carried out in conjunction with C squadron NORTHUMBERLAND HUSSARS	SSB
May 26th	A draft of 1 N.C.O and 6 men joined the Company this day.	SSB
May 27th	Nil.	SSB
May 28th	A reconnaissance scheme was carried out in conjunction with the Divisional Cavalry. 2 N.C.O's and 5 men this day rejoined the Coy. from the Base Depot at LE HAVRE	SSB
May 29th	Nil	SSB
May 30th	Lt E.S. MOLYNEUX proceeded to England on leave May 30th to June 5th both dates inclusive	SSB
May 31st 8 p.m. — 12 midnight	A tactical exercise was carried out in conjunction with the Divisional Cavalry. Lt SUMMIN and 30 men paraded at PONT LOOP as a working party under the 15th FIELD COY R.E, and were employed in carrying material from EBENEZER FARM to the left sector C line.	SSB

Ronald Hythe Heapthy Capt.
Comdg. 8th Divl. Cyclist Coy.

121/5871.

8th 15/1/1920

8th Divl: Cyclist Coy:

Vol VII June 1915

Army Form C. 2118.

WAR DIARY
or
INTELLIGENCE SUMMARY
(Erase heading not required.)

8/Divisional Cyclist Coy.

June, 1915

Army Form C. 2118.

WAR DIARY
or
INTELLIGENCE SUMMARY.
(Erase heading not required.)

Instructions regarding War Diaries and Intelligence Summaries are contained in F.S. Regs., Part II. and the Staff Manual respectively. Title pages will be prepared in manuscript.

Hour, Date, Place	Summary of Events and Information	Remarks and references to Appendices
June 1st.	nil.	
June 2nd	An advanced guard scheme was carried out in conjunction with the divisional cavalry. 2/Lt MURPHY was struck off the strength and returned to duty	SPB
June 3rd	nil.	SPB
June 4th	An outpost scheme was carried out in conjunction with the divisional cavalry	SPB
June 5th	2nd Lt E.S. MOLYNEUX returned from leave	SPB
June 6th	nil.	SPB
June 7th	A tactical scheme was carried out in conjunction with the divisional cavalry	SPB
	Major A.D. VAUGHAN, 14th Batt. NORTHUMBERLAND FUSILIERS, commanding 21/Divisional M.G. Troops, arrived from England to study conditions and methods of employing cyclists at the front.	SPB

WAR DIARY
or
INTELLIGENCE SUMMARY.

(Erase heading not required.)

Army Form C. 2118.

Hour, Date, Place	Summary of Events and Information	Remarks and references to Appendices
June 8th 9pm - 1am	2nd Lt. E.S. MOLYNEUX and 50 men paraded as a working party under the 15th Field Coy, R.E., and were employed in reconstructing captured GERMAN trenches S. of the MOATED GRANGE.	SB
June 9th	Major VAUGHAN left, having concluded his visit	SB
June 10th 8am	No 2 Section (No 1 Platoon) paraded and proceeded to be attached to 23rd Infy Bde. HQ Coy: they were for duty thenceforth	SB
June 11th	A tactical scheme was carried out in conjunction with the divisional cavalry	SB
June 12th	nil.	SB
June 13th	nil.	SB
June 14th	A tactical scheme was carried out in conjunction with the divisional cavalry.	SB
June 15th	nil.	SB
June 16th 7.30pm	2nd Lt PICKTHALL, 2nd Lt CASWELL and 100 other ranks proceeded to the trenches for trench duty with the 2/DEVONSHIRE REGT. They occupied part of F4 and part of P1.	SB
9.30pm	This party relieved the 2/WEST YORKSHIRE REGT in the above section of trench. Casualties:- nil.	SB

Army Form C. 2118.

WAR DIARY
or
INTELLIGENCE SUMMARY.
(Erase heading not required.)

Instructions regarding War Diaries and Intelligence Summaries are contained in F.S. Regs., Part II. and the Staff Manual respectively. Title pages will be prepared in manuscript.

Hour, Date, Place	Summary of Events and Information	Remarks and references to Appendices
June 17th	2nd Lt. Robson relieved 2nd Lt. Robson at No 2 Sector. 2nd Lt Robson at the 2nd Inf. Bde. Hd. Qrs. Trench party: - Improve trenches. Casualties: - Nil.	
June 18th 2.30 p-	Trench party: - strengthens parapet, put on new loopholes. Acquired 2 loopholes. Trenches were shelled. Parapet hit twice. Casualties: - Nil. 2nd Lt N.J. WILLANS, 8th Batt. K.R.R. joined the Coy for duty.	
June 19th 1 a.m.	Trench party. Cut trench grass in front of trenches. No firing. Casualties: Nil. Improved trenches during the Day.	
June 20th 2 p.m.	Trenches were shelled. Casualty: - 1 man wounded. Lt SWANN was granted 7 days leave of absence to England.	
June 21st 3 p-	Improve trenches. Germans shelled our trenches. Casualties - Nil.	
June 22nd 10 p-	Improve trenches. Relieved by 2/1 WEST YORKSHIRE REGT. Ration Party then returned to billets near DOULIEU	

Army Form C. 2118.

WAR DIARY
or
INTELLIGENCE SUMMARY.
(Erase heading not required.)

Instructions regarding War Diaries and Intelligence Summaries are contained in F.S. Regs., Part II. and the Staff Manual respectively. Title pages will be prepared in manuscript.

Hour, Date, Place	Summary of Events and Information	Remarks and references to Appendices
June 23rd	Nil.	SB
June 24th	Billets inspected by G.O.C. 8th Div. A draft of 5 men joined the Coy. for duty.	SB
June 25th	Nil.	SB
June 26th	Lt SWANN returned from leave. Lt W.E.C. PICKTHALL went on leave to ENGLAND	SB
June 27th	Nil.	SB
June 28th	A tactical scheme was carried out, in conjunction with the divisional cavalry.	SB
June 29th	Nil.	SB
June 30th	Nil.	SB

Ronald H Heath Captain
Comdg 8 Divl. Cycle Coy.

8th Division

121/6410

8th Div: Gen'l Cy
Vol XIII
From 15th to 31st July 1915.

Army Form C. 2118.

WAR DIARY
or
INTELLIGENCE SUMMARY. (SB)

(Erase heading not required.)

Instructions regarding War Diaries and Intelligence Summaries are contained in F.S. Regs., Part II. and the Staff Manual respectively. Title pages will be prepared in manuscript.

Hour, Date, Place	Summary of Events and Information	Remarks and references to Appendices
July 1st	No 4 section, no 1 platoon, relieved no 3 section at HQ Gro 23rd Inf. Bde.	SB
July 2nd	A tactical exercise was carried out in conjunction with the divisional cavalry	SB
July 3rd	Lt H.E. MURPHY and 50 men paraded as a working party under the 15th Field Coy. R.E. and were employed in digging trenches near TOUQUET. 1.36.a. (Ref Map B.36) Lt PICKTHALL returned from leave	SB
July 4th	Lt SAVILE went on leave to England, July 5th – July 12th both dates inclusive.	SB
July 5th	Nil.	SB
July 6th	1 man rejoined the Coy. from ROUEN	SB
July 7th	Lt CASWELL and 70 men paraded as a working party under the 15th Field Coy. R.E. and were employed in digging trenches near LA BOUTILLERIE, N.5.a. (Ref Map B.36)	SB

Army Form C. 2118.

WAR DIARY
or
INTELLIGENCE SUMMARY.
(Erase heading not required.)

Instructions regarding War Diaries and Intelligence Summaries are contained in F. S. Regs., Part II. and the Staff Manual respectively. Title pages will be prepared in manuscript.

Hour, Date, Place	Summary of Events and Information	Remarks and references to Appendices
July 8th	Nil.	S.B.
July 9th	A tactical scheme was carried out in conjunction with the divisional cavalry.	S.B.
July 10th	Nil.	S.B.
July 11th 9 p.m. — 1.15 a.m.	2Lt SWANN, 2Lt WILLANS and 70 other ranks paraded at CROIX BLANCHE as a working party, under the 15th Field Coy. R.E., and were employed in filling sandbags and widening communication trenches	S.B.
July 12th	Lt SAMLE returned from leave.	S.B.
July 13th	A tactical scheme was carried out in conjunction with the divisional cavalry.	S.B.
July 14th	Nil	N.C.

Army Form C. 2118.

WAR DIARY
or
INTELLIGENCE SUMMARY. 11/08

(Erase heading not required.)

Instructions regarding War Diaries and Intelligence Summaries are contained in F. S. Regs., Part II. and the Staff Manual respectively. Title pages will be prepared in manuscript.

Hour, Date, Place	Summary of Events and Information	Remarks and references to Appendices
July 15th	2nd Lieut E.S. Molyneut and 70 O.R. paraded at CROIX BLANCHE at a working party under Field Coy R.E. Work done — Carrying material up to 1st line. Straightening communication trenches.	K.W.T.
July 16th	Nil	K.W.T.
July 17th	A tactical exercise was carried out in conjunction with the divisional cavalry.	K.W.T.
July 18th	Nil	K.W.T.
July 19th	Nil	K.W.T.
July 20th	Nil	K.W.T.
July 21st	Capt. P.R. Hewitt D.S.O. proceeded to the U.K. on leave of absence.	K.W.T.
July 22nd	No 6 Section relieved No 5 Section at 23. H.P. 3rd Hyre. A tactical exercise was carried out in conjunction with the divisional cavalry. Lieut Barrow returned from leave.	K.W.T.

(73989) W4141—463. 400,000. 9/14. H.&J.Ltd. Forms/C. 2118/10.

WAR DIARY
or
INTELLIGENCE SUMMARY.

Army Form C. 2118.

(Erase heading not required.)

Hour, Date, Place	Summary of Events and Information	Remarks and references to Appendices
July 23rd	N.T.R.	W.O.S
July 24th RUE DU QUESNEZ	Lieut N.B.W. Sante and 70 o.r. paraded as a working party under 15th Field Coy. R.E.	W.O.S
July 25th	N.T.R.	W.O.S
July 26th	A Tactical exercise was carried out in conjunction with the Divisional Cavalry.	W.O.S
July 27th	N.T.R.	W.O.S
July 28th	N.T.R.	W.O.S
July 29th ELBOW FARM	Lieuts Sante, Murphy and 2nd Lieut Williams and 100 o.r. occupied the redoubt (Post 28) for the purpose of clearing the R. LAVES. There is some behind the line occupied by the Division.	W.O.S
July 30th	Capt R.R. Keatt returned from leave, and reported for duty at the 8th Divisional H.Q.	W.O.S

Army Form C. 2118.

WAR DIARY
or
INTELLIGENCE SUMMARY.
(Erase heading not required.)

Instructions regarding War Diaries and Intelligence Summaries are contained in F.S. Regs., Part II. and the Staff Manual respectively. Title pages will be prepared in manuscript.

Hour, Date, Place	Summary of Events and Information	Remarks and references to Appendices
July 31st	Nil	Nil

121/7051

8th Division

8th Divl: Cyclist Coy

Vol IX

Aug & Sep 15

Army Form C. 2118.

WAR DIARY
or
INTELLIGENCE SUMMARY.

(Erase heading not required.)

Instructions regarding War Diaries and Intelligence Summaries are contained in F.S. Regs., Part II. and the Staff Manual respectively. Title pages will be prepared in manuscript.

Hour, Date, Place	Summary of Events and Information	Remarks and references to Appendices
	War Diary for August & September. 1915	

Army Form C. 2118.

WAR DIARY
or
INTELLIGENCE SUMMARY.

(Erase heading not required.)

Instructions regarding War Diaries and Intelligence Summaries are contained in F.S. Regs., Part II. and the Staff Manual respectively. Title pages will be prepared in manuscript.

Hour, Date, Place	Summary of Events and Information	Remarks and references to Appendices
July 31st	Nil	Nil
August 1st	N.E.	Nil
August 2nd	N.E.	Nil
August 3rd	N.E.	Nil
August 4th	River LAYES working party was relieved	Nil
August 5th	The 20th Divl Cyclist Company (less 3 platoons) arrived this day, & be attached for Instructional purposes.	Nil
August 6th	N.E.	Nil
August 7th	N.E.	Nil
August 8th	N.E.	Nil
August 9th	A tactical exercise was carried in conjunction with the divisional cavalry and the attached platoons of the 20th Divl Cyclist Company.	Nil

R du LAYES

No 136 Pte Hopkins h. was wounded while working party.

(73989) W41141—463. 400,000. 9/14. H.&J.Ltd. Forms/C. 2118/10.

Army Form C. 2118.

WAR DIARY
or
INTELLIGENCE SUMMARY.

(Erase heading not required.)

Instructions regarding War Diaries and Intelligence Summaries are contained in F.S. Regs., Part II. and the Staff Manual respectively. Title pages will be prepared in manuscript.

Hour, Date, Place	Summary of Events and Information	Remarks and references to Appendices
August 10th	R. LAYES. Nothing particular was returned this day. Lieut N.E. Murphy proceeded to Ireland on leave of absence	NOS
August 11th	NIL	NOS
August 12th	3 platoons of the 25th Divl Cyclist Company arrived to be attached for instruction.	NOS
August 13th	A tactical exercise was carried out in conjunction with the divisional cavalry and 3 platoons 25th Divl Cyclist Company.	NOS
August 14th	A horse show was held by the 8th Division this day on the banks of the R. LYS. In an event for the best turned out cyclist in the division the following men gained the first three prizes — 7/Cpl Langton Pte Regan Pte Walker	NOS

Army Form C. 2118.

WAR DIARY
or
INTELLIGENCE SUMMARY.
(Erase heading not required.)

Hour, Date, Place	Summary of Events and Information	Remarks and references to Appendices
August 14th (Continued)	No 1345 - Cpl Horton & No 477 Pte Thompson proceeded to the base at ROUEN for discharge. No 355 - Capt Dyches took over the duties of Transport Capt vice Pte Phillips returned to duty.	N.S.
August 15th	Nil	N.S.
August 16th	R. LAVES working party was relieved this day. No 1458 Pte R. Grant wounded whilst working in R. LAVES	N.S.

Army Form C. 2118.

WAR DIARY
or
INTELLIGENCE SUMMARY.
(Erase heading not required.)

Instructions regarding War Diaries and Intelligence Summaries are contained in F. S. Regs., Part II. and the Staff Manual respectively. Title pages will be prepared in manuscript.

Hour, Date, Place	Summary of Events and Information	Remarks and references to Appendices
GRAND BAIS		
Aug 17th	Nil	hot
Aug 18th	Nil	hot
Aug 19th	Nil	hot
Aug 20th	Nil	hot
Aug 21st	Nil	hot
Aug 22nd	3 officers and 100 other ranks at work on River LAYES, GAdet in Post 29 (ELBOW FARM)	hot
Aug 23rd	Relief of River LAYES working party.	hot
Aug 24th	Work on River LAYES completed	hot
Aug 25th	Return of working party.	hot
Aug 26th	¾ hour G.S. BARROW (interpreter) proceeds to England on appointment to the R.F.A. (S.R.)	hot
Aug 27th	Nil	hot
Aug 28th	No 1 Platoon moves to new billet in the METEREN BECQUE road	hot
Aug 29th	Working party found by No 2 Platoon	hot
Aug 30th	Nil	hot
Aug 31st	Nil	hot

Army Form C. 2118.

WAR DIARY
or
INTELLIGENCE SUMMARY.

(Erase heading not required.)

Instructions regarding War Diaries and Intelligence Summaries are contained in F.S. Regs., Part II. and the Staff Manual respectively. Title pages will be prepared in manuscript.

Place	Hour, Date	Summary of Events and Information	Remarks and references to Appendices
GRAND BOIS	Sep 1st 6.45 p.m.	A working party of 70 NCOs & men paraded under Lieut MURPHY for work under the R.E.	NiF.
"	Sep 2nd 7.15 a.m.	A working party of 70 NCOs & men paraded under Lieut MOLYNEUX	NiF.
"	Sep 3rd	" " " " " SAVILE. The remainder of the ten(?) Company were at work on the ditches in the billeting area	NiF
BOIS	Sep 4th	The working parties (20 Y. 30 NCOs & men) paraded under Lieut CASSWELL for work under the R.E.	NiF
GRAND BOIS	Sep 5th	N.C.	NiF
	Sep 6th	Three working parties of 20 men paraded at 11.45 a.m. 1.45 p.m. and 3.45 p.m. respectively under Lieut PICKTHALL. They formed a carrying party under the supervision of the R.E. The remainder of the Company continued the work of clearing ditches & cutting wood for the improvement of billets	NiF

Army Form C. 2118.

WAR DIARY
or
INTELLIGENCE SUMMARY.

(Erase heading not required.)

Hour, Date, Place	Summary of Events and Information	Remarks and references to Appendices
CROIX ... Sept 7th 5·45 pm	Lieut WILLANS and 30 other ranks paraded for work under the R.E.	MS
GRAND BOIS Sep 8th 7·45 a.m.	The remainder of the Company continued the work of cleaning my ditches and cutting trees for repair of billets.	
	Orders having been received that the BECQUE DE BIEZ was to be cleared out from CROIX BLANCHE to the left of the DIVISIONAL Area, Lieut MURPHY and 30 other ranks paraded for the purpose of commencing this work.	MS
BECQUE ... Sep 9th	The above work was continued by Lieut SAVILE and 7s other ranks.	MS
... Sep 10th	The above work was continued by Lieut MOLYNEUX and 70 other ranks.	MS
... Sep 11th	The above work was completed by Lieut CASWELL and 50 other ranks.	MS

Army Form C. 2118.

WAR DIARY
or
INTELLIGENCE SUMMARY. five

(Erase heading not required.)

Instructions regarding War Diaries and Intelligence Summaries are contained in F.S. Regs., Part II. and the Staff Manual respectively. Title pages will be prepared in manuscript.

Hour, Date, Place	Summary of Events and Information	Remarks and references to Appendices
GRAND BOIS Sep 12th	M	
Sep 13th	Orders have been received that the RUE DES BASSIERES should be have the ditches cleared a both sides, the work being commenced at the N. end of the road. PICKTHALL and 70 other ranks.	KH
FORET DE HIRSON 20s	No 1 Platoon sent a party to cut wood in the FORET DE HIRSON for making billets for the winter.	KH

(73989) W4141—463. 400,000. 9/14. H.&J.Ltd. Forms/C. 2118/10.

Army Form C. 2118.

WAR DIARY
or
INTELLIGENCE SUMMARY.

(Erase heading not required.)

Instructions regarding War Diaries and Intelligence Summaries are contained in F. S. Regs., Part II. and the Staff Manual respectively. Title pages will be prepared in manuscript.

Hour, Date, Place	Summary of Events and Information	Remarks and references to Appendices
GRAND BOIS Sep 14th	A working party of 70 men under Lieut WILLANS paraded to clean ditches between RUE BATAILLE and CROIX BLANCHE	W.S.
FORT DE METEREN	No 3 Platoon went to cut wood for repairing the stables	W.S.
RUE DES BASSIERS Sep 15th	A working party (as above) paraded under Lieut MURPHY	W.S.
FORT DE METEREN	No 5 Platoon furnished a wood cutting party (as above)	W.S.
RUE DES BASSIERS Sep 16th	A working party of 70 men under Lieut SAVILE completed the work on the RUE DES BASSIERS.	W.S.
GRAND BOIS Sep 17th	Nil	W.S.
GRAND BOIS Sep 18th	Nil	W.S.
" Sep 19th	Lieut CASSWELL and 30 other ranks paraded for Divine Service at the Kiyn of the Died Mont Morfs.	W.S.
" Sep 20th	No 5 Platoon paraded as a working party. The work of cleaning out the METEREN BECQUE, and ditches in the Billeting area, was completed.	W.S.

Army Form C. 2118.

WAR DIARY
or
INTELLIGENCE SUMMARY.

(Erase heading not required.)

Instructions regarding War Diaries and Intelligence Summaries are contained in F.S. Regs., Part II. and the Staff Manual respectively. Title pages will be prepared in manuscript.

Hour, Date, Place	Summary of Events and Information	Remarks and references to Appendices
GRAND BOIS Sep 21st	[1st day of bombardment]. In accordance with orders received previous by, the following detachments left the company on this date — (a) L/Cpl VESSEY, and 5 men, to Adv. Divl. Hqrs. (b) 1 Section, No 6 Platoon, to 25th Infy Bde. (c) 1 Section, No 5 Platoon, to 24th Infy Bde.	Nil
5-45 pm	A working party of 3 NCOs & 8 men proceeded under Lieut CASSWELL	
GRAND BOIS Sep 22nd	[2nd day of bombardment] Nil	Nil
Sep 23rd	[3rd " " "] Nil	Nil
Sep 24th	[4th " " "] No 1 Platoon proceeded to Sq. H 29 central with orders to take over prisoners there, and march them to Adv. Corps Hqrs.	Nil
RUE BATAILLE Sep 25th 3-45 a.m.	The company (less 2 platoons) moved to the place previously pointed for the D.H.Q. AH Trench. No 6 Platoon occupied the dug-out & the redoubt. The remainder took cottages in the vicinity. Written last rain almost incessant. The new Burn Coat proved very useful in this weather.	Nil

Army Form C. 2118.

WAR DIARY
or
INTELLIGENCE SUMMARY.
(Erase heading not required.)

Instructions regarding War Diaries and Intelligence Summaries are contained in F.S. Regs., Part II and the Staff Manual respectively. Title pages will be prepared in manuscript.

Hour, Date, Place	Summary of Events and Information	Remarks and references to Appendices
RUE BATAILLE Sep 26th	The Divl Patrol Troops stood to arms at 4-15 a.m.	
2 p.m.	The company received orders to march back to forward billets.	
	There were no casualties during the operations.	
	No. 1 Platoon rejoined the company the next day	NP

Army Form C. 2118.

WAR DIARY
or
INTELLIGENCE SUMMARY.

(Erase heading not required.)

Instructions regarding War Diaries and Intelligence Summaries are contained in F.S. Regs., Part II. and the Staff Manual respectively. Title pages will be prepared in manuscript.

Hour, Date, Place	Summary of Events and Information	Remarks and references to Appendices
GRAND BOIS Sep 27th	NK.	NIL
" Sep 28th	NK	NIL
Sep 29th 8 a.m.	Lieuts PICKTHALL, MURPHY and MOLYNEUX, and 98 other ranks proceeded to FLEURBAIX as a working party under the orders of the 24th Infy Bde. The work consisted in completing the breastwork on the new obtained line between the BRIDOUX and WELL FARM salients. This night work in parties were shelled, but no casualties were sustained by this unit.	NIL
6 pm — 2 a.m. 10 a.m.	1 Section, No. 6 Platoon rejoined the company from 25th Infy Bde.	
GRAND BOIS Sep 30th	Major R.M. HEATH DSO. resumed command of the company. 1 Section No. 5 Platoon, rejoined the company from the 24th Infy Bde.	NIL
" Oct. 1st	Lieut CASSWELL and 24 other ranks paraded for Divine Service at the Hqrs of the DIVL MTD TPS.	NIL

Rwall for M Maj

"8th Division"

Div.

H Q 121/7781

Confidential

War Diary of
8th Divl. Cyclist Coy.

from 1st Oct. '15 to 31st Oct. '15

Vol X

Army Form C. 2118.

WAR DIARY
or
INTELLIGENCE SUMMARY. Nil.

(Erase heading not required.)

8th Regt Cyclist Coy

Hour, Date, Place	Summary of Events and Information	Remarks and references to Appendices
GRAND BOIS Oct 2nd	Detachment at FLEURBAIX worked on new breastwork, which was subjected to trench-mortar & rifle-grenade fire throughout the night. No casualties.	Nil.
" " Oct 3rd	Nil.	Nil
" " Oct 4th	Detachment at FLEURBAIX worked on new breastwork, which was subjected to trench-mortar & rifle-grenade fire throughout the night. No casualties.	Nil.
" " Oct 5th	Nil.	Nil
" " Oct 6th	Detachment at FLEURBAIX worked on new breastwork. No Casualties	Nil.
" " Oct 7th	Detachment at FLEURBAIX rejoined the Company.	Nil.
" " Oct 8th		Nil.
" " Oct 9th	A party of 2 officers and 100 O.R. were ordered to rendezvous at CROIX BLANCHE at 7 pm, for work under the 1st Rl Dragoon Coy. Lieuts SAVILE and WILLANS preceded both the party. No casualties. Lieut CASSWELL proceeded to England on leave	Nil.

Army Form C. 2118.

WAR DIARY
or
INTELLIGENCE SUMMARY.

(Erase heading not required.)

Instructions regarding War Diaries and Intelligence Summaries are contained in F.S. Regs., Part II. and the Staff Manual respectively. Title pages will be prepared in manuscript.

Hour, Date, Place	Summary of Events and Information	Remarks and references to Appendices
GRAND BOIS Oct 10th	NIL	NIL
" Oct 11th 7 a.m.	Lieuts PICKTHALL and MURPHY, and 80 other ranks proceeded to RUE PETILLON to work under R.E. The project of the 300 x line was built up.	NIL
" Oct 12th 5.30 p.m. 2.0 p.m.	Lieut MOLINEUX and 50 other ranks proceeded to ELBOW FARM to work under 1st H.C. Fld. Coy. R.E. No 2 Platoon found a party for bringing hurdles & firewood from the Foret de NIEPPE.	NIL
" Oct 13th	NIL	NIL
" Oct 14th	A tactical exercise was carried out in conjunction with the divisional cavalry. The G.O.C. was present during the operations. The weather was extremely foggy throughout.	NIL

Army Form C. 2118.

WAR DIARY
or
INTELLIGENCE SUMMARY. NWP

(Erase heading not required.)

Hour, Date, Place	Summary of Events and Information	Remarks and references to Appendices
GRAND BOIS Oct 15th	A working party of 50 men under Lieut SWANN was ordered to report to the 1st Home Counties Fld. Coy RE at CROIX BLANCHE. 100 x of parapet of DEVON AVENUE was completed into hurdle revetment. Time of work — 10 a.m. — 1 p.m.	NWP.
" " Oct 16th	The following working parties provided :— (i) 50 NCOs & men under Lieut WILLANS at 6.30 a.m. for 1st Home Counties Fld Coy RE at BAC ST MAUR. Bricks were unloaded from a barge on the R. LYS. Time of work — 8 a.m — 3 p.m. (ii) 50 NCOs & men under Lieut SAVILE at 7.30 a.m for 1st Bn Fld Coy RE at TIN BARN Tramway Terminus. Track was thrown out the front parapet of the 300th line. Time of work — 10 a.m — 1 p.m. A cinder path between hqrs of No. 1 & 4 Platoon Billets was commenced on CRANE. B Lieut MOLYNEUX proceeded on Leave.	NWP.

Army Form C. 2118.

WAR DIARY
or
INTELLIGENCE SUMMARY. KWF

(Erase heading not required.)

Instructions regarding War Diaries and Intelligence Summaries are contained in F. S. Regs., Part II. and the Staff Manual respectively. Title pages will be prepared in manuscript.

Hour, Date, Place		Summary of Events and Information	Remarks and references to Appendices
GRAND BOIS	Oct 17th	2/Lieut CASSWELL returned from leave. The construction of the cinder path between hypo & No 2 & 4 Platoon Billets was carried on later.	KWF
" "	Oct 18th	N.C.	KWF
" "	Oct 19th	The following working parties were ordered for this day:— (i) To parade at 6.30 a.m. Lieut MURPHY and 2/Lieut CASSWELL and 75 men. Rendezvous CROIX BLANCHE (ii) To parade at 7.30 a.m. Lieut PICKTHALL and 25 men. Rendezvous CROIX MARECHAL	KWF
" "	Oct 20th	N.C.	KWF
" "	Oct 21st	N.C.	KWF

WAR DIARY
or
INTELLIGENCE SUMMARY.

Army Form C. 2118.

Hour, Date, Place	Summary of Events and Information	Remarks and references to Appendices
GRAND BOIS Oct 22nd	Lieut MURPHY, 2Lieut WILLANS, and 70 other ranks paraded at 6:45 a.m. and proceeded to FLEURBAIX to work on DURHAM POST under the GLAMORGAN Fortress Coy RE.	WP
GRAND BOIS Oct 23rd	Working party as above, under Lieut SWANN and 2Lieut CALDWELL. 2Lieut WILLANS proceeded to ENGLAND on leave.	WP.
GRAND BOIS Oct 24th	Working party as above, under Lieut SAVILE & Lieut PICKNALL.	WP
GRAND BOIS Oct 25th	Working party as above, under Lieut SAVILE & Lieut MURPHY. Owing to bad weather - told to stand by at 9 a.m. but at 9.30 a.m. telephoned to return at 12.30 p.m. owing to weather. 2Lieut MOLYNEUX rejoined from leave.	WP
GRAND BOIS Oct 26th	Working party as above under Lieut SWANN & 2Lieut MOLYNEUX.	WP.

Army Form C. 2118.

WAR DIARY
or
INTELLIGENCE SUMMARY.

(Erase heading not required.)

Instructions regarding War Diaries and Intelligence Summaries are contained in F.S. Regs., Part II. and the Staff Manual respectively. Title pages will be prepared in manuscript.

Hour, Date, Place	Summary of Events and Information	Remarks and references to Appendices
GRAND BOIS Oct 27th	Working party as above under Lieut PICKTHALL and 2Lieut CASSWELL.	W.R.
" Oct 28th	Working party as above under Lieut SAMPLE and Lieut PICKTHALL — returned at 2-3.0 from owing to bad weather.	W.R.
" Oct 29th	Working party 10·0 other ranks under Lieut MURPHY and 2Lieut PICKTHALL	W.R.
" Oct 30th	Working party as above under Lieut SWANN and 2Lieut CASSWELL.	W.R.
" Oct 31st	Working party as above under Lieut SWANN and 2Lieut MOLYNEUX.	W.R.

Ronald M Heath Major
Comd 17th Divl Cycl Coy

1-11-15

121/7637

8th Divl Cyclist Co.

Nov. 1915

Vol XI

Army Form C. 2118.

WAR DIARY
or
INTELLIGENCE SUMMARY. hWS

(Erase heading not required.)

Instructions regarding War Diaries and Intelligence Summaries are contained in F.S. Regs., Part II. and the Staff Manual respectively. Title pages will be prepared in manuscript.

Hour, Date, Place	Summary of Events and Information	Remarks and references to Appendices
GRAND BOIS Nov 1st	A working party of 50 NCOs & men paraded at 7.45 a.m. under Lieut PICKTHALL for work on the defences of FLEURBAIX.	hWS
" Nov 2nd	Lieut SWANN proceeded to ENGLAND on leave. A working party of 70 (as above) paraded under Lieut MURPHY and Lieut MOLYNEUX.	hWS
" Nov 3rd	A working party of 50 (as above) paraded under Lieut MURPHY.	hWS
" Nov 4th	A working party of 70 (as above) paraded under 2Lieuts CASSWELL and WILLANS.	hWS
" Nov 5th	A working party of 50 (as above) paraded under Lieut SAVILE.	hWS
" Nov 6th	A working party of 70 (as above) paraded under 2Lieuts MOLYNEUX & WILLANS.	hWS

Army Form C. 2118.

WAR DIARY
or
INTELLIGENCE SUMMARY.
(Erase heading not required.)

Instructions regarding War Diaries and Intelligence Summaries are contained in F.S. Regs., Part II and the Staff Manual respectively. Title pages will be prepared in manuscript.

Hour, Date, Place		Summary of Events and Information	Remarks and references to Appendices
GRAND BOIS	Nov 7th	A working party (as above) paraded under Lieut PICKTHALL	AUS
"	Nov 8th	A working party of 45 (as above) paraded under Lieut MURPHY.	AUS
"	Nov 9th	The Divisional Snipers Corps, consisting of 2 Officers, 1 Sgt, 2 Cpls, & 33 O.R., Div. Cyclist Coy, and 6 O.R. Divisional Cavalry, was formed this day. The above details moved to FLEURBAIX, where they are now billeted under Lieuts SAVILE & PICKTHALL	AUS
"	Nov 10th	A working party of 45 (as above) paraded under Lieut WILLANS. Major R.R. Heath, D.S.O. returned both on the duties of 2nd in command of 2/Manch. Regt. from date	AUS
"	Nov 11th	A working party of 45 (as above) paraded under Lieut MOLYNEUX.	AUS

WAR DIARY
or
INTELLIGENCE SUMMARY.
(Erase heading not required.)

Army Form C. 2118.

Instructions regarding War Diaries and Intelligence Summaries are contained in F.S. Regs., Part II. and the Staff Manual respectively. Title pages will be prepared in manuscript.

Hour, Date, Place	Summary of Events and Information	Remarks and references to Appendices
GRAND BOIS 12th Nov.	A working party, as above, paraded under Lieut MURPHY. Owing to extremely bad weather, very little work could be done. Pte. SIMPSON, of the Sniping Corps, was wounded while walking up the BOIS GRENIER - BRIDOUX road.	K.E.
" 13th Nov.	A working party as above, paraded under Lieut CASWELL, but returned at once, owing to the state of the weather.	K.E.
" 14th Nov.	A working party, as above, paraded under Lieut WILLANS.	K.E.
" 15th Nov.	A working party, as above, paraded under Lieut MOLYNEUX. Lieut PICKTHALL proceeded to ENGLAND on leave. Lee Cpl HARDCASTLE, of the Sniping Corps, was wounded while constructing a sniping post.	K.E.
" 16th Nov.	A working party, as above, paraded under Lieut CASWELL. Tests of rifles fitted into telescopic sights, were carried out by the Sniping Corps at FLEURBAIX.	K.E.

WAR DIARY
or
INTELLIGENCE SUMMARY.

Army Form C. 2118.

(Erase heading not required.)

Hour, Date, Place	Summary of Events and Information	Remarks and references to Appendices
GRAND BOIS 17th Nov.	A working party, as above, paraded under Lieut WILLANS	WJS
" 18th Nov.	A working party, as above, paraded under Lieut MOLYNEUX. A report on roads between VIEUX BERQUIN and STEENBECQUE having been called for, this duty was carried out by Lieuts SHANN & CASSWELL, with a view to selecting march route between the above named places for the Division and its transport.	WJS
" 19th Nov.	A working party, as above, paraded under Lieut CASSWELL	WJS
" 20th Nov.	A working party, as above, paraded under Lieut MOLYNEUX	WJS
" 21st Nov.	A working party, as above, paraded under Lieut WILLANS	WJS
" 22nd Nov.	A working party, as above, paraded under Lieut CASSWELL. Notification was received by telegram that Lieut PICKTHALL, now on leave, had been granted Sick Leave	WJS

Army Form C. 2118.

WAR DIARY
or
INTELLIGENCE SUMMARY.

(Erase heading not required.)

Instructions regarding War Diaries and Intelligence Summaries are contained in F.S. Regs., Part II. and the Staff Manual respectively. Title pages will be prepared in manuscript.

Hour, Date, Place	Summary of Events and Information	Remarks and references to Appendices
GRAND BOIS Nov 22nd (Continued)	The Divisional Snipers rejoined the Company this day.	WF
" Nov 23rd	A working party, as above, paraded under Lieut CASSWELL. The 8th Division moved into GHQ Reserve this day. The Divl. Mtd. Troops (Cyclists & Yeomany) remained in trenches in GRAND BOIS.	WF
" Nov 24th	A working party, as above, paraded under Lieut MOLYNEUX. This is the last working party found by the Company until further notice.	WF
7 a.m.	Lieut CASSWELL & No 3 Platoon proceeded to BLARINGHEM, a few miles N. of AIRE, and reported to the Signal Company, 8 Division, quartered there.	WF
" Nov 25th	A period of 21 days' training was entered upon this day.	WF
" Nov 26th	Company training as per scheme of work.	WF

(73989) W4141—463. 400,000. 9/14. H.&J.Ltd. Forms/C. 2118/10.

Army Form C. 2118.

WAR DIARY
or
INTELLIGENCE SUMMARY.

(Erase heading not required.)

Instructions regarding War Diaries and Intelligence Summaries are contained in F.S. Regs., Part II. and the Staff Manual respectively. Title pages will be prepared in manuscript.

Hour, Date, Place	Summary of Events and Information	Remarks and references to Appendices
GRAND BOIS Nov 27th	Nil	NOF
" Nov 28th	Nil	NOF
" Nov 29th	Nil	NOF
" Nov 30th	No 2 Platoon proceeded to BLARINGHEM for duty at Divl Hqrs.	NOF

8th Div: Cyclists
December 1915
Vol. XII

Army Form C. 2118.

WAR DIARY
or
INTELLIGENCE SUMMARY.
(Erase heading not required.)

Instructions regarding War Diaries and Intelligence Summaries are contained in F.S. Regs., Part II and the Staff Manual respectively. Title pages will be prepared in manuscript.

Hour, Date, Place	Summary of Events and Information	Remarks and references to Appendices
GRAND BOIS Dec 1st	Nil	145 to S Lt
2nd	Lieut H.N. Swann joined detachment at Blaringhem BLARINGHAM. Lieut H.B.W. Savile taken over temporary command of the company	145 to S Lt
3rd	Nil	145 to S Lt
4th	1 Reinforcement joined the Company	145 to S Lt
5th	Nil	145 to S Lt
6th	Nil	145 to S Lt
7th	Lieut H.N.Swann returned from BLARINGHEM and resumed command of the Company	Nil
8th	Nil	Nil
9th	Nil	Nil
10th	During the night the METEREN BECQUE which has been flowing over (the?) area was considerably	

(73989) W4141—463. 400,000. 9/14. H.&J.Ltd. Forms/C. 2118/10.

WAR DIARY or INTELLIGENCE SUMMARY.

Army Form C. 2118.

(Erase heading not required.)

Hour, Date, Place		Summary of Events and Information	Remarks and references to Appendices
GRAND BOIS	10th (cont'd)	recent rains, flooding one road for over a quarter of a mile, and another road, entering the former at right angles, for the same distance.	W/S
"	11th Dec.	Roads still flooded. Water rather higher than yesterday. Bad weather still continues.	W/S
"	12th Dec	Roads still flooded. Wind went into the North. Heavy rain.	W/S
"	13th Dec	Floods partially subsided. Roads dry.	W/S
"	14th Dec	Lieut W.E.C. PICKTHALL rejoined the Company from Est Leave	W/S Addenda "Lieut de BELABRE, 9th Br. 5th Fusiliers, joined the Company" W/S
"	15th Dec	Nil	W/S
"	16th Dec	Nil	W/S
"	17th Dec	The O.C. Divisional Mounted Troops inspected the Company in marching order. He expressed his approval of the turn out and general appearance of the Company	W/S

Army Form C. 2118.

WAR DIARY
or
INTELLIGENCE SUMMARY. W.S.

(Erase heading not required.)

Instructions regarding War Diaries and Intelligence Summaries are contained in F.S. Regs., Part II and the Staff Manual respectively. Title pages will be prepared in manuscript.

Hour, Date, Place	Summary of Events and Information	Remarks and references to Appendices
GRAND BOIS 18th Dec	The Divisional Mounted Troops (1 Squadron, Northumberland Hussars, Divl Cyclist Company, less 2 Platoons) moved from present billets to LE CROQUET, in the vicinity of BLARINGHEM. Lieut. H.B.W. SAVILE was in charge of the Divisional Mounted Troops.	N.E.
LE CROQUET 19th Dec	N.E.	N.E.
LE CROQUET 20th Dec	Commencement of the Divisional Exercise. The Division marched on one road, protected by the Divisional Mounted Troops, who reached the hill SW of THEROUANNES by the evening of this day. On being relieved by the Infantry the Divisional Mounted Troops went into billets in the village of NIELE.	N.E.
NIELE 21st Dec	The march of the Division was resumed in the same form as before. By noon the head of the Main Column had reached the	

Army Form C. 2118.

WAR DIARY
or
INTELLIGENCE SUMMARY. WL

(Erase heading not required.)

Hour, Date, Place	Summary of Events and Information	Remarks and references to Appendices
Ratinghem 21st Dec	Hills surrounding RADINGHEM. The Mounted Troops withdrew to CAPELLE-SUR-LA-LYS, where they went into billets.	WL
CAPELLE-SUR-LYS 22nd Dec	Retirement of the Division on its lines of communication. The Mounted Troops arrived in their billets at the 8.15th instant at 6.30 p.m.	WL
LE CROQUET 23rd Dec	The Mounted Troops returned to the GRAND BOIS.	WL
GRAND BOIS 24th Dec	Roads in billets again flooded.	WL
" CHRISTMAS DAY	Floods partially subsided.	WL
" 26th Dec		WL
" 27th "		WL
" 28th "		WL
" 29th "		WL
" 30 "		WL
" 31st "		WL

Sir Dire Cyclist Co.
Jan 1916

XIII
vol

WAR DIARY
or
INTELLIGENCE SUMMARY. N.I.F.
(Erase heading not required.)

Army Form C. 2118.

Hour, Date, Place	Summary of Events and Information	Remarks and references to Appendices
GRAND BOIS 1916 NEW YEAR'S DAY	NIL	NIL
2nd	The promotion to rank of Captain of Lieut H.B.W. SAVILE was announced in the London Gazette of 31-12-15, dated 1-10-15. Captain K.B.W. SAVILE assumed command of the Company from this date	NIL
3rd	NIL	NIL
4th	NIL	NIL
5th	NIL	NIL
6th	NIL	NIL
7th	NIL	NIL

WAR DIARY or INTELLIGENCE SUMMARY.

Army Form C. 2118.

(Erase heading not required.)

Hour, Date, Place	Summary of Events and Information	Remarks and references to Appendices
GRAND BOIS Jan 8th	Nil	W/E
" 9th	Nil	W/E
" 10th	Lieut MOLYNEUX proceeded to take over command of the BLARINGHEM detachment, vice Lt CASSWELL, on leave.	W/E
" 11th	The abnormal snipers proceeded to FLEURBAIX, to commence active operations.	W/E
" 12th	Lieut BELABRE proceeded to FLEURBAIX for a course of bombthrowing.	W/E
" 13th		W/E
" 14th		W/E
" 15th		W/E
" 16th	Lieut N.J. WILLIAMS proceeded to ENGLAND on leave	W/E
" 17th	A working party of 50, to the setts, [?] proceeded R SMILY to unload timber from a barge; Lieut MOLYNEUX now in charge	W/E

Army Form C. 2118.

WAR DIARY
or
INTELLIGENCE SUMMARY.
(Erase heading not required.)

Instructions regarding War Diaries and Intelligence Summaries are contained in F.S. Regs, Part II. and the Staff Manual respectively. Title pages will be prepared in manuscript.

Hour, Date, Place	Summary of Events and Information	Remarks and references to Appendices
GRAND BOIS 18th Jan	NTR	
" 19th Jan	Working party, as above, returned under Lt MOLYNEUX	NTR
" 20th Jan	Lt CASSWELL returned from leave	NTR
" 21st Jan	Working party, as above, returned under Lt BELABRE	NTR
" 22nd Jan	NTR	NTR
" 23rd Jan	Lt MOLYNEUX proceeded to ENGLAND on leave. Working party, as above, paraded under Lt CASSWELL	NTR
" 24th	NTR	NTR
" 26th	2/Lt WILLANS returned from leave. Working party, as above, paraded under Lt BELABRE	NTR
" 27th	NTR	NTR

Army Form C. 2118.

WAR DIARY
or
INTELLIGENCE SUMMARY.
(Erase heading not required.)

Instructions regarding War Diaries and Intelligence Summaries are contained in F.S. Regs., Part II and the Staff Manual respectively. Title pages will be prepared in manuscript.

Hour, Date, Place	Summary of Events and Information	Remarks and references to Appendices
GRAND BOIS 29th Jan	Lieut SWANN proceeded to ENGLAND on leave. 1 man was hit by the Divisional Snipers	WJF
" 29th	The Divisional Snipers hit two (2) the enemy and caused a party who were passing to get to better cover.	WJF
" 30th	Orders to fight for safety. Went over shown on patrol.	WJF
" 31st	Ten men have left G Divisional Snipers.	WJF

Feb & March 1916

8

8 Div Cyclist Coy
Feb
Vol XIV

Army Form C. 2118.

WAR DIARY
or
INTELLIGENCE SUMMARY.

(Erase heading not required.)

Instructions regarding War Diaries and Intelligence Summaries are contained in F.S. Regs., Part II and the Staff Manual respectively. Title pages will be prepared in manuscript.

Hour, Date, Place	Summary of Events and Information	Remarks and references to Appendices
GRAND BOIS Jan 1st	1st MALVAGNY returned from leave	
2nd	enemy were hit by Divisional Snipers	hit
3rd	enemy were hit by Divisional Snipers	hit
4th	enemy were hit by Divisional Snipers	hit
	one officer and [illegible]	hit
5th	enemy hit by Divisional Snipers	hit
6th	enemy hit by Divisional Snipers	hit
7th	enemy hit by Divisional Snipers	hit
8th	Lieut. [illegible] to hospital for [illegible]	hit
	Lieut SWANN returned from leave	hit

(73989) W 4141—463. 400,000. 9/14. H. & J. Ltd. Forms/C. 2118/10.

Army Form C. 2118.

WAR DIARY
or
INTELLIGENCE SUMMARY.
(Erase heading not required.)

Instructions regarding War Diaries and Intelligence Summaries are contained in F.S. Regs., Part II and the Staff Manual respectively. Title pages will be prepared in manuscript.

Hour, Date, Place	Summary of Events and Information	Remarks and references to Appendices
23rd Feb.	Snipers shot 2 Germans. Working Party of 20 men for 605th at BAC-ST-MAUR. Working Party of 10 men for SAILLY CHURCH. Three reinforcements joined the Company	ASMH.
24th "	NIL.	ASMH.
25th "	Working Party of 50 men in two reliefs for SAILLY BRIDGE	ASMH.
26th "	Snipers shot 1 German. Capt. H.B.W. Savile rejoined the 2nd Bn. MIDDLESEX REGT. 2/Lt. E.D.S. Caswell took over Temporary command	ASMH.
27th "	NIL.	ASMH.
28th "	Working Party of 50 men in two reliefs for SAILLY BRIDGE.	ASMH.
29th "	Snipers shot 4 Germans. Five reinforcements joined the Coy. Lieut. H.C. Murphy took over command of the Coy. Lieut. W.F.C. Pickthall proceeded to take over command of IIIrd Corps Sniping School.	ASMH.

Army Form C. 2118.

WAR DIARY
or
INTELLIGENCE SUMMARY.
(Erase heading not required.)

Hour, Date, Place	Summary of Events and Information	Remarks and references to Appendices
9th Feb	2nd Lt. A.N. Strace joined order 5 & 3rd Corps	KWPh
10th	Working Party 30 men SAILLY BRICK FIELDS. Sniper hit 2 Germans	KWPh
11th	Nil	KWPh
12th	Working Party 30 SAILLY BRICK FIELDS	KWPh
13th	Nil	KWPh
14th		KWPh
15th	Snipers Hit 2 Germans	ASHH
16th	Working party 30 men, in two reliefs SAILLY BRICKFIELDS	ASHH
17th	Snipers Hit 1 German	ASHH
17th	Working Party 30 men, in two reliefs SAILLY BRICK FIELDS	ASHH
18th	Snipers Hit 1 German	ASHH
19th	Snipers constructed three new posts. Working Party 30 men in two reliefs SAILLY BRICKFIELDS. Lieut. W.E.C. Tickhall proceeds on leave from 19th – 26th	ASHH
20th	Snipers Hit 3 Germans & constructed three new posts.	ASHH
21st	Snipers Hit 5 Germans & constructed three new posts	ASHH
22nd	Snipers constructed three new posts.	ASHH

Cyclist Coy

Vol XV

Army Form C. 2118.

WAR DIARY
or
INTELLIGENCE SUMMARY.
(Erase heading not required.)

Instructions regarding War Diaries and Intelligence Summaries are contained in F.S. Regs., Part II. and the Staff Manual respectively. Title pages will be prepared in manuscript.

Hour, Date, Place	Summary of Events and Information	Remarks and references to Appendices
1st March	Snipers hit 2 Germans. Two reinforcements that Toy: missed. Lt: O: Dobbs proceeded to the cadet school at St OMER, prior to his obtaining his commission.	A.S.H.H.
2nd "	Snipers hit 1 German.	A.S.H.H.
3rd "	Working party of 50 men, in two reliefs at SAILLY BRIDGE	A.S.H.H.
4th "	Nil.	A.S.H.H.
5th "	2/Lt: V: Mc Bride proceeded to School of instruction at NOUVEAU MONDE.	A.S.H.H.
6th "	Snipers hit 2 Germans. Working party of 50 men in two reliefs at SAILLY BRIDGE	A.S.H.H.
7th "	Nil.	A.S.H.H.
8th "	2/Lt: N.F. Williams proceeded to FLEURBAIX to take over command of Batt: Sniping Corps, vice 2/Lt: C.S. Holyoake to duty with Company. Working party of 50 men, in two reliefs at SAILLY BRIDGE. Snipers hit 4 Germans.	A.S.H.H.
9th "	Snipers hit 4 Germans.	A.S.H.H.

Army Form C. 2118.

WAR DIARY
~~INTELLIGENCE SUMMARY.~~
(Erase heading not required.)

Instructions regarding War Diaries and Intelligence Summaries are contained in F.S. Regs., Part II. and the Staff Manual respectively. Title pages will be prepared in manuscript.

Hour, Date, Place	Summary of Events and Information	Remarks and references to Appendices
10th March	Working party of 50 men in two reliefs at SAILLY BRIDGE. Snipers hit 3 Germans.	A.P.M. H.
11th "	Snipers hit 4 Germans, including one officer.	A.P.M. H.
12th "	Snipers hit 4 Germans. Snipers also discovered a German field battery, which was reported to Artillery Observer, who had it promptly put out of action.	A.P.M. H.
13th "	Working party of 50 men, in two reliefs at SAILLY BRIDGE. One NCO & 4 men proceeded A.P.M. at SAILLY for instruction in traffic duty. Snipers hit 12 Germans.	A.P.M. H.
14th "	Snipers hit 2 Germans.	A.P.M. H.
15th "	Four officers & 30 other ranks of 39th Divl. Cycle Coy. were attached to the Company for instruction. Working party of 50 men in two reliefs at SAILLY BRIDGE. Snipers claim 2 Germans.	A.P.M. H.
16th "	One man proceeded to base for discharge. Snipers hit 2 Germans.	A.P.M. H.

WAR DIARY
or
INTELLIGENCE SUMMARY.
(Erase heading not required.)

Army Form C. 2118.

Hour, Date, Place	Summary of Events and Information	Remarks and references to Appendices
17th March	Working party of 50 men in two reliefs at SAILLY BRIDGE.	A.S.M.H.
18"	Snipers hit 1 German.	A.S.M.H.
19"	Snipers hit 1 German.	A.S.M.H.
20"	Working party of 50 men in two reliefs at SAILLY BRIDGE. Snipers hit 6 Germans. 2/Lt R.L. Campbell Bras. joined Company.	A.S.M.H.
21st	Lieut. A.E. Murphy proceeded on Leave from 21st to 28th March.	A.S.M.H.
22nd	Working party of 50 men in two reliefs at SAILLY BRIDGE.	A.S.M.H.
23rd	Snipers shot 1 German.	A.S.M.H
24th	Working party of 50 men in two reliefs at SAILLY BRIDGE. Snipers rejoined Company from FLEUR BAIX.	A.S.M.H.
25"	Lieut. N.E. Critchall rejoined Coy from Ill to B.W. Sniping School at NORBECQUE.	A.S.M.H.
26"	The Company moved from DOULIEU to CALONNE.	A.S.M.H
27"	The Company entrained at HERVILLE & detrained at LONGEAU, & proceeded from there to OLINCOURT.	A.S.M.H.
28"	Lieut. A.E. Murphy returned from leave.	A.S.M.H.

Army Form C. 2118.

WAR DIARY
or
INTELLIGENCE SUMMARY.
(Erase heading not required.)

Instructions regarding War Diaries and Intelligence Summaries are contained in F.S. Regs., Part II. and the Staff Manual respectively. Title pages will be prepared in manuscript.

Hour, Date, Place	Summary of Events and Information	Remarks and references to Appendices
March 29th	Nil.	A.S.M.H.
30th	Nil.	A.S.M.H.
31st	Nil.	A.S.M.H.

April - May 1946

Confidential 8/ac/2141

Officer i/c
A.G's Office
Base

Herewith War Diary of the
8th Divl Cyclist Coy for the month of
April

W. Cohn Pickthall
Lieut
3-5-16 Cmdg 8th Divl Cyclist Coy

Army Form C. 2118.

WAR DIARY
or
INTELLIGENCE SUMMARY.
(Erase heading not required.)

Instructions regarding War Diaries and Intelligence Summaries are contained in F.S. Regs., Part II. and the Staff Manual respectively. Title pages will be prepared in manuscript.

Hour, Date, Place	Summary of Events and Information	Remarks and references to Appendices
April 1st	Combined scheme with NORTHUMBERLAND HUSSARS.	#SMH:
" 2nd	Nil.	ASMH:
" 3rd	Nil.	#SMH:
" 4th	2/Lt. V.H. de Belabre proceeded on leave from 5th + 14th. The Company moved from OLINCOURT into billets at HENENCOURT.	#SMH:
" 5th	1 reinforcement joined the Company.	#SMH:
" 6th	Nil.	#SMH:
" 7th	Nil.	#SMH:
" 8th	35 N.C.O's own proceeded on detachment to FLESSELLES for work under officer in charge of remounts details.	#SMH:
" 9th	Nil.	#SMH:
" 10th	Working party of 1 officer + 20 O.Rs for work under the officer in charge No 6 R.E. Park at MERICOURT.	#SMH:
" 11th	4 N.C.O's Proceeded on detachment for Traffic duty under the A.P.M. at HENENCOURT. Working party of 1 officer + 30 O.Rs for work under the officer in charge No 6 R.E. Park at MERICOURT.	#SMH:

April 11th: Two N.C.O's + 20 men proceeded on detachment to ALBERT for traffic duty under the Town Major. #SMH:

WAR DIARY
or
INTELLIGENCE SUMMARY.

(Erase heading not required.)

Army Form C. 2118.

Hour, Date, Place	Summary of Events and Information	Remarks and references to Appendices
April 12th	Lieut. P.O.P. Caswell proceeds on leave from 12th to 21st. Lieut. M'Ingnew, Sgt Drumm & Pte Harris, G.M.H. & the Brigade Snipers proceeds on detachment to ALBERT. Working party at HERICOURT, same as for previous day.	A.S.M.H.
" 13th	Working party at HERICOURT, same as for previous day.	A.S.M.H.
" 14th	1 Reinforcement joined the Company. Working Party HERICOURT, same as for previous day.	A.S.M.H.
" 15th	Working party HERICOURT, same as for previous day. Orders received for all Officers, N.C.O's & men to be recalled off leave by April 18th.	A.S.M.H.
" 16th	Working party HERICOURT, same as for previous day.	A.S.M.H.
" 17th	Working party HERICOURT, same as for previous day.	A.S.M.H.
" 18th	Working party HERICOURT, same as for previous day. Two Reinforcements joined the Company.	A.S.M.H.
" 19th	Working party HERICOURT, same as for previous day.	A.S.M.H.
" 20th	Working party HERICOURT, same as for previous day.	A.S.M.H.

WAR DIARY
or
INTELLIGENCE SUMMARY
(Erase heading not required.)

Army Form C. 2118

Place	Date	Hour	Summary of Events and Information	Remarks and references to Appendices
In the field	April 21st		Working party HERICOURT same as for previous day	A.E.M.H.
"	22nd		2/Lt V.H. de Belabre proceeded to ALBERT to join Div: Sniping Corps	A.E.M.H.
"	23rd		One man proceeded to the Base for discharge, on completion of 4 years in special Reserve. One reinforcement joined the Company. Snipers claim 3 Germans.	A.E.M.H.
"	24-4-16		34 N.C.O's & men proceeded to AGNICOURT. Snipers claim 1 German.	A.E.M.H.
"	25-4-16		Nil.	A.E.M.H.
"	26-4-16		A Tactical scheme with the N.H. 35 N.C.O's & men rejoined the Company from FLESSELLES 2/Lt C.D.S Caswell & 2/Lt N.T. Willans proceeded on leave from 26th April - May 5th. Snipers claim 3 Germans.	A.E.M.H.
"	27-4-16		Snipers claim 2 Germans.	A.E.M.H.
"	28-4-16		Snipers claim 1 German	A.E.M.H.
"	29-4-16		Snipers claim 1 German	A.E.M.H.
"	30-4-16		32 N.C.O's & men proceeded to ALBERT to join Div: Sniping Corps	A.E.M.H.

Confidential
Officer i/c
A.G's Office
Base

Herewith War Diary for the
Month of May 1916

2-6-16   H.E. Murthly. Lieut
                COMDG. 8TH CYCLIST CO.

WAR DIARY
or
INTELLIGENCE SUMMARY

(Erase heading not required.)

Army Form C. 2118

Instructions regarding War Diaries and Intelligence Summaries are contained in F. S. Regs., Part II. and the Staff Manual respectively. Title Pages will be prepared in manuscript.

Place	Date	Hour	Summary of Events and Information	Remarks and references to Appendices
In the Field	May 1st		Nil.	A/1914
"	2-5-16		1 NCO. proceeded to FRANVILLERS Locale attached to Div. Supply Column for scouting	A/1914
"	3-5-16		Nil	A/1914
"	4-5-16		Nil.	A/1914
"	5-5-16		Snipers claim 1 German.	A/1914
"	6-5-16		Lieut. E.S. McGhee proceeded to leave to England. Lce-Corporal Henderson R. is sent to private e'ment. Snipers claim 1 German. Working party of 1 NCO & 5 men proceeded to 8th Divl. Amm. Sub. Park.	A/1914
"	7-5-16		Working party same as for previous day. Snipers claim 1 German.	A/1914
"	8-5-16		Working party same as for previous day.	
"	9-5-16		Working party same as for previous day.	EDSC
"	10-5-16		Working party same as for previous day.	EDSC
"	11-5-16		Nil	EDSC
"	12-5-16		Company moved to BEAUCOURT to join 3rd Corps Cyclist Bn. 2nd Lt Campbell Ross proceeded to 4th Div. Family Hostov School.	EDSC
"	13-5-16		Nil.	EDSC
"	14-5-16		Nil.	EDSC
"	15-5-16		Nil	EDSC
"	16-5-16		Nil.	EDSC
"	17-5-16		Nil.	EDSC
"	18-5-16		Nil.	EDSC

Army Form C. 2118

WAR DIARY
or
INTELLIGENCE SUMMARY
(Erase heading not required.)

Instructions regarding War Diaries and Intelligence Summaries are contained in F. S. Regs., Part II. and the Staff Manual respectively. Title Pages will be prepared in manuscript.

Place	Date	Hour	Summary of Events and Information	Remarks and references to Appendices
In the field	19-5-16		1 Officer & 26 O.R. rejoined the company.	EDSC.
" "	20-5-16	Nil.		EDSC.
" "	21-5-16	Nil.		EDSC.
" "	22-5-16		2nd Lt. E.S. Holyoak proceeded to Albert in relief of 2nd Lt. V.M. de Belabre who rejoined the company.	EDSC
" "	23-5-16		46 NCO's and men proceeded to join Royal Berkshire Regiment.	EDSC
—	24-5-16		2nd Lt. V.M. de Belabre and 2nd Lt. R.L. Campbell Browne with 6 O.R. proceeded to ROUEN as first line reinforcements.	EDSC
	25-5-16	Nil.		EDSC
	26-5-16	Nil.		EDSC
	27-5-16	Nil.		EDSC
	28-5-16	Nil.		EDSC
	29-5-16	Nil.		EDSC
	30-5-16	Nil.		EDSC
	31-5-16	Nil.		EDSC

8TH DIVISION TROOPS

5TH BRIGADE R.H.A.
NOV 1914-DEC 1916

To 4th Army

121/3933

8th Division

5th Brigade R.H.A.

Vol I. 4.11 — 31.12.14

War Diary

5th Brigade R.H.A

Nov. 4th 1914 – Dec 31st 1914

Hour, date, Place	Summary of Events	Remarks and references to Appendices
10:30 am Nov 4th Hursley Park	Received orders to embark for France	
11:30 pm to 5 am Nov 5th	Marched off by batteries. G Battery & Bde H.Q. first. Embarked at Southampton on S.S. Minneapolis.	Very wet & dark night
6:30 pm	Sailed	
12 noon Nov 6th Havre	Disembarked & marched up a very steep hill to Rest Camp. The whole Brigade was encamped by about 2 am Nov 7th	No tents pitched. Had to draw them somewhat closer quarters
6 am Nov 10th Havre	Began to entrain. The Brigade occupied 5 trains. The ammunition column did not start until 9 p.m.	
Nov 11th	Brigade detrained at STRAZEELE, MERVILLE and BERGUETTE and marched to billets at CAUDESCURE.	O.72 had a 3 mile march in absolute pitch dark.
Nov 14th CAUDESCURE	After receiving various somewhat	

Hour, date, Place	Summary of Events	Remarks and references to Appendices
9.30 p m LEVANTIE	contradictory orders the Brigade started at 9.30 pm & marched about 11 miles to near LEVANTIE when it took over the positions of the 42nd Bde R.F.A.	
Nov. 15th 6.0 am.	The Brigade took up positions as shewn in accompanying sketch. Observation was done by officers right up in advance near the Infantry trenches. Bde Headquarters were	appendix A
Nov. 16th.	comfortably esconced in a good house in the RUE DE PARADIS where stabling accommodation was available for the horses. Enemy fired some shell from howitzer batteries of the variety locally and familiarly known as 'Whistling Willies' but failed to locate the batteries & did no damage	

Hour, date, Place	Summary of Events	Remarks and references to appendices
12 noon. Nov 17th LEVANTIE	Enemy's Heavy Howitzers shelled the area occupied by the Brigade vigorously, some of the shell dropping within 80 yards of Bde. H.Q. but no damage was done. G Battery succeeded in locating a house in which the Headquarters of a German unit was situated. They got 3 direct hits on the house, which the Germans hurriedly evacuated.	
8.30 p.m. Nov. 18th LEVANTIE	All 3 Batteries shelled some houses in which it was believed Germans slept. A motor car & a considerable number of Germans were 'bolted'.	
9 p.m. 12 m.n. 2 a.m Nov 19th	Shelled town of NEUVE CHAPELLE to cover an infantry working party digging fresh trenches. The trenches were successfully dug. During the night preparations were	

Hour, Date, Place	Summary of Events	Remarks and references to Appendices
	made with a view to bringing a gun of O Battery into a position close to the infantry trenches, whence it could enfilade roads leading into NEUVE CHAPELLE.	
Nov. 19th	Quiet day.	
8 p.m. Nov. 20th	gun of O Battery put in action at D this gun successfully shelled the roads leading into NEUVE CHAPELLE withdrawing at night without casualties. The infantry, particularly the DEVON Regiment appear to object strongly to gun being brought close up complaining that they draw fire. It is difficult to see how artillery can effectively support infantry if the latter object to their presence.	Appendix A. Square J.8.A
Nov. 21st – Nov. 23rd	No change in situation. Z Battery advanced & took up a position near l'EPINETTE farm	

Date	Summary of Events	Remarks and references to appendices
Nov 24th	G Battery left to join 3rd Cavalry Division. O Battery advanced & took up a position near WANGERIE	
Nov. 25th	Quiet day. The limitations placed on the expenditure of ammunition prevented any offensive action being taken by the Brigade. The enemy's artillery appears to be numerically inferior to our own & given a supply of ammunition it would apparently be possible to keep them entirely in check & to considerably harass & annoy them, thus creating an opportunity for the infantry to advance.	
Nov 26th	57th (How) Battery R.F.A. arrived & came under orders of O.C. 5 Bde R.H.A	
Nov. 27th 8pm	57 (How) Battery took up position S.E. of RUE DE BACQUEROT. One section was detached and attached	

Hour, Date, Place	Summary of Events	Remarks and references to appendices
	to 33rd Bde R.F.A. & two guns are temporarily unserviceable leaving only one complete section in action.	
Nov. 28th	O Battery shelled TRIVELET & 57th Bty a house near NEUVE CHAPELLE. in both cases fire appeared to be effective.	
	Z Battery registered German trenches in front of D lines & O those in front of C lines.	
2 p.m.	No 12 anti aircraft section consisting of one anti-aircraft 18 pr. under Capt WADE-GERY R.G.A. it billetted & came into action at A	Appendix A square 6 C 23 A
Nov. 29th	Quiet day	
Nov. 30th	Section 57th Bty shelled Germans in house near HT. POMINEREAU causing an enormous burst of flame suddenly to leap up from just behind house &	

Hour. Date. Place	Summary of Events	Remarks and references to Appendices
	giving rise to the hope that an ammunition wagon may have been destroyed.	
	Germans shelled field near brewery at LAVENTIE very heavily with heavy howitzers - did no actual damage.	
2 p.m.	With their heavy field howitzers they shelled Bde. H.Q. Though they came unpleasantly close no actual damage was done	
Dec. 31st	57th How. Battery shelled TRIVELET. Their fire was accurate, the observing officer being in Vicarage near FAUQUISSART church.	
	German artillery replied & put several shell very near battery position, which however suffered no casualties	
Dec. 2nd	57th Battery withdrawn & put into billets in second line at NEUF BERQUIN	
Dec. 3rd - 5th	Quiet days. Batteries registered points on German trenches	

Hour. Date. Place	Summary of Events	Remarks and references to Appendices
Dec. 6th	German aeroplane passed over. Was fired at by anti-craft gun but escaped. It subsequently passed over HAZEBROUCK when it dropped bombs on the station killing 8 people	
Dec. 7th 6.a.m	No 12 Anti-aircraft section withdrawn from the Brigade & sent to HAZEBROUCK.	
5.30 p.m.	Alarm of night attack. Infantry sent up red rockets & Brigade came into action on German trenches in front of C & D lines – firing a total of 76 rounds. The alarm came to nothing & was probably the outcome of an action that had been arranged between the Rifle Brigade & Capt. Grosvenor, Z Bty. who had assumed command of two old trench mortars, dating from 1810, which had been attached to Bde. on Dec 1st & had thrown bombs	

Hour, Date, Place	Summary of Events	Remarks and References to appendices
	into the German trenches with varying effect	
Dec 8th - 15th	Quiet days	
Dec 16th	Supported attack of INDIAN CORPS on GIVENCHY by five attacks at intervals, on a The result of attack of Indian Corps was not made known to the Brigade.	Appendix II
12 midnight	Sentry of O Battery on duty at Gun Park near Bde. H.Q shot in finger by a sniper	
Dec 17th	Shelled German trenches.	
Dec 18th		
4.15 pm	Shelled German trenches heavily to prepare for attack by 23rd Inf Bde.	Appendix III
4.30 pm	Devons attack & captured portion of trench in Z I3 A. The attack on trench ~~running from I 13 B to I 23 D was~~ Y not pressed, as the Devons encountered the barbed wire & suffered heavy casualties	Appendix I

Hour, Date, Place	Summary of Events	Remarks & references to appendices
	from machine gun fire. 20 prisoners were taken, as well as two wounded officers. There was no attempt at counter-attack, probably owing to the heavy shellfire brought to bear on area over which supports would have to advance.	
Dec 19th	Infantry report that the Germans suffered many casualties from shellfire.	
7.30 am	Infantry forced to evacuate captured trench by German bombs.	
Dec 20th 3 p.m.	Information received that 23rd Inf. Bde anticipated attack. Preparations made to shell approaches near MOULIN du PIETRE. The attack did not come off but approaches were searched with shrapnel during the night.	
Dec. 21st 1.15 pm	Orders to cooperate with Indian Corps in counter-attack received	Appendix IV

Hour, Date, Place	Summary of Events	Remarks & references to Appendices
	Brigade fired bursts of fire on area around MOULIN DU PIETRE	
7.30 pm	Instructions received to again bring reserve sections into action	
8.15 pm	Information received that NEUVE CHAPELLE was full of GERMANS at 9.45 pm a burst of fire from all available guns was opened on the village. It is not known whether any damage was done.	
Dec 22nd 11.15	Information received that large bodies of enemy were collecting about HAUT POMMEREAU. A burst of fire was brought to bear on approaches to AUBERS & NEUVE CHAPELLE & the whole Brigade stood to their guns	
Dec 23rd & 24th	Quiet days - batteries fired a few bursts of fire during the night at trenches & approaches	

Hour, Date, Place	Summary of Events	Remarks & references to appendices
Dec. 25th	Christmas day – No firing on either side.	
Dec. 26th	During day some blind shell fell very near to Z Battery, one shell actually hitting ground line of house where men were billeted but without bursting no damage was done. At night information was received at Divl. H.Q. from a deserter that an attack on our lines had been arranged for 12.15 a.m. (German time – 11.15 p.m. Greenwich time). At 11.30 p.m. all the batteries opened fire on German trenches & approaches. The promised attack did not take place.	
Dec. 27th	Quiet day. The above mentioned deserter stated that reinforcements for the trenches would be marching along the ~~Aubers~~ AUBERS – TRIVELET – FAUQUISSART road between	

12

Hour, date, place	Summary of Events	Remarks and references to appendices
	10 pm and 12 mn. Bursts of fire were accordingly brought to bear on this road at 10.30 pm, 11.0 pm & 11.30 pm. The results of the fire are not known.	
Dec 28th	Quiet day. Sentry on duty Z Battery guns wounded by spy	
Dec. 29th 30th	Quiet days	
Dec. 31st	A French howitzer, which is attached to Brigade & under the command of Capt GROSVENOR, Z Battery was moved to A lines to engage a house occupied by snipers	
12 noon	Hostile artillery abandoned their continued silence & put a number of shells into the neighbourhood of LA FLINQUE	

H. Umiacke
Lt Col RHA
Cmdg 5th Bde RHA

Appendix I

NOT TO SCALE

APPENDIX II

Instructions for Action 8th Divisional Artillery.

16th December, 1914.

Reference 1/80,000 sheet St.OMER, ARRAS, and LILLE and country S.W. of ARMENTIERES.

1. The LAHORE division is attacking GERMAN trenches opposite GIVENCHY this morning.
   This attack will afterwards be pressed on RUE D'OUVERT.
   The MEERUT division are cooperating with a fire attack by bursts of fire.

2. The 8th Division will support operations of Indian Corps by heavy fire attacks at intervals throughout the day.

3. 5th R.H.A. Bde. - "O" Battery, to search trench in P 10.

   57th Battery to search trench from TRIVELET to T of FAUQUISSART.

   33rd R.F.A. Bde. - To search German trenches in P 9 d and P 10.

   45th R.F.A. Bde. To concentrate on German trench between TRIVELET and T of FAUQUISSART.

   8th Heavy Bde. Section at St. VAAST - to search German trenches in square P 10 with shrapnel.
   Remainder to await further orders.

   All firing to commence at 11.0.a.m. and to be continued by bursts in cooperation with the infantry throughout the day.
   Ammunition to be expended up to limit allowed none to be retained for night firing.

R H Johnson
Major. R.A.

Brigade Major 8th Divisional Arty.

Issued at 10.45 am

"A" Form. Appendix Army Form C. 2121
MESSAGES AND SIGNALS.

Prefix	Code	Words	Charge	This message is on a/c of:	Recd. at m.
Office of Origin and Service Instructions.		Sent			Date
		At m.		Service.	From
		To			By
		By		(Signature of "Franking Officer.")	

TO { MAJOR DOBSON
     5TH RHA Bde.

| Sender's Number | Day of Month | In reply to Number | AAA |
| SF 86 | 18TH | | |

Herewith a diagram of cme. showing arrangements made for proposed attack to night, ~~which it~~ In the event of operation taking place our H.Q. will be at the RED BARN. The 24th Bde will be in Reserve to us. and our Reg"s as follows.
"A" lines 2 Middlesex
"B" lines 2 Scottish Rifles
"C" lines 2 Devon's Reg" who commence the attack and will be supported by 2 West York's Reg".
When joined up your line will run through the PC line to RED BARN as shown on diagram. One telephone will be left here for cme with Divn. Copies of diagram have been sent to YH, ZX, ZY.

From SIGNALS ZW   9.40 a
Place
Time

Censor.   Signature of Addressor or person authorised to telegraph in his name.

5 - A + B Bde.   Appendix III

COPY No. 8

8th Div. Operation Orders No. 5.

18th December, 1914.

Reference Map 1/40,000.

1. In conjunction with attacks along general front of Allies ; portions of enemy's trenches will be attacked by 4th Corps at dusk to-day.

2. Main objective of 8th Div. attack NEUVE CHAPELLE and trench running generally N. and S. to East of that village atv one time occupied by British Troops.

3. 23 Inf. Bde.
23rd Inf. Bde. and 15th Field Coy. R.E. will attack enemy's trenches opposite "C" Lines at 4-30 p.m.
First objective, enemy's front trench in neighbourhood of "Moated Grange".
One Bn. 24 Inf. Bde, will be at C.Os quarters "A" Lines at 4 p.m. and will come under orders of G.O.C. 23rd Inf. Bde. at that hour.
After enemy's front trench has been secured the attack will be continued on the main trench in rear.

24th Inf. Bde.
24 Inf. Bde., less one Bn., will be in Div. Reserve at ROUGE CROIX at 4 p.m.

25th Inf. Bde.
25 Inf. Bde. will demonstrate with view to supporting 23 Inf. Bde. and keep enemy engaged in fron of D, E, F, Lines.

Div. R.A.
Attack of 23 Inf. Bde. will be preceeded by Artillery bombardment commencing at 4-15 p.m.

Div. Mtd. Troops.
Div. Mtd. Troops will move to LA FLINQUE cross roads arriving there 5 p.m. as Div. Reserve.

4. Hd. Qrs. Inf. Bdes. from 4 p.m.

23 Inf. Bde. at RED BARN just North of ROUGE CROIX on LA BASSEE Road.

24 Inf. Bde. - same as 23 Inf. Bde.

25 Inf. Bde. - House on LAVENTIE - LA FLINQUE Road just NORTH of Ft. d'ESQUIN.

5 REPORTS to present Div. H.Q.

Issued at 4 p.m.

W.H. Anderson Colonel, G.S.
8th Div.

Received at 7.5 pm !

Appendix III

Instructions 8th Divisional Artillery
for Action Night 18th-19th December, 1914.

Reference Map Country S.W. of ARMENTIERES $\frac{1}{40,000}$.

1. The following instructions are issued in confirmation of verbal instructions given this morning.
   Please acknowledge receipt on annexed slip.

2. The Primary objective is the hostile trench P 5 to J 21.
   The Secondary objective is the hostile trench P 5 to P 20. Subsequent action will be dictated by the course of events.

3. The 33rd F.A. Bde. To open fire at 4.15 p.m. on enemy's trench P 5, J 21 C and D, P 9, and P 14.
   At 4.30 p.m., or as requested by G.O.C. 23 rd Inf. Bde., fire to be concentrated towards P 14 and J 21 C and D and to the EAST of these points.
   The section 57 th Howitzer battery near CROIX BARBEE will be under the tactical control of the O.C., 33rd F.A. Bde., and will cooperate in the execution of the tasks allotted to that Bde.

4. The 5th H.A. Bde. and 1st and 57th Field Batteries to open fire at 4.15 p.m. on hostile trench P 5 to P 15 and on NEUVE CHAPELLE.
   At 4.30 p.m., or as requested by G.O.C., 23rd Inf. Bde., fire to be switched rather to the EAST to search the trench P 5 to P 15 and the approaches to this trench from the EAST.
   It will also be necessary at 4.30 p.m. to concentrate some fire towards TRIVELET and LES MOILLES Pe.
   It is suggested that 57th battery will be suitable for this task and that its fire should be reserved for that purpose.

5. The 45th F.A. Bde. (less 1st battery) will act in cooperation with 25th Inf. Bde.
   It will open fire at 4.15 p.m. on hostile trenches from T of FAUQUISSART to the junction of our lines with the 7th Division.

6. 8th Heavy Bde. to open fire at 4.15 p.m. and search square P 10 - At 4.30 p.m. or as requested by G.O.C. 33rd Inf. Bde., the three roads leading to the hostile trenches at TRIVELET, MIN DU PIETRE and NORTH of NEUVE CHAPELLE will be searched with shrapnel.
   The Heavy batteries will act primarily against any hostile guns which are reported to be harassing our infantry, such guns must be engaged at once.

7. The 7th Mountain Battery — The two guns already in action will act as called upon by the G.O.C. 23rd Inf. Bde. or by the battalion commander they are in immediate touch with.

   The remainder of the battery will be held in readiness about square O 1 A communication being maintained with Headquarters R.A., through section 118th battery at BOUR DEVILLE.

8. The 5th H.A., 33rd F.A., and 8th Heavy Brigades, will maintain close touch with the G.O.C., 23rd. Inf. Bde. at RED BARN at whose Headquarters they will be represented by an Officer.
   Similarly 45th F.A. Bde. will establish connection with 25th Inf. Bde.

9. Brigade Commanders are not to consider themselves bound by these instructions but will act in entire cooperation with the Infantry Brigade Commander concerned. They will further take whatever action is deemed necessary on reports received from their own observation officers forthwith.

10. Reports of the situation as affecting the Artillery will be made to Headquarters, R.A. every two hours or on the occurrence of any important event.

11. The support of the Infantry is of primary importance and for this purpose bursts of fire must be intense.
    Economy in expenditure of ammunition must however be looked to when it can be done without prejudice to the attainment of the above object.

R T Johnson Major. R.A.

Brigade Major 8th Divisional Artillery.

18.12.14.

Issued at 2.30 pm.

CONFIDENTIAL

Commanding 5th H.A. Bde.   Appendix IV

A counter attack against the enemy is going to be made in the GIVENCHY and FESTUBERT area this afternoon.

The G.O.C. 8th Division wishes to occupy the enemy in our front by fire.

The crisis of the attack is expected to take place between 3 pm and 5 pm this afternoon and the maximum expenditure of ammunition should be between those hours.

5th H.A. Bde. — To search enemy's trenches in front of C and D lines and the approaches by Mⁿ DU PIETRE and just NORTH of NEUVE CHAPELLE.
Bursts of fire to be employed up to 20 rounds per gun.
Sf Battery not to fire without urgent necessity.

45th F.A. Bde. — To search enemy's trenches in front of E and F lines and the approaches by RUE D'ENFER and F^{me} DELAVAL.
Bursts of fire to be employed up to 15 rounds per gun.

33rd F.A. Bde. — To concentrate on enemy's trenches in P.19 B., P.20 A and C, and P.24 B.
Bursts of fire to be employed up to 20 rounds per gun.

In all cases fire should be opened as soon as possible but the maximum intensity is to take place between 3 and 5 pm.

21 XII 14
12.30 pm

R.T. Johnson Major
B.M. R.A. 8th D.

8th, Division.

5th, Bde. R. H. A.

January, 1915.

8th Division

5th Bde: R.H.A.

Vol II. 28-12-44 — 31-1-15

121/4194

Hour, Date, Place		Remarks and references to appendices
	Summary of FVO's	
	10 p.m. to 12 mn. Quite if fair morn accordingly bombed Khan in this road at 10.30 pm. 11.0 pm & 11.25 pm. The results of firing are not known	
Dec 28th, 29th, 30th Dec. 31st	Quiet days. Seeing no Z Battery was wounded by spy. A Lunch, Kurutzer, which is attached to brigade trench command of Capt. GROSVENOR, Z Battery was moved to a line to enjoy a home occupied by snipers. Took a killing advanced their continued silence & put a large number of shell in the neighborhood of LA FLINQUE.	
12 noon		
Jan 1st 1915	Quiet day. The trench bombers under Capt Grosvenor & Scott have been attached to the Brigade moved along to A line & attempted to destroy a house that is occupied by snipers - so far we have not acquired the preparation of trench bombs & the fire has been ineffective	

Hour, Date, Place	Summary of Events	Remarks and references to appendices
Jan. 2nd.	Quiet day. Our forward observing officers assisted in registering targets for the 5th siege battery & 3rd F.A. Battery. This proved rather a high trial for the telephone communications but was nevertheless successfully carried out. It was reported that reliefs to Fromelles were being carried out between 10 pm & 12 mn. Accordingly bursts of fire from all batteries were brought to bear at 10.30pm, 11.0pm & 11.30pm on the roads immediately North & West of NEUVE CHAPELLE in hopes of catching the reliefs. The result is not known.	
Jan 3rd 10.45 am 11.15 am	Orders received to concentrate all available guns on AUBERS. Then orders received to switch on to NEUVE CHAPELLE. Both concentrations were successfully carried out. It is not known whether	

Hour. Date Place	Summary of Events	Remarks and references to appendices
	any damage was done to the Germans. Our own infantry state that some shell fell among them, but portions of shell found proved to be of German origin – the back blast possibly accounting for error.	
4th	Uneventful day. Z Battery shelled LE PLOUICH producing a prompt reply from hostile artillery, which however did no harm as they had got position of Z Battery wrong	
5th	similar to 4th	
6th	Quiet day. O & Z Batteries both shelled LE PLOUICH, immediately getting a reply out of the German artillery, who never notice our shelling any other place. O Battery informed that they constitute part of the Corps reserve & must	

Hour, Date, Place	Summary of Events	Remarks and references to Appendices
	be ready to move to join corps reserve in an emergency.	
10 pm	Trench mortars succeeded in bringing down snipers house, & it is hoped inflicted damage on enemy. Capt GROSVENOR received congratulations of B.G.C.R.A. 8th Division	
7th	O & Z Batteries shelled hostile trenches & LE PLOUICH	
10 pm	Trench howitzers succeeded in destroying another house that was supposed to shelter a maxim gun	
8th	Orders received to concentrate all efforts on annoying & wearing out Germans in NEUVE CHAPELLE area. Batteries ordered to undertake as many private enterprises as possible in cooperation with affiliated infantry battalions. Batteries ordered to search the PIETRE road between 10 pm & 12 mn every night	Appendix 5

Hour	Date	Place	Summary of Events	Remarks and references to appendices
11 am	9th		Enemy placed some shell in LAVENTIE but did us serious damage. 7 Battery fired at LE PLOUICH and at our own reply. Press of shell rounds showed that Germans were using 11.5 cm. French Howitzer. Expenditure of ammunition limited to 40 rounds per gun. The 57th Battery not allowed to fire owing to shortage of ammunition	
3 pm	9th			
12 nn	10th		Ordered Batteries one to fire on LE PLOUICH area & fire switches on trenches North of NEUVECHAPELLE. A sausage shaped captive balloon, which had several times been seen before was again observed in neighbourhood of HAUT POMMEREAU Trench mortar howitzers succeeded in destroying a house opposite B	
1.35 pm				

Hour date place			Remarks & references to appendices
11/R	11:15am	Summary of Event: Line occupied by enemy's snipers fire of O & Z Batteries concentrated on trenches near TRIVELET & Praelize was carried out in the afternoon with new trench mortars — result entirely unsatisfactory — One had 7 other rounds dangerous	
	11:45am	O & Z Batteries concentrated on trenches North of NEUVECHAPELLE. Nothing special. O & Z Batteries fired on enemy trenches — slight return fire from enemy guns & trenches.	
	12/R	trench howitzer succeeded in silencing an the hostile snipers, have infact	
	13/R 2am	By an arrangement with West Yorkshire Regt. O Battery & 36 R Battery shelled hostile trenches in front of O lines. The West Yorks then cheered & raised a heavy fire in hope of making enemy show themselves.	
	5:45am		

Hour. Date. Place	Summary of Events	Remarks & references to appendices
13th	in anticipation of attack. The result seemed to shew that enemy were not holding their advanced trenches. Nothing special. O & 2 Batteries co-operated with infantry shelling trenches west of Pietre.	
14th	O & Z Batteries shelled RUE D'ENTIER & PIETRE ROAD. Enemy's guns replied & for the first time appeared to find our gun positions dropping shell in to 15K.O & Z Batteries. Z Battery had one man slightly wounded. This first casualty from shell fire suffered by Brigade.	
15th	Battery searched for bttrs O & Z but did not succeed in inflicting any damage on them.	
16th	Shelled approaches to trenches. Z Battery engaged some houses in trenches in	

and had place | Summary of Events | Remarks & references

| | front of 7 a.m. — They succeeded in putting in appearance
17th | 7 succession shell through our horses.
| Damage done unknown.
| Whilst the Artillery Advisers to the 4th
| Corps were inspecting the trench numbers
| near L Battery, a german shell passed
| him to quit.
| Quiet day. Batteries fired on trenches
| & LA MOTTE farm with the object of
| keeping down sniping
18th 11 a.m. | D Battery in conjunction with West
| York & 36th Battery shelled trench
| near CHAPIGNY, with the object of making
| German sharpshooters rg in a large
| to infantry. No known results of fire
| This 9 batteries are limited to 5 rounds
| per gun per diem by ordrs of GHQ.
19th south | No section to A/Kh digging at a
| redoubt for the infantry near FAUQUISSART
| church. Gr Symns, 57th Battery was

Date	Place	Summary of Events
20 R. 21st		Slightly wounded in the sub-maxillary No incident to report. Trench mortars shelled mines & trenches Opposite D have knocking down several traverses & causing during considerable damage to the trenches.
22nd & 23rd		Quiet days. On 23rd experimental practice with 3.7 trench heavy mortar, using electric tubes. The results were satisfactory – Black powder & trench tubes were used.
24 R. & 25 R.		Quiet days Sherwood Foresters from right of Division reported that they were suffering heavily from trench – trench mortar detachment went out to patrol in A lines with 1 4" Trench howitzer & 1 or 3.7" trench howitzer The 3.7" trench howitzer burst on the

Return to references to trajectories

Hour, date, place		Remarks & references to Appendices
16th	Summary of Front. Armor it is evening. The "mules" turned out with high explosn Shrapnel fired by guns at close range	
26th 8.0 pm	Quiet day — Battery party digging at redoubt near FAUQUISSART church had 6 high explosn shrapnel fired at or near them. No casualties were suffered.	
27th 11.00 am	Kaiser's birthday. O Battery fired 56 minute fuzes at LA PLOUICH.	
12 noon	Z Battery gunfire scattering shrapnel on various pts of German trenches reported.	
1.15 pm	Germans shelled Z Battery with H.E. shrapnel, though their shooting was accurate Z Battery suffered no casualties	
28th 4.15 pm	Germans fired a few H.E. shrapnel	

Hour. Date. Place	Summary of Events	Remarks to References to Appendices
	& common shell in to the RUE DE PARADIS - no harm was done. Detached section 57th Battery rejoined unit	
29th	'O' Battery and 'Z' Battery fired on enemies trenches during the day. 'O' also fired on NEUVE CHAPELLE. Captain A.K. Main joined the Brigade as Adjutant in relief of Major M.C. Dobson who proceeded to England on posting to the New Army.	
30th 11.35 A.M.	Observation Station 'M1' was shelled. Quiet day. Batteries shelled hostile trenches and approaches on C & D lines.	
31st 8 A.M.	'Port Arthur' was shelled for about an hour by field guns	
4 p.m.	A few time shrapnel burst E. of LAVENTIE apparently fired at infantry reliefs.	
6 p.m.	A few more shell fell round 'PORT ARTHUR'	

Hour. Date. Place	Summary of Events	Remarks to References to Appendices
	'O' Battery fired on house on PIETRE Road - 'Z' Battery fired on hostile trenches opposite 'D' lines. 57th Battery registered hostile trenches opposite D and E lines.	
2/2/15.	[signature] Major R.H.A. Commanding 5th Bde. R.H.A.	

A 2

121/4508

8th Division

5th Bde: R H A.

Vol III 1 — 28.2.15

Army Form C. 2118.

WAR DIARY
or
INTELLIGENCE SUMMARY

(Erase heading not required.)

Instructions regarding War Diaries and Intelligence Summaries are contained in F. S. Regs., Part II. and the Staff Manual respectively. Title pages will be prepared in manuscript.

Hour, Date, Place	Summary of Events and Information	Remarks and references to Appendices
1st February	Bn. still hold E. of LAVENTIE in the morning & again about 4.15 p.m.	
9.20 p.m.	'O' & 'Z' fired on hostile approaches and trenches during the day	
	'Z' fired two bursts at machine gun in house at M20a H7 Exactly by infantry and previously reported by Z.	
2nd Feb.	'O' and 'Z' fired on trenches & houses at POMMEREAU. An increase in machine gun fire at night Batty.	
3rd Feb.	Same objectives during the day as on the 2nd — Somewhat intermittent during the West trenches opposite Co 'D' lines were being relieved at night.	
9.15 p.m.	Both batteries in engagement with 57s & remaining Divisional Artillery opened fire in locality described by describer five rounds per gun —	
4th Feb.	'O' and 'Z' fired on enemy trenches and houses in neighbourhood of PIETRE during the day —	
3.30 p.m.	'Z' Gun position and billets were heavily shelled by H.E. Howrs from the direction of LE PLOUICH. Enemy fire very accurate but no damage. R.Bde asked for a concentration on LE PLOUICH about 3.30 p.m. next day	
5th Feb.	'Z' fired on approaches, hostile trenches 'O' on AUBERS and neighbourhood RUE D'ENFER during the day.	
1 p.m.	Enemy shelled RUE PARADIS with shrapnel and HE. — One driver of 'O' Killed.	
6th Feb.	During the day 'O' fired on PIETRE, LARUSSIE, and PIETRE road. 'Z' on enemy approaches. Nothing to report. Major D.C. Spencer-Smith and Major H.P.S. Cadell returned to England & posting to Home Establishment for Home Army. Lieuts. A. Sudbury and Edye joined 'Z'. L.P. Wayburg joined 'O'.	

WAR DIARY or INTELLIGENCE SUMMARY

Army Form C. 2118.

Instructions regarding War Diaries and Intelligence Summaries are contained in F. S. Regs., Part II. and the Staff Manual respectively. Title pages will be prepared in manuscript.

(Erase heading not required.)

Hour, Date, Place	Summary of Events and Information	Remarks and references to Appendices
7th Feb 2	'O' fired on RUE D'ENFER and Enemy Trenches. 'Z' on occupied houses at road junction of RUE D'ENFER and AUBERS ROAD — 4 direct hits. 57F Enemy Breastwork opposite C Redn. Captain Stannock went posted as Adjutant 33rd Bde. R. F. A.	
8th Feb 2	'O' & 'Z' fired on AUBERS — 57F on Enemy Trenches. 2nd New Territorial Officers arrived for attachment to the Brigade to gain experience before Enemy put them in units. LA FLINQUE CROSS ROADS and LAVENTIE were shelled by Enemy during the day.	
9th Feb 2	Signal 'S.O.S.' was introduced throughout the Division to denote to Enemy attack + a call for Artillery support. Practice at getting Artillery support at various parts of the line was carried out through the day. 'Z' held the record – 30 seconds from call to fire RCB Batteries fired on Enemy Trenches during the day.	
10th Feb 1	'Z' fired on Enemy Trenches and PIETRE road. Nothing to report. Lieutenants J.d. Lee, D.D.V. Carden and H.J. Pearse arrived about 10 p.m. to be attached to the Brigade.	
11th Feb 2	'O' 'Z' and 57F fired on Enemy Trenches and approaches. Enemy shelled	
3.15 p.m.	Enemy shelled LAVENTIE.	
12th Feb 4	'O' 'Z' & 57F fired on Enemy Trenches + approaches.	
13th Feb 2 10 a.m.	Concentration of Heavy Artillery of 7th, 8th and present Divisions on LE PLOUICH and POINT POMMEREAU gun positions.	
10.30 a.m.	'Z' turned on to hostile on RUE D'ENFER. This shown fire at once from that direction on to RUE TILLELOY. O.C. 115th 13th R.F.A. turned his Brigade on to Enemy which immediately silenced their fire.	
2 p.m.	RUE du PARADIS and LAVENTIE shelled by Enemy.	

1247 W 3299 200,000 (E) 8/14 J.B.C. & A. Forms/C. 2118/11.

Army Form C. 2118.

WAR DIARY
or
INTELLIGENCE SUMMARY

(Erase heading not required.)

Instructions regarding War Diaries and Intelligence Summaries are contained in F. S. Regs., Part II. and the Staff Manual respectively. Title pages will be prepared in manuscript.

Hour, Date, Place	Summary of Events and Information	Remarks and references to Appendices
14th Feb. 11.30 am	57th fired on LES MOTTES FERME, reported to be headquarters of a hostile battalion, obtaining 5 direct hits on the building and finally setting on fire a post seen endeavouring to put the fire out was disposed with shrapnel. "O" located an observation post on a haystack and engaged it, knocking 76 top portion of stack. Two figures were seen hurriedly escaping.	
15th Feb.	"O" and "Z" fired on hostile trenches, RUE DE BACQUEROT  shelled by the enemy. Some shells fell close to "Z" Batterys guns.	
16th Feb.	"O" fired on hostile trenches. 57th and "Z" fired on LES MOTTES FERME. "Z" was shelled in the afternoon but without damage being done.	
17th Feb. 18th Feb.	"O" and "Z" fired on approaches to hostile trenches in the neighbourhood of PIETRE crossroads. "O" and "Z" fired on approaches to hostile trenches about a dozen shells fell round "Z" battery and three on the RUE DE PARADIS. The 57th battery left the brigade to join the 8th division, its place being taken by the 9th battery but the latter is not attached to this brigade.	

WAR DIARY or INTELLIGENCE SUMMARY

Army Form C. 2118.

(Erase heading not required.)

Instructions regarding War Diaries and Intelligence Summaries are contained in F. S. Regs., Part II. and the Staff Manual respectively. Title pages will be prepared in manuscript.

Hour, Date, Place	Summary of Events and Information	Remarks and references to Appendices
19th Feb.	"C" and "Z" fired on hostile trenches. Both Batteries were shelled during day on a stationary observed. The shrapnel falling near "Z".	
20th Feb.	"O" and "Z" fired on trenches in front of C and Dhour. a few enemy shell fell short of the RUE DE PARADIS	Snow, Rain & gale in the evening.
21st Feb.	Nothing to report. Batteries fired on Trenches.	Snow early, aft. fine.
22nd Feb.	" "	
23rd "	" "	
24th "	" "	Very fine
25th Feb.	"Z" were shelled during morning by field guns from direction of AUBERS. No damage. "O" replied. Both Batteries shelled Enemy Trenches and approaches during the day.	
26th Feb.	Lt Col Unwicke Commanding the 13th at they returned to proceed to G.H.Q. on special duty. Batteries shelled enemy Trenches & approaches. G.S. wagon of Hd Bn Column blown up & day while carrying Trench [?] Down H.Q. Hd Trench in wagon – 2 men & Pte Brown cycling [?] were severely wounded. Right drivers of the wagon only slightly – whilst horses also slightly. Wagon nothing left. L Col Unwicke promoted Brigadier-General to command 2 Gp[?] G.H.Q. Artillery. Batteries fired on enemy Trenches & approaches.	Dull
27th Feb.		

Army Form C. 2118.

WAR DIARY
or
INTELLIGENCE SUMMARY

(Erase heading not required.)

Instructions regarding War Diaries and Intelligence Summaries are contained in F. S. Regs., Part II. and the Staff Manual respectively. Title pages will be prepared in manuscript.

Hour, Date, Place	Summary of Events and Information	Remarks and references to Appendices
26th Feb.	Nothing to report. Officer on PIETRE road (between cross roads) and AUBERS. 2 enemy flashes.	None

A. Newmarch
Capt Adjt
5. Bde. R. H.A.

8th, Division.

5th, Bde, R. H. A.

March, 1915.

8th, Division.

~~Bdes.Bde., R. H. A.~~

Army Form C. 2118.

WAR DIARY
or
INTELLIGENCE SUMMARY

(Erase heading not required.)

Instructions regarding War Diaries and Intelligence Summaries are contained in F. S. Regs, Part II. and the Staff Manual respectively. Title pages will be prepared in manuscript.

Hour, Date, Place	Summary of Events and Information	Remarks and references to Appendices
1st March	'O' & 'Z' engaged hostile trenches	Fine except for two heavy showers.
2nd "	'O' & 'Z' engaged hostile trenches. Lieutenant Ussher left the Brigade on appointment as A.D.C. to Brig. Gen. of 2nd Group. C.H.O. A. Elkest.	Fine
3rd "	'O' & 'Z' fired on AUBERS and enemy trenches. 'O' prepared position for 'Z' battery. The following Batteries are attached to XXIII & Division Temporarily and turned with the Brigade viz: H.A. Group under Lt Col H Rouse D.S.O. - 'A','Q','W' and F & 7. - The two last Bring the 14th D.A R.H.A. under Major H.A. Tiston.	Very wet.
4th "	'O' & 'Z' did not fire. 'J' & 'T' registered. 'Q' & 'W' moved into position at dark.	Fine
5th "	'O' & 'Z' did not fire. 'J' & 'T' registered. 'Q' & 'W' registered. 'A' moved into position at dark being shelled more than usual chiefly LA FLINQUE, CROIX MARIE and BAC QUEROT.	Fine
6th "	'O' & 'Z' fired on AUBERS & enemy trenches to cover A's registration. A without success. Clothutz was shelled not + chiselled to change position to night. Lt Col A. T. Butler arrived and took over command of 5th B.R.H.A.	Very wet & cold
7th "	'O' & 'Z' did a little registration. Remain Batteries completed registration.	
8th "	General programme for attack received. Nothing doing.	

Army Form C. 2118

WAR DIARY
or
INTELLIGENCE SUMMARY
(Erase heading not required.)

Instructions regarding War Diaries and Intelligence Summaries are contained in F.S. Regs., Part II. and the Staff Manual respectively. Title pages will be prepared in manuscript.

Hour, Date, Place		Summary of Events and Information	Remarks and references to Appendices
9th		'O'+'Z' did further registration for combining with 7th Divn attack. Final orders to morrow received.	Appendix (4)
10th	7.30 a.m.	Wire cutting & heavy guns commenced bombardment.	
	7.40 a.m.	'O'+'Z' in combination with remaining Artillery commenced 1st phase of bombardment. 2.10 guns in action.	Appendix (1)
	8.5 a.m.	'O'+'Z' turned on to second phase covering left of attack.	" (1)
	8.35 a.m.	'O'+'Z' turned on to 3rd phase covering area to prevent counter attack.	" (1)
	11.5 a.m.	All R.H.A. Batteries concentrated on point 93	" (2) and (6)
	11.30 a.m.	Bombard 'O'+'Z' on RUE D'ENFER at slow rate of fire.	" (3)
	2.30 p.m.	Stop firing.	
	3. p.m.	Re-opened fire at slow rate.	
	6 p.m.	7th + 8th Division infantry held the line left on German trenches at Junction A C + D thence thence F & D on PIETRE ROAD + on E. A. NEUVE CHAPELLE. Stop firing ordered.	" (5)
	8 p.m.	Orders for the night received.	" (5) + (7)
11th	6.45 a.m.	Z + O opened fire in accordance with 7th Divn instructions.	" (8)
	7.30 a.m.	Turned on to 2nd phase at slow rate of fire. Remained on it for remainder of day except for small occasional changes.	

Army Form C. 2118.

WAR DIARY
or
INTELLIGENCE SUMMARY

(Erase heading not required.)

Instructions regarding War Diaries and Intelligence Summaries are contained in F. S. Regs., Part II. and the Staff Manual respectively. Title pages will be prepared in manuscript.

Hour, Date, Place	Summary of Events and Information	Remarks and references to Appendices
11th Corps H.Q.	At the end of the day night lines were laid out as in the Appendix	Appendix (9)
12th 5.30 am	Enemy counter attacked from N.E. of BOIS DU BIEZ and from W. Enemy repulsed. On cooperation with 22" Inf Bde hrs in TRIVELET.	
11.30 am	Bombardment for attack at 12.15 Inf Bde Attack succeeded in getting to N.E. of PIETRE ROAD. 7th Division took two prisoners. 2nd & 6th fired throughout the day on various zones in support of attack.	(10)
	Copy of order taken in German Artillery Officer dated 3/1/15 ordered Special attacks to be directed on advancing Battalions at L'Epinette (Z's position throughout the mmts.)	"
1 p.m.	Batteries of B.A.H.Q. moved to rear position in M 20. Regs and M 26a. F.8 + returned to command of 8th Division moved B Group (each with 3 Hows.)	
13th	Batteries report the morning firing up Observation stations in NEUVE CHAPELLE – very hard to hit. Enemy threatened counter attack from BOIS DE BIEZ at 2 p.m. On Z turned on N.W. Edge of Bois & N.W. Edge A.A. Bursts of fire. Counter attack did not develop and the Batteries spent the rest of daylight registering.	
14th 10 am	On Z started registering on the new trips & held by 25th Inf & 8th Division stations had to find & were constantly cut.	
	But R. Batteries registered	"
15th	"	"
16th	"	
17th	"	heavy premature owing to the few unwrapped fuzes.

WAR DIARY or **INTELLIGENCE SUMMARY**

(Erase heading not required.)

Army Form C. 2118

Instructions regarding War Diaries and Intelligence Summaries are contained in F. S. Regs., Part II. and the Staff Manual respectively. Title pages will be prepared in manuscript.

Hour, Date, Place	Summary of Events and Information	Remarks and references to Appendices
18th March 10 a.m.	Test of O.P. sent up by Rifle Brigade; was well executed. Batteries reduced by order to reduced expenditure of ammunition. Limit fixed to a gun a day. This we have to thank the Stankers at home for. No more firing during the day. Day's allowance gone in shoot.	Somewhat gale.
19th "	No firing. NEUVE CHAPELLE shelled &. Rifle guns and a trench 5.9	
20th "	No firing. A certain amount of hostile in our right front at night - in front of Indian corps.	Fine.
21st "	No firing.	
22nd " 11.30 pm	'D' & 'Z' each fired a salvo of six guns on enemy digging party in combination with Berkshires who also opened with heavy rifle fire.	Fine.
23rd "	No firing.	Fine - a wet evening.
24th "	Z fired 6 rnds at sniper houses.	
25th "	Capt. B. L. Burke 10th set off from Isap A.V. train bolted & 27 Squadn. Lieut Lucas (O.O.) S.V. to Ambulance - etc Rennes - from attached to Z. Came as O.O. Z did not fire. D did not fire -	No raids.
26th "	No firing. Amn Col moved in 3pm to G 29 d. O + Z moonlit nights new positions H 20 + 27. Relieved B to H 27 B	fine moonlight night.

Army Form C. 2118.

WAR DIARY
or
INTELLIGENCE SUMMARY

(Erase heading not required.)

Instructions regarding War Diaries and Intelligence Summaries are contained in F. S. Regs., Part II. and the Staff Manual respectively. Title pages will be prepared in manuscript.

Hour, Date, Place	Summary of Events and Information	Remarks and references to Appendices
27th March.		
28th. 12. noon.	Batteries arrived at Nieuport about 1.30 am. no firing – German aeroplane over about 9 am. Quiet.	
6. pm.	About 10 shells fell near Haendert Cross Rds from Ramelles direction.	
Sunny day	About 15 5.9 Shells fell near Z fires from Ramelles direction.	
29th.	Both batteries registered squares N.5. N.6. No. X11. – O'Brakie gun near La Vovie at N5 D 3,2. and a Cupola at N5 D.4.2.	
	'O' moved to new night 29/30 and to H 33 C.4.7.	
	'Z' registered – fired 15 rounds.	
7–8 p.m.	'O' moved to new position.	
30th.	'Z' registered – fired 13 rounds.	
	'O' prepared new position & dug in.	
	3 shells fired at Klinkart about 2.30 pm – probably 59".	
31st.	'Z' ordered to send forward 1 gun to N 4 a.1.1. 2nd Canadian Bde having heavy gun fire. This move was carried out 8.30 pm.	
	'Z' fired 15 rounds. 'O' 25 rounds registering.	

M Dunlap
Adj. 5th Div RHA.

31.3.15.

"B"

Ref:-
maps:-
FRANCE
Sheet 36 S.W.
1/20,000
Special maps
issued by 8th
& 7th Divisions
respectively.

Detailed Report dealing with the operations
of 10th to 14th March 1915, as carried out by
5th Brigade Royal Horse Artillery.

5th Brigade R.H.A. (O & Z batteries) were placed
under the command of H.A. Group for the
operations pending.

10th March 1915

7.40 am — 5th Brigade R.H.A. in combination with all other
Artillery commenced 1st phase of 8th Division
bombardment. Objective area (7)(3)(4).

8.5 am — Turned on to 2nd phase. Objective (79) to (4) and
search back 300x.

8.35 am — Turned on to 3rd phase. Objective (94) to (96) search
300x.

11.5 am — Concentrated with remaining R.H.A. batteries on
point (93).

~~H.A. Group came under command of B.G.C.R.A.
VIIth Division of B.U.R.A.D. not commenced 1st phase
7th Div bombardment~~

11.30 am — Turned on to RUE d'ENFER at slow rate of
fire.

2.30 pm — Stop firing.

3 pm — Re-opened fire at slow rate on RUE d'ENFER.

6 pm — 7th and 8th Divisions held the line left on German
trenches at division of C & D lines - Thence to elbow
on PIETRE road & on E of NEUVE CHAPELLE.

6 pm — Stop firing.

8 pm — Orders for night received ~~from~~ O Battery on (113), 'Z' Battery
on track running N.W. from N.E. exit from AUBERS.
These were allotted by H.A. Group. 'O' Battery to be
also prepared to concentrate on 144.

11th March 1915

6.45 am — 'O' & 'Z' opened fire in accordance with 7th Divn R.A.
instructions on area allotted by H.A. Group: Viz- the
front MOULIN DE PIETRE — TRIVELET dividing this
front with remaining batteries of H.A. Group, searching
from RIVIERE DES LAYES back to within safe
distance of our trenches. Rate of fire Section fire 30 seconds.

7.30 am — 2nd phase of 7th Divn bombardment 'O' & 'Z' on same
area as for 1st phase. 'O' having orders to be careful
not to fire W. of (06). Rate of fire Sect. fire 2 minutes.

11th March 1915
cont. — 'O' & 'Z' on 2" phase for remainder of day except for small occasional changes. Rate of fire was normally Section fire 5 minutes. Occasionally increased for special objectives in the same area.

6.30 pm. — Orders for night received. 'O' & 'Z' were expected to move to VIIIth Division Area. They were ordered to be laid with central lines on PIETRE up till time of movement. They did not move.

12th March 1915
5.30 am. — Enemy counter-attacked from due W. and from N of BOIS DU BIEZ. 'O' Battery in co-operation with 22" Infy. Bde opened fire at once on TRIVELET and neighbouring trenches. 'Z' also switched on. Counter-attack easily repulsed.

11.50 am. — O & Z assisted in bombardment preparatory to 7th Div attack. They fired on area 106, 107, 110. Rate of fire Sect: fire 2 minutes.

12.30 pm. — Same objectives same rate. Attack reported to have got to N.E. of PIETRE ROAD. O & Z fired for remainder of day — constantly switching in support of attack.
Throughout the day information was very difficult to obtain as to movements of Infy. as F.O.O's were very hampered by mist.

7 pm. — Brigade H.Q. and batteries moved to new positions in M20 C 97 and M26 b a 88 & returned to the command of the 8th Division. Joined B Group (Askwith's Horse)

13th — Batteries spent the morning in finding observation stations in NEUVE CHAPELLE. Time allotted by B Group for registering 2 pm to dusk.

2 pm. — Report from F.O.O. Meerut Divn. that enemy were collecting, a few at a time, in trenches N.W. of BOIS DE BIEZ. Counter-attack expected. O & Z ordered to fire on N.W. edge. Did so by the map. Bursts of fire. Counter-attack did not develop & batteries spent remainder of daylight registering.

14th March
10 am. — Batteries continued registering. Time allotted by B group 10 am to 2 pm. During this time all essential points ordered to be registered, were done.

A. T. Butler
Lt Col R.H.A
Comd 5th Bde R.H.A

Bde H.Q.
18/3/15

From O.C. "O" RHA

To Adj. 5th D.A. RHA

Sir

I have the honour to report that "O" Battery

March 10th — Opened fire on the area 3.4.7 at 7.40 a.m. for 25 mins. Fire was then lifted to area 4.7.9 searching back 300 yds for 30 minutes.
An order was then received from 5th HA Brigade turning fire on to 106, 107 & 110 and fire was continued at a slow rate on this area & the RUE D'ENFER for the remainder of the day.
2 Lieut LUCAS was in observation at M 23 A.3.5. and kept me constantly informed of the position of the VEREYS lights & flags on the left of the attack which got as far as the junction of C & D Lines.

March 11th — The fire of the Battery was directed all day on the 106, 141, 110, 114, 113, 108 being switched to different portions of it by order of the 5th HA RHA. As it was rather foggy 2 Lt LUCAS was advanced to a stack at M 23 D.3.5. from which he was able to give me constant information of the Left Attack which he reported as stationary about the junction of C & D Lines. He also reported that apparently the GERMANS were using VEREYS lights when bombarded.

March 12th — About 5 a.m. the GERMAN guns shelled heavily & there were all the indications of a GERMAN counter-attack. A message was received by telephone from General LAWFORD's HQ that the enemy were in considerable

March 12th — numbers in TRIVOLET & the trenches in the neighbourhood & requesting me to open fire at once.

Fire was immediately opened on TRIVOLET & the trenches & report sent to 5th Bde that this had been done as well as forwarding General LAWFORDS message.

Owing to the fog 2/Lt LUCAS was ordered to the neighbourhood of the RUE TILLELOY & took up an observation post in a house about M 23 D 8.4 whence he could see well.

During the morning a message was received to be forwarded on to the Brig. Genl. Cg. 20th Infy. Brigade.

This message was sent on to 2/Lt LUCAS by telephone & carried by orderly to the 20th Infy. Brigade HQ near the MOATED GRANGE.

The Bombardment for the 20th Infy. Brigade attack began at 11.50 a.m.

Immediately after the bombardment 2/Lt LUCAS reported that a considerable number of GERMANS in the trenches SE of the X roads M 23 D had surrendered.

Immediately afterwards he was knocked over by a shell striking the wall behind which he was observing but beyond a bad shaking he was unhurt.

Shortly afterwards 2/Lt LUCAS reported that the left attack had crossed the MIN DU PIETRE Road but that the GUARDS had swung swung round behind our trenches & were lying down in front of his observation station in the RUE TILLELOY.

2/Lt LUCAS also stopped some GRENADIER GUARDS who had lost their direction & were moving behind the RUE TILLELOY.

The RUE TILLELOY was heavily shelled at this time & the telephone wire had twice to be mended

March 12th. Under heavy fire. Qr Humphrey went out on each occasion
The Battery continued to fire all day on various
points of the area 141. 106. 107. 108. 110. 111.
112. 113. 118. 119 as directed by 5th Bde RHA
At dusk the Battery was moved into the area
of the 8th division & its position was handed over
to the 12th Battery R.F.A.
 I have the honour to be
  Sir
   Your obedient servant
    LL Tilney Major RHA
     Cd O. RHA

From O.C. Z Battery RHA
To Adjutant 5th Bde RHA

Z Battery RHA
H.Q./5th Bde RHA.
14-3-15

Sir,

With reference to the operations of March 10th & 12th. I have not retained a copy of the orders received for alteration of line & range. I have never out of touch with your Head Quarters by telephone so that in that respect I have nothing to add to what you already know. 2nd Lt R.C. Lyons was sent out as forward observing officer to the purposes of transmitting information direct to the Divl Artillery Head Quarters. His line was attached to that of the 2nd Siege Battery. No messages were received in on March 11th & 12th. Lindsay was at the Observation Station at FAUQUISSART & although communication was maintained with Q of 30th could be sent as the attack of the 7th Division did not develop.

I was in communication with 2nd Lieut. Q.O. Battery RHA at intervals during the three days. The report on what that officer did has already been forwarded to you by his Commanding Officer.

Lieutenant Major RHA Commanding Z Battery RHA

The accompanying tasks for the attack on NEUVE CHAPELLE are forwarded.

All previous instructions on this subject are to be destroyed.

These instructions and tasks are to be treated as SECRET and be carefully safeguarded.

The Bombardment for the 1st Phase lasts 30 minutes in the case of the Siege batteries, with the exception of 5th Siege which fires for 35 minutes, and for 25 minutes in the case of Horse and Field Guns and Howitzers, when the first lift takes place.

The Bombardment for the 2nd Phase similarly lasts for 30 minutes where the second lift takes place and the 3rd Phase commences.

The 3rd Phase continues until we have consolidated ourselves in the enemy's position.

Tasks for covering any subsequent advance will be allotted later.

Although tasks and times are allotted and these (especially the times) are to be rigidly adhered to, until orders for a change are issued; it is always the unexpected which happens in War and Battery Commanders must be prepared for both change of tasks and for being kept longer on certain zones or brought back to zones which they have quitted.

These changes depend on the information received during the action, and all ranks must be prepared for these changes

R H Johnson

Major. R.A.

Brigade Major 8th Divisional Artillery.

1st PHASE

The Bombardment   30 Minutes

	A M	A M		Ammunition deemed sufficient.
5 Siege Battery	8.0 to 8.20	8.21 to 8.35	Post (27) Trench (33) to (34)	30 rounds per gun
6 Siege Battery	8.5 to 8.20 8.21 to 8.35		Trench (27) to (37) Trench (34) to (72)	do.
Siege Battery M 15 c	8.5 to 8.20 8.21 to 8.35		Trench (72) to (74) Trench (38) to (82) (1 Section on (17) from 8.21 - 8.35)	do.
4 Siege Battery	8.5 to 8.20 8.21 to 8.35		Trench (74) to (76) Front trench Trench (82) to (75) Rear trench	do.
Siege Battery M 10 a	8.5 to 8.20 8.21 to 8.35		Trench (76) to (20) Trench (75) to (77)	do.

4.5" Howitzers

	A M	A M		
35 5th Battery R.F.A.	8.10 to 8.35	8.10 to 8.35	(58) to (40) 1 section on (27)	40 rounds per gun
55 5th do.	8.10 to 8.35		(40) to (41)	do.
31 1st do.	8.10 to 8.35		(75) to (77)	do.

1st Phase (Continued)

13 and 18 Pounders

	A.M.	A.M.		Ammunition deemed sufficient

"A" Group

33rd and 45th Brigades.	8.0 to 8.15	Firecutting 200x at (15) and 75x SOUTH + 150x NORTH of road (34)	40 rounds per gun
33rd Brigade (14)(Guns)	8.16 to 8.35	(27) to (17) and search back 400x	20 rounds per gun
45th Brigade (22 Guns)	8.16 to 8.35	(17) to (20) and search back 400x	

"B" Group

Z Batteries 22nd Brigade	8.5 to 8.35	Trench (33) to (44) and trenches (58) to (70) and (69) to (71)	20 rounds per gun H.E.
1 Battery 22nd Brigade	8.5 to 8.35	(27) and search back 300x	20 rounds per gun Shrapnel *to search*
35th Brigade	8.5 to 8.35	(33) to (17) and search back 400x	10 rounds per gun H.E.
			20 rounds per gun shrapnel to search.
"X" and "Y" Batteries	8.5 to 8.35	Search roads running into BOIS DU BIEZ at (36), (97), and (98)	30 rounds per gun
"N" Battery	8.5 to 8.35	area (7) (3) (4)	do.
118th Heavy Battery	8.20 to 8.35	Post (27)	10 rounds per gun
"Z" and "O" Batteries	8.5 to 8.35	Area (7) (3) (4)	30 rounds per gun
"A" "C" "U" Batteries	8.5 to 8.35	Bursts of fire on "A", (86), (94), (98), search and sweep	20 rounds per gun
"F" and "T" Batteries	8.5 to 8.35	Trench (3) to (4)	20 rd do.

NOTE. On all occasions when shelling troops under cover, one section should fire High Explosive if such ammunition is available.

2nd PHASE.   30 Minutes Bombardment.

6" Howitzers.

	A.M. to A.M.		Ammunition deemed sufficient
5th Siege Battery	8.35 to 9.5	NEUVE CHAPELLE area (62) (32)	30 rounds per gun
6th Siege Battery	8.35 to 9.5	do do.	do.
4th Siege Battery	8.35 to 9.5	(19) and trenches 150x to NORTH of it	do.
Siege Battery M 15 c	8.35 to 9.5	(5) and trench 75x on either side of it	do.
Siege Battery M 10 a	8.35 to 9.5	(4) and 150x of trench to SOUTH of it	do.

4.5" Howitzers

35th Battery	8.35 to 9.5	Trench (4"), .6 (72)? and Cross roads (18)	30 rounds per gun
31st Battery	8.35 to 9.5	Post (16) and trenches (4) to (3)	20 do.
55th Battery	8.35 to 9.5	Trenches EAST of road (18) to (66)	30 do.

13 and 18 Pounders

Wirecutting Group (32nd and 33rd Batteries)	8.35 to 9.5	(62) to (26) and search back 300x	30 rounds per gun
36th Battery	8.35 to 9.5	Trench (2) to (3) and search back 400x	do.
45th Brigade R.F.A.	8.35 to 9.5	From (19) to 400x SOUTH and search back 400x	do.

"B" Group

22nd Brigade, R.F.A.	8.35 to 9.5	(57) to (65) and search back 400x	40 rounds per gun
35th Brigade, R.F.A.	8.35 to 9.5	(18) to (67) and search back 400x	do.
"N", "A" and "V"	8.35 to 9.5	(6) to (9) and search back 400x	do.

Horse Artillery Group.

"O" and "Z" batteries	8.35 to 9.5	(79) to (4) and search back 300x	
"A" "O" "U" "F" and "T"	8.35 to 9.5	Bursts of fire on "A", (86). (94)	
	8.5 8.35	(98) search and sweep	20 rounds a gun

NOTE.   On all occasions when shelling troops under cover one section should fire High Explosive if such ammunition is available.

3rd PHASE after trench is taken.   Ammunition deemed sufficient.

6" Howitzers.

5th Siege Battery	(97)	
6th Siege Battery	(98)	These points to be
7th Siege Battery M 15 c	} on trenches (2) to MOULIN de PIETRE road	shelled periodically
Siege Battery M 10 a		and watched.

4.5" Howitzers.

35th Battery	(94)	30 rounds per gun
55th Battery	(86)	do.
33rd Battery	Point "A"	do.

13 and 18 Pounders.

"A" Group.

32nd }
33rd } Batteries   Watch front (30) to (31) and search back 400x   40 rounds per gun
1st }

3rd }
5th } Batteries   Watch front (5) to (3) and search back 400x   40 rounds per gun
36th }

"B" Group.

"F", "V",
22nd Brigade R.F.A.   Watch front (31) to (5) and search back 400x   40 rounds per gun
35th Brigade R.F.A.   Watch front (30) to (31) and search back 400x   do.
                       Watch front (5) to (3) and search back 400x   do.

H.A. Group.   H.A. batteries will continue on zone "A",   40 rounds per gun.
               (86), (98), (96), and (94)

NOTE.   On all occasions when shelling troops under cover one section
         should fire High Explosive if such ammunition is available.

30 rounds per gun.

F.T. 'A' + 'B'.
Search F.
0, 2, 94, 96. 300x front.
A.Q. to 86, 94, 98. 300x front.

SECRET

H. A. Group.

Herewith copy of amended Time table of tasks for Artillery 1st Army.

Please acknowledge

R H Johnson Maj RA

9.3.15

SECRET.

AMENDED TIME TABLE.
(TIMING 30 MINUTES EARLIER THAN PREVIOUS TABLE).

FIRST PHASE.

Description of Gun.	Objective.	Time. Commence.	Cease.
15" Howitzer.	AUBERS and guns round AUBERS and POMMEREAU.	7.30 a.m.	
9.2" Howitzers. Three.	NEUVE CHAPELLE & outskirts.	7.30 a.m.	8.5 a.m
One.	Railway triangle under orders of 1st. Corps.	7.30 a.m.	As required.
6" Howitzers.	One battery. Ind. Corps. To shell selected spots.	7.30 a.m.	7.40 a.m
18 pounders.	9 batteries. Ind. Corps. Wire-cutting.	7.30 a.m.	7.40 a.m
-Ditto-	6 batteries, 4th. Corps. Wire-cutting.	7.30 a.m.	7.40 a.m
6" Howitzers.	4th. Corps. Shell selected spots.	7.30 a.m.	7.40 a.m.
13 pounder. 1 baty.) 4.7" One Xn.)	Three roads & trench running N.W. from BOIS de BIEZ.	7.35 a.m.	8.5 a.m.
4.7". One Xn.	"Gap" between Corps.	m7.40 a.m.	8.5 a.m.
4.5" Howitzers.	Three batteries. 4th. Corps. Enemy trenches.	7.40 a.m.	8.5 a.m.
-Ditto-	Three batteries. Ind. Corps. Enemy trenches & flank.	7.40 a.m.	8.5 a.m.
6" Howitzers.	Five batteries. 4th. Corps. Enemy trenches.	7.40 a.m.	8.5 a.m.
-Ditto-	One battery, Ind. Corps. Enemy trenches.	7.40 a.m.	8.5 a.m.
18 pounders.	Twelve batteries. 4th. Corps. Covering areas & flank.	7.40 a.m.	8.5 a.m.
-Ditto-	Eighteen batteries. Ind. Corps. Covering areas & flank.	7.40 a.m.	8.5 a.m.
13 pounders	Three batteries. 4th. Corps. Covering areas.	7.40 a.m.	8.5 a.m.
-Ditto-	Six batteries, 4th. Corps. Belt of fire East.	7.40 a.m.	8.5 a.m.
4.7". One battery.	Trenches 4th. Corps. Point 27.	7.55 a.m.	8.5 a.m.
	Roads & trench from BOIS de BIEZ.	8.5 a.m.	To end.

COUNTER BATTERIES.

6" B.L. Gun.	Counter batteries, AUBERS Ridge.	7.35 a.m.	
60 pr. Gun.	Counter batteries, under 1st. Corps. Area N. of Canal to BEAU PUITS, S. 30.	7.35 a.m.	
4.7". 6 batteries.	Counter batteries.	7.30 a.m.	
4.7" 1 battery.	Counter battery.	8.5 a.m.	
One 6" Gun %) Armoured(Two 4.7" Guns.) Train ((% possibly) (two 6" guns.)	AUBERS and guns near there.	7.35 a.m.	

===
Pack Artillery. 4th. Corps. Two Xns. R. Column, one Xn. Left Column and to push forward.
Pack Artillery. Ind. Corps. Two guns close up in orchard, & both push forward.
===

SECRET.

SECOND PHASE.

8.5 a.m.

Description of gun.	Objective.	Time. Commence.	Cease.
15" Howitzer.	AUBERS and guns there.	8.5 a.m.	
9.2" Howitzers.	Two on NEUVE CHAPELLE.	8.5 a.m.	8.35 a.m.
	One on NEUVE CHAPELLE. and turn on to:-	8.5 a.m.	8.35 a.m.
	Two N.W. edge of BOIS de BIEZ	8.35 a.m.	9 a.m.
	One available for AUBERS, or continue at NEUVE CHAPELLE, if required.	8.35 a.m.	9 a.m.
6" Howitzers.	4th. Corps. Lift as shewn.	8.5 a.m.	8.35 a.m.
-Ditto-	Indian Corps. Right flank.	8.5 a.m.	As required.
4.5" Howitzers.	4th. Corps. Lift as shown.	8.5 a.m.	8.35 a.m.
-Ditto-	Indian Corps. Lift as shown.	8.5 a.m.	As required.
18 pounders.	4th. Corps. Lift as shewn.	8.5 a.m.	8.35 a.m.
-Ditto-	Indian Corps. Lift as shewn.	8.5 a.m.	8.35 a.m.
-Ditto-	Indian Corps. One battery, on approaches of BOIS de BIEZ.	8.5 a.m.	8.35 a.m.
13 pounders.	4th. Corps. Lift as shewn.	8.5 a.m.	8.35 a.m.
4.7" One battery.	BOIS de BIEZ.	8.5 a.m.	To end.

COUNTER BATTERIES.

4.7". Seven batteries.) 6" B.L.. One battery.)	Counter batteries, mainly AUBERS Ridge.		
60 pr. Two batteries.	Counter batteries under 1st. Corps one covering area up to S. 30.		
One 6" gun) Armoured (Two 4.7" guns) Train. (3 possibly 2/ 3" guns.	AUBERS.	7.35 a.m.	To end.

THIRD PHASE.

All 13 and 18 pounder batteries establish belt of fire round front of the position.
One 4.7" battery - BOIS de BIEZ approaches.
Counter batteries)
Armoured Train   )   As before.

(1) Copy No. 10.

INSTRUCTIONS FOR ACTION
8th Division and attached Artillery.

Reference Maps - Belgium and France Sheet 36 S.W. $\frac{1}{20,000}$
and NEUVE CHAPELLE $\frac{1}{5,000}$

9-3-15.

1. The 4th and Indian Corps are to carry out a vigorous attack on the enemy ~~on a date and at an hour to be notified later.~~ tomorrow at 8-5 am.
The first objective is the capture of NEUVE CHAPELLE, after which a further advance will be made to gain the line AUBERS - LE PLOUICH - LA CLIQUETERIE FERME - LIGNY LE GRAND.

2. The attack on the village of NEUVE CHAPELLE will be carried out in two stages by the 8th Division.

    First Objective - The enemy's front and support trenches opposite "B" lines.

    Second Objective - Eastern edge of NEUVE CHAPELLE village on the right to ORCHARD No.6. and the MOATED GRANGE on the left.
    The point of Junction with the Indian Corps will be at the S.E. corner of the Village Point No.80

    The INDIAN CORPS will make a simultaneous attack on NEUVE CHAPELLE from the SOUTH.

3. For the attack on NEUVE CHAPELLE village, the Artillery of the 7th and 8th Divisions, less the 4.7" Heavy Batteries, will be grouped under the orders of the G.O.C. 8th Division; the 4.7" batteries of the 7th and 8th Divisions together with certain heavy batteries will form a group under the orders of 1st Army.

4. The 23rd and 25th Infantry Brigades will carry out the attack of the 8th Division until the capture of the village is completed.
The 25th Infantry brigade will be on the RIGHT and the 23rd Infantry Brigade on the LEFT.
The dividing line between the brigades will be the road (14) (17) (18) (19) (31) for which the left brigade will be responsible.

5. The action of the 8th Division and attached artillery to support this attack will be as laid down in table of tasks already issued to all concerned.

No. 5 MOUNTAIN BATTERY.

No 5 MOUNTAIN BATTERY (less 1 section) will accompany the Right attack and act under the orders of the G.O.C. 35th Infantry Brigade.

1 Section No.5 MOUNTAIN BATTERY will accompany the left attack and act under the orders of the G.O.C. 23rd Infantry Brigade.

6. POSITION OF WAGON LINES.

During the attack on NEUVE CHAPELLE the position of the Gun and Wagon teams will be as follows:-

Unit	Position
1st Indian Cavalry Division Artillery) 5th Brigade, R.H.A.)	M 3 b
2nd Indian Cavalry Division Artillery)	R 6 d
22nd Brigade, R.F.A.	R 6 c
35th Brigade, R.F.A.	R 5 d
33rd Brigade, R.F.A.	M 1 d and M 2 a
45th Brigade, R.F.A.	M 2 a, M 2 b, M 2 c
57th Field Howitzer Brigade, R.F.A.	L 34 d and G 32 b (31st Battery).

All other teams of the remainder of the Artillery units will remain with their respective wagon lines.

(3)

7. Bombing Parties will mark their position in captured trenches by blue signalling flags.

The Grenadiers of the INDIAN CORPS are using Pink flags for the same purpose.

During their advance the Infantry will indicate their position as they get forward by the use of VEREYS lights.

8. Regimental Aid Posts will be established at following places.

(a) Four hundred yards SOUTH of ROUGE CROIX (M 27 b) on LA BASSEE Road.

(b) "C" lines Headquarters M 22 central

(c) "D" lines Headquarters M 23 a.

Advanced dressing stations on LA BASSEE road one mile SOUTH of railway crossing M 8 b.
This will also be used as a Divisional Collecting Station to which wounded men, able to walk should be directed.

9. Headquarters R.A. 8th Division will remain in its present position.

R H Johnson
Major. R.A.
Brigade Major 8th Division Artillery.

Issued at 4.45 pm

Copy No. 13

Further Instructions for Action
8th Division and attached Artillery
after the capture of NEUVE CHAPELLE.

References to Maps — Belgium and France Sheet 36 S.W. $\frac{1}{20,000}$

and NEUVE CHAPELLE $\frac{1}{5,000}$

1. As soon as the village of NEUVE CHAPELLE has been captured and made good, the 7th and 8th Divisions, supported by the INDIAN CORPS on their right, will be ordered by the CORPS COMMANDER to press forward to capture the high ground AUBERS – LA CLIQUETERIE FERME – and LIGNY LE GRAND.

First Objective

7th Division   From German trenches on road due SOUTH of CHAPIGNY to Cross-roads WEST of "P" in PIETRE exclusive.

8th Division   From Right of 7th Division to NORTH EAST corner of copse NORTH EAST of BOIS DU BIEZ exclusive.

INDIAN CORPS   From Copse NORTH EAST of BOIS DU BIEZ inclusive.

SECOND Objective.

7th Division   From the road junction NORTH - WEST of ROUGES BANCS to road junction 350 yards SOUTH-by-WEST from "P" in LE PLOUICH.

8th Division   From the Right of 7th Division to a point 250 yards SOUTH of LA CLIQUETERIE FERME.

INDIAN CORPS   From the Right of the 8th Division through LIGNY LE GRAND to the marsh at RUE DES TRONCBANI

(2)

2.	When the CORPS COMMANDER issues instructions to the 7th Division to attack, the following artillery units will come under the orders of the G.O.C. 7th Division :-

The 4th, 59th, and 81st SIEGE BATTERIES,

111th and 112th Heavy batteries.

"F" and "T" batteries.

"A", "Q" and "U" batteries.

"O" and "Z" batteries, but not to be moved from their present positions without reference to the G.O.C. 8th Division.

31st Howitzer battery.

One section No.5 Mountain Battery previously working with 23rd Infantry Brigade.

22nd Brigade, R.F.A.

35th Brigade, R.F.A.

Telephonic messages to 6th Siege battery will then be transmitted via 37th Brigade, R.F.A. H.Q.

Headquarters 5th Brigade, R.H.A. must maintain communication with H.Q. R.A. 8th Division.

Such Forward observation officers of the 22nd and 35th Brigades, R.F.A. as have been sent forward to NEUVE CHAPELLE should rejoin their batteries if such a course is possible.

3.	Instructions for the action of the Artillery to support the projected movements will be issued as information of the course of events becomes available.

R H Johnson

Major. R.A.

Brigade Major 8th Division Artillery.

issued at 8 p.m.

Ref:—
maps
FRANCE
Sheet 36 S.W.
1/20000
Special maps
issued by 8th
& 7th Divisions
respectively.

Detailed report dealing with the operations of 10th to 14th March 1915, as carried out by 5th Brigade, Royal Horse Artillery.

5th Brigade R.H.A. "O" & "Z" Batteries were placed under the command of H.A. Group for the operations pending.

10th Mch. 1915. 7-40 a.m.	5th Bde. R.H.A. in combination with all other Artillery commenced 1st phase of 8th Division bombardment. Objective area (Y) (3) (H)
8-5 a.m.	Turned on to 2nd Phase. Objective (79) to (H) and search back 300x
8-35 a.m.	Turned on to 3rd phase. Objective (94) to (96) search 300x
11-5 a.m.	Concentrated with remaining R.H.A. Batteries on point (93)
11-30 a.m.	Turned on to RUE d'ENFER at slow rate of fire.
2-30 p.m.	Stop firing.
3-0 p.m.	Re-opened fire at slow rate on RUE d'ENFER.
6-0 p.m.	7th & 8th Divisions hold the line left on German trenches at division of C & D lines – thence to elbow on PIETRE road & on E of NEUVE CHAPELLE.
6-0 p.m.	Stop firing.
8-0 p.m.	Orders for night received. "O" Battery on (113), "Z" Battery on track running N.W. from N.E. exit from AUBERS. These were allotted by H.A. Group. "O" Battery to be also prepared to concentrate on 144.
11th Mch. 1915. 6-45 a.m.	"O" & "Z" opened fire in accordance with 7th Divn. R.A. instructions on area allotted by H.A. Group, viz: the front MOULIN de PIETRE – TRIVELET dividing this front with remaining Batteries of H.A. Group & searching from RIVIERE DES LAYES back to within safe distance of our trenches. Rate of fire, Section fire 30 seconds.
7-30 a.m.	2nd phase of 7th Divn. bombardment. "O" & "Z"

11th Mch. cont'd	on same area as for 1st phase, "O" having orders to be careful not to fire W of (106). Rate of fire, Section fire 2 minutes.
	"O" & "Z" on 2nd phase for remainder of day except for small occasional changes. Rate of fire was normally Section fire 5 minutes. Occasionally increased for special objectives in the same area.
6-30 p.m.	Orders for night received. "O" & "Z" were expected to move to 8th Divn area. They were ordered to be laid with central lines on PIETRE up till time of movement; they did not move.
12th Mch. 1915. 5-30 a.m.	Enemy counter-attacked from due W. & from N. of BOIS DU BIEZ. "O" Battery in co-operation with 22nd Inf. Bde. opened fire at once on TRIVELET & neighbouring trenches. "Z" also switched on. Counter-attack easily repulsed.
11-50 a.m.	"O" & "Z" assisted in bombardment preparatory to 4th Divn attack. They fired on area 106, 107, 110. Rate of fire, Section fire 2 minutes.
12-20 p.m.	Same objective, same rate.
	Attack reported to have got to N.E. of PIETRE road. "O" & "Z" fired for remainder of day, constantly switching in support of attack.
	Throughout this day information was very difficult to obtain as to movements of Infantry as F.O.Os were very hampered by mist.
7-0 p.m.	Brigade Head Qrs. & Batteries moved to new positions in M.20.c.9.2 & M.26.a.8.8 & returned to the Command of the 8th Divn. Joined B Group (Askwith's Horse)
Mch. 13th 1915.	Batteries spent the morning in finding observation stations in NEUVE CHAPELLE. Time allotted by B Group for registering 2 p.m. to dusk.
2-0 p.m.	Report from F.O.O. Meerut Divn that enemy were collecting, a few at a time, in trenches N.W. of BOIS DU BIEZ. Counter-attack expected. "O" & "Z" ordered to fire on N.W. edge. Did so by the map. Bursts of fire. Counter-attack did not develop & Batteries spent remainder of daylight registering.

14th March
10-0 a.m. Batteries continued registering. Time allotted by B Group 10-0 a.m. to 2-0 p.m. During this time all essential points ordered to be registered were done.

18/3/15

(sd.) A. T. Butler, Lt. Col. R.H.A.
Comdg. 5th Brigade, R.H.A.

TO: RHA Group
~~35 F A Bde~~
~~7th Siege Brigade~~

Sender's Number: BM 17
Day of Month: 10th
AAA

Our 21st Inf Bde is on the general line of the road 86 – 103 – 102 aaa Night lines are allotted as follows aaa 35th F.A. Bde to cover front of 21st Inf. Bde aaa RHA group one battery on 144 one ~~battery~~ on 143 one on 113 one on track running N.W. from N.E. exit from AUBERS one on ROE DELEVAL one on track running S.E. from FERME DELEVAL one on track running S.E. from ROUGES BANCS aaa 7th Siege Brigade one battery on 113 one ~~battery~~ on 115-116 one on 200 (road junction 500 S.W. of 116) aaa 31st How battery one section on N.E. exit from AUBERS one on road angle 130 one on road angle 450 yards N.E. of 130 aaa 22nd FA Bde one battery on AUBERS CHURCH one on ~~Ro Deleval~~ 130 one on ROUGES BANCS

From: Seventh Div Arty

MESSAGES AND SIGNALS.

Received From: (6)

TO H.A. Group

Sender's Number: BM 499 **Day of Month:** 10TH **In reply to Number:** AAA

Situation at 12.30 PM AAA Our Inf hold points 78, 18, 31, 80 and to the EAST of 80 AAA INDIAN hold 30 to PORT ARTHUR AAA Enemy reported advancing from HT POMMEREAU towards BOIS DU BIEZ AAA

FROM: 8TH Div Arty
PLACE & TIME: 12.31 PM

"A" Form.   Army Form C. 2121.
MESSAGES AND SIGNALS.   No. of Message _____

Prefix ___ Code ___ m.	Words.	Charge.	This message is on a/c of:	Recd. at ___ m.
Office of Origin and Service Instructions.	Sent		⑦	Date ___
	At ___ m.		Service.	From ___
	To ___		(Signature of "Franking Officer.")	By ___
	By ___			

TO   Z, O + 14th Bde.

Sender's Number	Day of Month	In reply to Number	AAA
	Tenth		

21st Infn Brigade now holds position left resting on German trench M29b central thence to road angle M30c thence South to M36A central AAA. Three trains arrived at WAVRIN AAA Night attack most probable AAA Attack from PIETRE may develop during night. AAA Night lines will be laid as follows AAA Battery on 144 U Battery on 143 O Battery on 113 Z battery on track running N.W. from N.E. exit from AUBERS Q Battery on RUE DELAVAL 14th Brigade R.H.A. one battery on track running S.E. from Farm DELAVAL and one battery on track running S.E. from ROUGES BANCS AAA. A, U + O Batteries

From			
Place			
Time			

The above may be forwarded as now corrected.   (Z)

Censor.   Signature of Addressor or person authorised to telegraph in his name

* This line should be erased if not required.

"A" Form.   Army Form C. 2121.

MESSAGES AND SIGNALS.   No. of Message _____

To be prepared to concentrate on 144 ~~antiaircraft under~~ AAA (A) Battery will fire 4 times before 4 am on ~~B~~ 144 using 15 rounds per battery on each occasion.

From: H.A. Group
Time: 8.40 p.m.

A Mann
Capt

SECRET

④

ARRANGEMENTS for ARTILLERY
Support of VII Division

Ref. Numbered Trench Map
1/10,000.

1st Objective   Line of road from PIETRE to German Trenches at ⑩⑩

Ⓐ Siege Bty   road between points ㊐ + ㊏ and houses.

4th Siege Bty   points ㊨㊨ ⑩⑩ ⑩①
     Two communication Trenches + breastwork
     + houses 141 MOULIN DU PIETRE

Ⓑ Siege Bty   points ⑩② ⑩③ + houses along road.

31 How. Bty   communication trench ① to ㊼
     and two houses at bend of road
     N of where communication Trench runs into road.

13 Pounder Batteries R.H.A.

   2 Brigades (5 Batteries) ② to ⑩⑩
     + search back to road ⑭④ ⑭③

   one Brigade searching communication trench
     ⑩⑤ to ⑭②

36th Bde R.F.A.
     Covering advance on line ⑩⓪ to ⑭④

O+Z   2–100
Search back   9–101

A.Q.V.   9 to 101
Search back to ⑭④ ⑭③

2nd objector
  0 + 2   (H2) Front Book
 113 112
            back seat to (113)

A.G.U. (113) to (113)

2.

The Batteries will open fire at a slow rate from the time they come under the orders of B.G.C. R.A. 7th Div.

Fire will be continued for twenty minutes from the time the XXI Inf. Bde begins its advance.

This time will be notified by the 7th D.A. H.Q.S. If the forward obs. off in observation post near Mir sees that the Inf. advance is not up to the road at the end of this twenty minutes he will communicate to 7th D.A. H.Q. who will order fire to be kept up for further periods of 5 minutes at a time.

As soon as the F.O.O. is satisfied that no further fire is required he will notify 7th D.A. H.Q. who will then order batteries to switch on to the second objective.

N.B. 31st How. Battery will fire for the first ten minutes after the infantry advance begins on the communication trench ① to ⓔⓔ, afterwards on to the houses just N of where communication trench runs on to the road—

2nd objective

    A. Siege   LES MOTTES FARM.

    4. Siege   points (115) to (116) in AUBERS VILLAGE.

    3rd Siege   group of buildings about 600 yds S.W. of point (116) (hereafter called (200))

    31 How.   communication trenches running from point (106) (107) (108)

    111th Hvy Batty   Houses on RUE D'ENFER. from point (113) to point (115)

    13 Pr Batteries R.H.A.   Search area from points (107) to (119) Back to AUBERS

    18 Pr 35th Bde   Cross Roads RUE D'ENFERS left (200).

    Arrangements for timing as in case of 1st Objective

3rd Objective.

  A. Siege. TRIVELET Area

  4 Siege N. road of AUBERS village.

  B Siege South road of AUBERS village up to the church.

  31st How Batt POINT (125) AUBERS VILLAGE ~~south and east of the South road~~ + area points (120) to (128) (Church)

  111th Hvy Point (117)

  18 Pdrs. RUE DELAVAL ~~AUBERS~~
  ~~18 Pdrs~~
  13 pdrs (1) area (120)-(128) (2)(127)-(140)

An officer from the R.H.A group, Siege and How group + 35th Bde R.F.A will report to Brig. Com. XXI Inf Bde at his temporary H.Q.S. on M 2/8.d. and an officer of the R.H.A. group also to Brig Gen Com. XXII Inf Bde. at his HQS at M 11 D 8.2 or M 18 C 8.7

  & Search forward to track 1000x behind RE DELAVAL.

Neuve Chapelle

REFERENCE
Wire Entanglement
Chevaux de frise { Single
Double

"A" Form. Army Form C. 2121.
MESSAGES AND SIGNALS.

Day of Month: 11/3/15

Instructions for IIIrd Divisional and Attached Artillery.

Ref 1/8000 Numbered Trench map and 1/20000 Sheet 36 S.W. FRANCE.

(1) The IIIrd Division is to continue the attack AUBERS to-day.

(2) The first objective of XXI Infᵗ Bᵈᵉ will be the PIETRE - Mᶦⁿ de PIETRE road, against which it will advance at 7 a.m.

(3). At 6.45 a.m. the Artillery will bombard its FIRST OBJECTIVE

(c) R.H.A. Group (105) to (119) searching back to RIVIERE DES LAYES.

(4) FIRE on first objectives will cease at 7 a.m. unless otherwise ordered.

"A" Form.   Army Form C. 2121.
MESSAGES AND SIGNALS.   No. of Message_____

Prefix___ Code___ m.	Words.	Charge.	This message is on a/c of:	Recd. at___ m
Office of Origin and Service Instructions.	Sent At___ m. To___ By___		Service. (Signature of "Franking Officer.")	Date___ From___ By___

TO {

| Sender's Number | Day of Month 11 | In reply to Number | AAA |

(5) Orders will then be issued from this office as to time of opening fire on SECOND OBJECTIVE which will be as follows:—
(c) R.H.A. Group As for first objectives, para 3(c), but guns therein detailed to fire (105)–(106) will now search (112) to (114), and no fire will be applied West of (106).

(6) During this phase the right batteries of the R.H.A. group must carefully watch the progress of the left of the XXI Inf. Bde as it advances on LES MOTTES FARM.

(7) ~~Third Objectives~~ THIRD OBJECTIVES will be engaged when ordered as under:—

From_____
Place_____
Time_____
The above may be forwarded as now corrected.   (Z)
Censor.   Signature of Addressor or person authorised to telegraph in his nam
* This line should be erased if not required.
(24473). M.R.Co.,Ltd. Wt.W4843/541. 50,000. 9/14. Forms C2121/10.

"A" Form.   Army Form C. 2121.
MESSAGES AND SIGNALS.   No. of Message _____

Prefix _____ Code _____ m. | Words. | Charge. | This message is on a/c of: | Recd. at _____ m.
Office of Origin and Service Instructions. | | | | Date _____
                              | Sent | |
                              | At _____ m. | ...Service. | From _____
                              | To _____ | |
                              | By _____ | (Signature of "Franking Officer.") | By _____

TO {   ② ③

* er's Number | Day of Month | In reply to Number | AAA
              | 11 | |

⑦ (c) R.H.A. Group, 1 Brigade RUE
DE LAVAL
Remainder search area between N. & S.
roads A AUBERS.
⑨ Rate of fire For first objective
(5 minutes bombardment) ammunition
allowed as follows:—
13 pounders:— 15 rounds per gun.
⑩ H.Q.S. 7 D.A. remain as at present
⑪ All telephone lines must be
constantly patrolled and immediately
repaired when necessary.
All Brigades and Groups will call
up H.Q. at least once every hour
                    Sd. S.W. Rawlins Maj R.A.
                    Bde Maj. 7th D.A.

From _____
Place _____
Time _____
The above may be forwarded as now corrected. (Z)
                                    Censor. Signature of Addressor or person authorised to telegraph in his name

"A" Form.   Army Form C. 2121.

MESSAGES AND SIGNALS.

Prefix____ Code____ m.	Words.	Charge.	This message is on a/c of:	Recd. at____ m
Office of Origin and Service Instructions.	Sent			Date____
	At____ m.		F Service	From____
	To____			
	By____		(Signature of "Franking Officer.")	By____

TO {

Sender's Number	Day of Month	In reply to Number	AAA
	11/3/15		

Instructions for R.H.A. Group in compliance with 7th D.A. instructions. FIRST OBJECTIVE ③(c) H.A. Group will fire on the zone TRIVELET – Road elbow N19C32 – MOULIN DE PIETRE. Batteries will divide this zone in the following order :– U, O, Z, Q, 14th Bde R.H.A. 'A' Battery will direct its fire on MOULIN DE PIETRE, Q battery on road elbow N19C32, left battery 14th Brigade on TRIVELET. Remaining batteries dividing the front. All batteries will search from RIVIERE DES LAYES back to within safe distance of our trenches. Rate of fire section fire 30 seconds.

From
Place
Time

The above may be forwarded as now corrected. (Z)

Censor.   Signature of Addressor or person authorised to telegraph in his name

* This line should be erased if not required.

"A" Form.   Army Form C. 2121.
MESSAGES AND SIGNALS.   No. of Message _____

Second Objective 'A' and 'U' Batteries search RUE D'ENFER from LES MOTTES FARM to 200 yards S.E. of the cross-road S.E. of LES MOTTES FARM.
Remaining batteries as for first objective 'O' battery being careful not to fire W. of (10b) vide § 5(c) 7th Divn Instructions.
Attention of all is drawn to § 6 of those instructions.
Rate of fire Section fire 2 minutes.
Third Objective 14th Bde R.H.A. RUE DELAVAL.
Remaining batteries await orders.
Watches will be synchronised with H.A. Group at 6 a.m.
           A. Mann
           Capt R.H.A.
           H.A. Group.

"A" Form.　　　　　　　　　　　　　　Army Form C. 2121.

MESSAGES AND SIGNALS.

Prefix	Code	m.	Words.	Charge.	This message is on a/c of:	Recd. at____m
Office of Origin and Service Instructions			Sent At ___ m. To ___ By ___	(9)	_____ Service. (Signature of "Franking Officer.")	Date____ From____ By____

TO: R. A. Group

Sender's Number	Day of Month	In reply to Number	A A A
*BM 28	11TH		

Lines for tonight as follows one Bty 144 one Bty 143 one Bty 113 one Bty on track running NW from NE from AUBERS one Bty on TRIVELET AAA O and Z Btys will very likely move and therefore should not be selected for any of the above but will both be ldid with central lines on PIETRE up to such time as they may be ordered to move AAA Please acknowledge

158
4"

From
Place: 7TH DIV ARTY
Time: 6.28 PM

"A" Form.
MESSAGES AND SIGNALS.
Army Form C. 2121.

Prefix	Code	m.	Words	Charge	This message is on a/c of:	Recd. at	m.
Office of Origin and Service Instructions.			Sent At 1.10 A.m. To 14th Z + O By Cpl Mayus		(10) Service. (Signature of "Franking Officer.")	Date 12.3.15 From By	HE

TO { Z/O 14th Bde

Sender's Number	Day of Month	In reply to Number	AAA
	Twelfth		

Attack will be made by 20th Inf. Brigade (2 battalions) to day on points 103, 104, 102, 101, 100, Big house, and 105. AAA. Artillery bombardment commences 7.30 am. A, Q, and U batteries Search area 104, 105, 143 AAA Z + O area 106, 107, 110, AAA 14th Bde R.H.A. area 107, 108, 112, 113 AAA Bombard Rate of fire Section fire two minutes AAA Bombardment ceases at 8. am. but all batteries continue on same areas at same rate of fire except A. Q + U which come off 104 and 105 + continue on area from elbow road elbow just North of P in Min du PIETERE to 143 AAA Synchronise watches with here at 7 a.m.

From H.A. Group
Place 12.20 A.m
Time

The above may be forwarded as now corrected. (Z)
Bombardment was postponed till 11.50 am.
Censor. Signature of Addressor or person authorised to telegraph in his name

This line should be erased if not required.

8th, Division.

5th, Bde..R. H. A.

April, 1915.

121/5195

8th Division

5th Bde R H A.
Vol I 1—30.4.15

Army Form C. 2118.

WAR DIARY
or
INTELLIGENCE SUMMARY

(Erase heading not required.)

Instructions regarding War Diaries and Intelligence Summaries are contained in F. S. Regs., Part II. and the Staff Manual respectively. Title pages will be prepared in manuscript.

Hour, Date, Place	Summary of Events and Information	Remarks and references to Appendices
April 1st	"O" registered fired 13 rounds. "Z" registered fired 13 rounds. Battery limits to 18 mr. 2 deg. All Canadian artillery intensive in evening from behind our line.	Quiet
2nd	"O" + "Z" registered	do
7.20 pm 10.10 pm	Test SOS signal sent out by 85 Div A.L.Q. "Z" + "O" fired to program. do.	
3rd 12.20 am	Test SOS signal sent to "Z" by infantry in trenches. "Z" fired 1 rd. program. "O" + "Z" both registered. keep line of "O" + "Z" rounds to H 13/7/9	do
4th	Easter Sunday. "O" + "Z" both registered.	
5th 2 pm	Fleurbaix crossroads shelled by 5.9" from near Fromelles - about 12 shells. "Z" did not fire. "O" 12 rounds at Fromelles. Very few reported a German observation station in Fromelles church tower - 2nd line positions for Batteries chosen. 38 rounds 5.9" into Fleurbaix during morning	not a ready all day
6th		quiet
7th	Moved HQ + horses [?] from Fleurbaix. "O" + "Z" registered. Lt. A.R.F. Lucas (O.O.) rejoined from H. aspl.	

WAR DIARY or INTELLIGENCE SUMMARY

Army Form C. 2118.

(Erase heading not required.)

Hour, Date, Place	Summary of Events and Information	Remarks and references to Appendices
8 hr	Pos'n for 4 gun Bty chosen in front of O.	Quiet
9 hr	Both batteries fired 12 rounds. Z at machine gun emplacement sqt 2 directhit not registered	do
10 hr	Z did not fire. D registered	do
	Both batteries registered. 25 rounds fired at Croix Blanche about 3 pm near O's hut.	do
11 hr	Both batteries registered. Brigade HQ shelled about 12 noon by 5"9". Zn first shell hit kitchen, killed one man, wounded another. Started firing 4, 5"9 shells. They changed to 4"2 Bangcoul & continued whole afternoon for two hours firing steady.	do
	Moved B'd HQ to H 26.a 4.4.	
8 pm	Both batteries registered.	
12 hr	do do do. Lieut D'M'V Craven to hospital. Sick	do
13 hr	do do do.	do
14 hr	do do do.	do
15 hr	Increase of sniping at O's observing St's. Both batteries registered.	do

Army Form C. 2118.

WAR DIARY
or
INTELLIGENCE SUMMARY

(Erase heading not required.)

Instructions regarding War Diaries and Intelligence Summaries are contained in F. S. Regs., Part II. and the Staff Manual respectively. Title pages will be prepared in manuscript.

Hour, Date, Place	Summary of Events and Information	Remarks and references to Appendices
Apl. 15th	Both batteries registered.	Quiet
17th	do. 2 L.G., 2 Edge Hospital rick.	do
18th	do.	do
19th	Test S.O.S. sent to Ö by Infantry at 12.5 am. Ö prepared to fire into wireless aeroplane at 5.30 pm but operator failed to see aeroplane signals. Both batteries registered. 3 pm 30 H.E., 15 shr shells fired at Croix Blanche.	
20th	Batteries ordered to include Aubers in their area, its regular fire. Owen had previously been from Le Maisnil at Lennington A.V.C. Lt.-R. Brigade (England). Both batteries registered. At Rouge Blanches and + 2 detonement	do
21st	Neither Battery fired.	do
22nd	Both registered.	do
23rd	O + Z btn. registered. Have a lot of firing apparently rear Bois Grenier.	do
24th	I action exc g A. O. + U took acting Fein Am Cdr placed under orders of O.C. 5th Brigade, on their other guns were back away.	

Army Form C. 2118.

WAR DIARY
or
INTELLIGENCE SUMMARY

(Erase heading not required.)

Instructions regarding War Diaries and Intelligence Summaries are contained in F. S. Regs., Part II. and the Staff Manual respectively. Title pages will be prepared in manuscript.

Hour, Date, Place	Summary of Events and Information	Remarks and references to Appendices
Apr. 25th	Sections of A.Q & U placed in one position at H.34.a.8.5. Lt Austin A.V.C. joined.	Quiet.
Apr. 26th	A.Q.V. Batteries registered and observed for 119th Heavy Bty, attempting at a German 15th Battery whose flashes were visible. 2.30 pm "Q" received Trent S.O.S. from Infantry. Q fired a few rounds at Sniper's house. Rather some firing from until our front during night 26/27th	do
Apr. 27th	Q & U did not fire. A.Q.V. registered	do
Apr. 28th	Q & O did not fire. A.R.V. reg. Cross Roads? Where Rifling Bde came into position near H.Q. Z who lifted from ammunition parade	Quiet
Apr. 29th	"Z" did not fire. "Q" and A.Q.V. registered. Flandrin shelled by 5.9" from 10 a.m. - 1 p.m.	Quiet
Apr. 30th	The Brigade moved known tonight & tomorrow night to leave C divn 8th Divn. near Neuve Chapelle. AQU Batteries leaving to Bde & joining 14th Bde R.H.A. 4 guns each J.O.&Z to one position at M.21.a.5.2 and M.21.b.I.7. Heymarcha at 8.30 p.m. 1 section A.330 marched alternatively.	Quiet

Metcalfe Capt
Ra, 5th Bde R.H.A.
30/4/15

8th, Division.

5th, Bde. R. H. A.

May, 1915.

121/5556

8th Division

5th Bde: R.H.A.

Vol VI 1 — 31.5.15

WAR DIARY or INTELLIGENCE SUMMARY

Army Form C. 2118.

(Erase heading not required.)

Instructions regarding War Diaries and Intelligence Summaries are contained in F. S. Regs., Part II. and the Staff Manual respectively. Title pages will be prepared in manuscript.

Hour, Date, Place	Summary of Events and Information	Remarks and references to Appendices
May 1st 4-4.50am	Neuve Chapelle heavily shelled - attack expected - Bde guns Each O + Z went to new positions O with Z at night - O at M21a5.2 Z at M14.7.7. Bde at and the two guns of each battery moved into new positions at 8 pm. Bde HQ being at M3d5.1.	
2nd	The officer of our Battery tub fired some 30 rounds about 5 am. Bde Batteries registered during the day. O's West knick hit by 4.2 shells. Z registered 8 detonators fire.	
3rd 4 pm	The Brigade about to move back to near Rhadaik the position left last Sunday. O. at H33c.3.8. Z at H33a.8.8 Bde HQ at H26a4.4. The move was completed by 1 am. today.	
4th	O + Z each fired 3 rounds at enemys front trench at 4.15, and 2nd Lt A.S. Dallas and 10 men from RFA attached for 14 days from England	
5th	O fired 3 rounds ——— at 4.30 am.	
6 pm	1st Bde RHA. 5th Bde RHA and 1st West Riding Bde RHA(T) formed into C group under Command of Col. Rouse DSO RHA. O + Z checked registration.	
6th	Z fired 4 rounds at enemys front trench.	

Army Form C. 2118.

WAR DIARY
or
INTELLIGENCE SUMMARY
(Erase heading not required.)

Hour, Date, Place	Summary of Events and Information	Remarks and references to Appendices
January 7th 1916 9"	O. fired 3 rnds. And Z 15 checking registration. Z fired 3 rnds. Attack on trenches W. of Gordonnerie Farm. 5.10 am — Bombardment began by 5th Bde RHA fired on 883, 882 and contact of communication trenches 831. 3rd RC. fired on F.O.O hits left attack. addition by F.O.O. of each Battery. (1st phase — up to 5.25 am, 20 rds a gun) 5.25 am No dispose reported. Some 3 of Cliffe crews dropping short behind our trenches. 5.40 am — 5.50 am. 5th Bde RHA on 832 — 829 sweeping back to 816 (10 rds a gun) 5.50 am No dispos opposite left half ground front trenches 5.50 — 6.5 am. 5th Bde RHA on LE HAYEM trench and sweeping (2nd phase) back to 780. (30 rds a gun. rate of fire) 6.3 am No dispos reported heavy torpedoes rifle/m. in left of attack. 6.5 — 6.20 am. 5th Bde RHA on LE HAYEM trench and sweeping back to 780. (3rd phase) (20 rds a gun) 6.18 am O.C. D infantries Centre our infantry on line 826 and 827.	Reference Bois Grenier, Fromelles, Helies and Bois des Près Sheets. 1/10.000

WAR DIARY
or
INTELLIGENCE SUMMARY

(Erase heading not required.)

Army Form C. 2118.

Instructions regarding War Diaries and Intelligence Summaries are contained in F. S. Regs., Part II. and the Staff Manual respectively. Title pages will be prepared in manuscript.

Hour, Date, Place	Summary of Events and Information	Remarks and references to Appendices
May 9th (Contin)		
6.20 – 6.40 am (4th phase)	5th Bde RHA aw 749 – 745 – Barrage. (20 yds a gun)	
6.45 am	Order received addressed to O & Z "At end of 4th phase uppers seconds phase slow bursts. rate of fire. Section fire 5 mins."	
7.21 am	Report from O.C. "Z" Rifle Bde toward point 827 have entered for further infantry support MMG. Section rifles just moving out front line Nq 9.6." (report sent from Cellar farm.)	
9.45 am	Bde keeping up fire as at 6.45 am.	
11.20 am	5th Bde RHA formed arcs 832 – 829 and search back to 816 "Commencing at same rate Section fire 2 mins."	
12.5 pm	"Section fire 5 minutes" ordered.	
12.25 pm	Stop firing. Stand ready."	

Army Form C. 2118.

WAR DIARY
or
INTELLIGENCE SUMMARY
(Erase heading not required.)

Instructions regarding War Diaries and Intelligence Summaries are contained in F. S. Regs., Part II. and the Staff Manual respectively. Title pages will be prepared in manuscript.

Hour, Date, Place	Summary of Events and Information	Remarks and references to Appendices
May 9th (contd)		
12.32 pm	"Commence firing - section fire 5 minutes"	
1.15 pm	Tasks as above (at 11.20 am)	
1.30 pm	do	
1.50 pm	"Bombard front trenches 879 to 876 and search back to 878. Continue firing for 15 mins; heavy repeats to be counter attacking - Batteries ordered to fire Battery fire at 15 seconds.	
2.25 pm	Order received "Stop firing & watch the area."	
3.30 pm	Order received - "Fire on 883 & 829 and search back to 831 and 830"	
3.33 pm	"Section fire 3 mins."	
3.55 pm	Enemy reinforcements reported marching on Fromelles. Section fire 5 mins ordered	
4.35 pm	X ordered fire along road 795 - 791. O along road 791 to 788 - section fire 5 mins	
7.10 pm	Batteries ordered to stop firing.	
8.30 pm	Right line on 879 inclusive to 881 exclusive.	

Army Form C. 2118.

WAR DIARY
or
INTELLIGENCE SUMMARY
(Erase heading not required.)

Instructions regarding War Diaries and Intelligence Summaries are contained in F.S. Regs., Part II. and the Staff Manual respectively. Title pages will be prepared in manuscript.

Hour, Date, Place	Summary of Events and Information	Remarks and references to Appendices
May 9th (contd) 9.30 pm	Orders received to commence firing at 4 am 10th.	Each Battery fired about 1050 rounds during the day.
10.55 pm	Above order cancelled — 4 men in 2 and 1 man in O wounded today.	
May 10:		
8.5 am	No more firing before 2 pm except for defensive reasons.	
8.21 am	Tactical control of all batteries of 8th Bde and attached artillery passes to 7th Divl Artillery.	
	Lt. APF Bacon (wireless officer) sick Ehospital. 2d R.S. Duke RFA from attached 'O' BtyRAHQ as wireless officer.	
1 pm.	Knight time rifle to be 2nd wave 2 and 3 am Army 8th — it. Coming face of next Riding Sign.	
6 pm.	Control of 8 B.E. Bde Artillery back to BGC RA 8th Divn. Neither Battery fired today.	
May 11:	Each Battery fired 150 rounds at 882 – 832 and checked registration of night lines. 'O' had Lieut killed by shrapnel in their billet. Lt Dalton back to 'O'. 2 Lts my hugh KHO a wireless officer.	
May 12:	Each Battery fired about 15 rounds at front line trenches.	

Army Form C. 2118.

WAR DIARY
or
INTELLIGENCE SUMMARY

(Erase heading not required.)

Instructions regarding War Diaries and Intelligence Summaries are contained in F. S. Regs., Part II. and the Staff Manual respectively. Title pages will be prepared in manuscript.

Hour, Date, Place	Summary of Events and Information	Remarks and references to Appendices
May 13th	Heavy firing to the South all day. Z fired 6 rounds on German front line trenches.	
May 14th	1. a.m. Heavy guns and Infantry fire from some 7 minutes by our Infantry + guns (except O + Z) firing a triumph attack. 2 p.m. Our Guns again fired for some 3 minutes (except O + Z) Wagon lines moved from H.19.a to H.30.a. Neither Battery fired.	
May 15th	Neither battery fired. Bombardment by our guns at 12 midnight.	
May 16th	Either battery fired. (Bn HQ moved to G.35.c.6.3 - 0 to M.5.d.9.9. 2 to M.6.d.8.8 cancelled) 5th Bde RHA comes under Tactical Control of B.G.C.R.A. 49th (West Riding) Division - The 2nd & 7th of this division are in Sections 1.2.3.4.5.6. The 5th Bde arrives in Covering Sections 3 and 4.	
May 17th	Z fired rounds at night when Infantry sent Tem SOS 3Q.	

Army Form C. 2118.

WAR DIARY
or
INTELLIGENCE SUMMARY

(Erase heading not required.)

Instructions regarding War Diaries and Intelligence Summaries are contained in F. S. Regs., Part II. and the Staff Manual respectively. Title pages will be prepared in manuscript.

Hour, Date, Place	Summary of Events and Information	Remarks and references to Appendices
May 18th	Neither Battery fired.	
May 19th	Neither Battery fired.	
May 20th	do. do. do.	
May 21st	Lts. Speer and Dakes who have been attached since 6th May, returned to England. Neither Battery fired.	
May 22nd	Neither Battery fired.	
May 23rd	do. do. do.	
May 24th	9 a.m. Six 5.9 Shells fell near Z gun. At midnight bombarded "O" 8 p.m. 10-12 Green. Notstanding Div Artillery bombarded enemy punitive trenches. Lees 6.	Neither Onor Z fired.
May 25th	8 a.m. & 12 noon. do. 6. 5.9 shells fell very close to Z billet.	
May 26th	German 5.9" Howrs active yesterday & today. A gun set on fire further west. Two German Observation balloons up today.	

Army Form C. 2118.

WAR DIARY
or
INTELLIGENCE SUMMARY
(Erase heading not required.)

Instructions regarding War Diaries and Intelligence Summaries are contained in F.S. Regs., Part II. and the Staff Manual respectively. Title pages will be prepared in manuscript.

Hour, Date, Place	Summary of Events and Information	Remarks and references to Appendices
May 27th	Neither Battery fired. The Brigade moved back to G.21 with H.Q. at 8.30 pm and 9 pm. G.14.b. for refitting. The first time O has been out again since November - (Z had 3 days out in December). Be more complete by 11 pm. No Battery picture allowed. Fires kept in case of return.	
May 28th	Batteries drilling.	
May 29th	do. Painting & overhauling all vehicles.	
May 30th	do.	
May 31st	The Brigade moved back into action, taking over from 3rd Regt RHA. O at M.11.c.6.4. Z at M.15.b. central. Battle HQ at M.4.c.0.2. Move complete by 10 pm.	

M. D. Lee Capt.
Adj, 5th Bde R.H.A.

8th, Division.

5th, Bde. R. H. A.

June, 1915.

121/3935

8th Division

5th Bde R.H.A.
Vol XII 1 — 30.6.15.

a²
a/6

Army Form C. 2118.

WAR DIARY
or
INTELLIGENCE SUMMARY 5th Bde RHA

(Erase heading not required.)

Instructions regarding War Diaries and Intelligence Summaries are contained in F. S. Regs., Part II. and the Staff Manual respectively. Title pages will be prepared in manuscript.

Hour, Date, Place	Summary of Events and Information	Remarks and references to Appendices
June 1st	Neither Battery fired.	
2nd	do	
3rd	do	
4th	do. Front D/E guns shelled by 4·2 in afternoon (O's position)	
5th		
6th	9.45 am German aeroplane active. Neither Battery fired	
7th	do	
8th	do	
9th	do	
10th	The Brigade issued with 18/pr guns. One section 18/pr in each Battery in action. 'O' and 'Z' registration with new 18/prs. 2 more 18/prs in to position in each Battery at 9 pm. The change from 13/pr to 18/pr to completed. Instructions from Bde + Div Am Col awaiting Return a forward slaving officer.	
11th	Both batteries registered. Notification received that No 34263 Gunner T. Humphrey 'O' Bty had been awarded D.C.M. 'Z' moved section from keep line into action at M. 23a. 5.8 at 10 pm.	
12th	Z registered with Battery and forward section. All 13/pr equipment sent away - guns were on to being been handed into R.T.O. La Gorgue. Sent back to Div Am Col. Ammunition	

WAR DIARY or INTELLIGENCE SUMMARY

Army Form C. 2118.

(Erase heading not required.)

Hour, Date, Place	Summary of Events and Information	Remarks and references to Appendices
13th	Neither Battery fired.	
14th	4/pm. "O" fired 60 rds. shrapnel at German wire from 316 for 100 yds to the N.E.	
	9/pm. each Battery fired 4 rds shrapnel per gun. { O at 316 and 100ˣ to N.E. { Z at 316 for 200ˣ to South	
	11/pm. do – do – do – do	
	1.am. and 3.am. do – do – do	
15th	4 am. "O" fired 60 rds. shrapnel at same as above –	
	4.10 am bombardment of 20 rds a gun – both batteries – same targets as above.	
	11.am. 1/pm. 3/pm. } "O" fired 2nd a gun each time at 316 and 100ˣ N.E. 5/pm.	
	6/pm – 6.20/pm. O & Z same targets a above. 60 /per gun shrapnel.	

WAR DIARY
or
INTELLIGENCE SUMMARY

(Erase heading not required.)

Army Form C. 2118.

Hour, Date, Place	Summary of Events and Information	Remarks and references to Appendices
16th	10.pm Trenches Z & RUE BACQUEROT withdrawn to the wagon line.	
17th	Neither Battery fired.	
	8am Test S.O.S. E to sent out by Inf.L. O'fired round.	
18th	2/Lt J.A. Sanger joined the Brigade and attached to O.	
	Z fired 5 rounds at request of Infantry	
19th	Both batteries registered trenches right-of-left opposite own front.	
20th	Neither Bty fired. Percentage of HE, lyte kept up, only 5%.	
21st	Z fired 11 rounds registered. O did not fire.	
	2/Lt Packman Charn F.O. to A Battery. O to Column.	
22nd	Neither Bty fired.	
23rd	do do	
24th	do do — 8.30pm 1 section of one Battery from wagon line went into action D at H.33 c central. Z at H.33a.9.8. The two Batteries only left here position 21st May.	

WAR DIARY
or
INTELLIGENCE SUMMARY

Army Form C. 2118.

(Erase heading not required.)

Hour, Date, Place	Summary of Events and Information	Remarks and references to Appendices
25th	One section Highland Battery came into Z's disposition.	Remaining two sections of
26th	marched Knox Blancs about midnight 26/27.	Highland Bty remain in order till 8 am 28.
27th	One section T.O. went into Maude's posn 26/27. and section of a Highland Bty sent to B's disposition.	
	9.30 p.m. remaining section of T.O. moved to m.g. line H.19.a.	
28th	6 a.m. defence of Tanguissart. Chopitour line handed over to 1st Highland Bde RFA and S.	
	Bde RHA took over defence of Sections 3 and 4 (about N.10 & N.6)	
	Both batteries visited. Battle moved to H.26.d. Cross roads.	
29th	Both batteries visited.	
30th	do. do. Battle moved to H.20.c. Central.	

M.O.Rhu Capt.
Adj. 5 RHA.

8th, Division.

5th, Bde. R. H. A.

July, 1915.

8th/5 Division

151/6292

5th Bde. R # A.

Vol VIII

1-15-7-15

Army Form C. 2118.

WAR DIARY or INTELLIGENCE SUMMARY

5th Bde RHA

(Erase heading not required.)

Instructions regarding War Diaries and Intelligence Summaries are contained in F. S. Regs., Part II. and the Staff Manual respectively. Title pages will be prepared in manuscript.

Hour, Date, Place	Summary of Events and Information	Remarks and references to Appendices
July 1st	Bde batteries registered. Ammn field supplemented 3 rounds shrapnel. Col. Butler returned from 7 days leave.	Preparing Bay.
2nd	Bde batteries registered - working parties of 1 NCO + 6 men from each about night for work in improving trenches about 9 p.m. The Brigade finds an officer for these eg alternate times.	Bde + the Chinese parade every day.
3rd		
4th	Lt A. Bull posted RHA Aircraft + left for Rota.	W. Party 9 p.m.
5th	Alternate position chosen near east Bty position of 'J' gun registered from same.	W. Party. —
6th		W. Party. —
7th	1 gun continuing registering from east Battery's alternate position. Lt. T. J. Teeling (Special Reserve R.F.A) posted to the Brigade.	W. Party. —
8th	Bde batteries fired few rounds at enemy working parties during day.	W. Party. —
9th	'O' fired few rounds at working party.	
10th	Both batteries fired a few rounds.	W. Party —
11th	Neither battery fired. Lt. S.J.K. Calkins posted to the Brigade from Sin Arm Co.	
12th	Each battery fired a few rounds. Lt. W.E. Bowman from 'O' Bty/an orderly officer	W. Party 9 p.m.
13th	Each Bty fired a few rounds at working parties. Major N.E. Tidney posted from O bty bde SV. Major W Stirling posted from 32nd Bde, RFA to O.	W. Party 9 p.m.

Army Form C. 2118.

5th Bde RHA

WAR DIARY
or
INTELLIGENCE SUMMARY

(Erase heading not required.)

Instructions regarding War Diaries and Intelligence Summaries are contained in F.S. Regs., Part II. and the Staff Manual respectively. Title pages will be prepared in manuscript.

Hour, Date, Place	Summary of Events and Information	Remarks and references to Appendices
14th	Neither battery fired. First wet day for about a month. Working party at 5 p.m.	working party 9 p.m.
15th	Z fired a sh at regd of Infantry	working party 9 p.m.
16th	Neither battery fired	
17th	do do	
18th	"O" did not fire – Z fired 12 rds at regd of Infantry	working party 9 p.m.
19th	neither Bty fired	
20th	"O" fired with aeroplane scheme. registered 5 points. Z did not fire	working party 9 p.m.
21st	Z registered with aeroplane. 7 p.m. "O" did not fire.	
22nd	Neither Battery fired	working party 9 p.m.
23rd	"Z" fired 12 rounds. "O" did not fire.	do – do
24th	"O" registered with aeroplane 7 p.m. Z did not fire	w. party 9 p.m.
25th	"O" fired 2 rounds. Z did not fire	do do
26th	neither Battery fired	do do
27th	Each Battery fired a few rounds	

Army Form C. 2118.

WAR DIARY
or
INTELLIGENCE SUMMARY

(Erase heading not required.)

5th March 1915

Instructions regarding War Diaries and Intelligence Summaries are contained in F.S. Regs., Part II. and the Staff Manual respectively. Title pages will be prepared in manuscript.

Hour, Date, Place	Summary of Events and Information	Remarks and references to Appendices
28th	Both batteries fired a few rounds at working parties etc.	working party 9 p.m.
29th	do	
30th	do. do. Lt Inybrogh with his section in action at M.5.a.	working party 9 p.m.
31st	2 rifle into Saagtafe from Scholbsday line position	
	Everything has been very quiet during the last month here.	
		Major Capn Maj. S. McD...

8th, Division.

5th, Bde. R. H. A.

August, 1915.

121/6587

8th Division

5th Bde: R.H.A.
Vol IX
From 1- 31. 5. 15

Army Form C. 2118.

WAR DIARY
or
INTELLIGENCE SUMMARY

(Erase heading not required.)

Instructions regarding War Diaries and Intelligence Summaries are contained in F. S. Regs., Part II. and the Staff Manual respectively. Title pages will be prepared in manuscript.

Hour, Date, Place	Summary of Events and Information	Remarks and references to Appendices
August 1st	Captain Cooper RFA(T) from Northumberland attached the Bde for 4 days -	
2nd	Each Battery fired a few rounds — at working parties or taking prize BS.	
	"O" fired a few rounds — 2 officers 4.23 other ranks attacked "E.O" for 3 days from 9th Bde R.F.A (2nd New Army)	
	8.45 p.m. working party 3 N.C.Os + 23 men doing trenches whilst Infantry.	
3rd	"O" fired a few rounds. "Z" did not fire.	
4th	"O" fired a few rounds. "Z" did not fire — away	
	In detached action of "O" retinier the Bty 9.30 pm	
	Next working party at 8.45 pm.	
5th	"O" fired a few rounds and replied to hostile one gun from "Schilchny line forts".	
	"Z" did not fire. working party 8.45 pm	
6th	Capt. B. Cooper RFA(T) attacked, Sick to Fld. Ambulance. 2 Officers 23 other ranks 9th Bde to p.O.	
	each Bty fired a few rounds. working party 8.45 pm	
7th	"Z" fired 18 rounds at request of Infantry at some snipers houses. Ordhouse set on fire.	

Army Form C. 2118.

WAR DIARY
or
INTELLIGENCE SUMMARY

(Erase heading not required.)

Instructions regarding War Diaries and Intelligence Summaries are contained in F. S. Regs., Part II. and the Staff Manual respectively. Title pages will be prepared in manuscript.

Hour, Date, Place	Summary of Events and Information	Remarks and references to Appendices
8.	Each Bty. fired a few rounds.	Working party 8.45 p.m.
9.	do - do.	do.
10.	do - do. G.O.C.R.A. inspected wagon lines.	Working party 8.45 p.m.
10.	do - do. G.O.C. 35 Bn. inspected wagon lines.	Working party 8.45 p.m.
11.	"O" fired a few rounds "Z" did not fire.	Working party 8.30 p.m.
12.	Both Btys fired a few rounds at German working parties.	do do do
13.	do. do.	do. do. do.
14.	neither Bty fired. Divisional Horse show.	Working party 8.45 p.m.
15.	"O" fired 3 rounds. "Z" did not fire. Both batteries preparing positions in case of retirement.	do do do
16.	"O" fired 3 rounds attempt "Z" didn't fire	do do do
17.	"O" did not fire "Z" fired 15 rounds	Working pty - 8.30 p.m.

WAR DIARY
or
INTELLIGENCE SUMMARY

(Erase heading not required.)

Army Form C. 2118.

Hour, Date, Place	Summary of Events and Information	Remarks and references to Appendices
18th	Neither Battery fired	
19th	"O" Bty did not fire. "H" Bty fired 5 rounds	Working Pty 2.0 P.m
20th	2nd Lieut F. Chaplin to Hospital sick, injury to wrist & concussion caused by shell "O" Battery off through the wood struck him. Neither Bath fired	"
	Capt. Hon. R.E. Grosvenor left to join 164th Brigade R.F.A 7th Division	
21st	"O" fired 10 rounds checking parallelism to "Z" fired 12 rounds Bat 6.9 German Bty near la Hr. Rue	
22nd	Neither Bty fired. Bty.C.R.A. inspected s-line positions Major Shirley returned to Bty. in evening.	Working Pty 8.0 P.m
23rd	"Z" Bty fired 6 rounds at W.P.	
24th	"O" Bty did not fire "Z" fired 8 rounds at W.P.s Capt Barrow-Gill took over as temporarily R.A. and left to S.Christophe attached to Centre Army for a few days whilst Maj. Hongon Capt. Adjutant R.A. was on leave.	Working Pty 7.10 P.m
25th	"O" Bty fired 4 rounds at W.P. "Z" Bty fired 8 rounds Details below.	
26th	"O" Bty fired 3 rounds at W.P. "Z" Bty " 15 rounds shelling "	
27th	"O" Bty fired 7 rounds at, and dispersed a working party at N.S.D 21. Z did not fire - Usual working party at 7.10 pm.	

WAR DIARY or INTELLIGENCE SUMMARY

Army Form C. 2118.

Hour, Date, Place	Summary of Events and Information	Remarks and references to Appendices
28th	'O' fired a few rounds. 'Z' did not fire.	heard nothing if Oct 7. 10 p.m.
29th	About 6 rounds from each AG from the German batty positions within the harvest daily since 15th August. Neither Battery fired. Everything has been quiet during the last month. A new million strongpoint for "Z" Bty near Wye Farm.	
30th	'O' fired a few rounds. 93rd Bde RFA Head quarters moved to Fleurbaix, Z Bde in Batterie HQ. C+D going to Port à Cloud during nights 30/31st.	
31st	Z preparing position, also Batteries of 93rd Bde. AOB near CROIX MARECHAL, C+D in H 28 A. For tactical employment 'Z' Bty leaves the Brigade and Battalion Group (once AT Rulli) consisting of O Bty and two to Batteries of 93rd Bde RFA (M.G.) is formed consisting of	

M. J. H. Capt.
Bde. 5th Bde RFA

8th, Division.

5th, Bde. R. H. A.

September, 1915.

1699/T.1

8th Division

6th Brigade R.H.A.
Vol X
Sept. 15

WAR DIARY or INTELLIGENCE SUMMARY

Army Form C. 2118.

5th Bde RHA

Hour, Date, Place	Summary of Events and Information	Remarks and references to Appendices
September 1st	"O" Bty reconnoitred position for signallers in front trenches. "O" Bty's drawing station shelled by 77 rounds 4.2" Howr.	
2nd	2 Batteries of 93rd Bde moved into action during the day moving by single carriage into position. "O" Bty did not fire in trenches. Section Z's no. "O" fired.	
3rd	B/93 registered. "O" Bty reg'd. D/93 ditto. A/93 and C/93 moved into action.	
4th	A/93 and C/93 registered. B/93 moved one section forward their position coming under GRAHAM'S GROUP.	
5th	93rd Bde registered.	
6th	93rd Aeroplane Column and 5th Bde RHA Am Col moved up to S. of R. Lys. "O" fired 17 rounds checking one Right line Registration/fires - "Z" moved two others & fires to new position at 7 pm. 93rd AC RFA registered.	
7th	"O" fired afternoon heavy at request of Infantry - ale Batteries of 93rd Bde registered evening machine gun emplacements with shrapnel & H.E. Wires laid during the last 3 days to two observation stations. Silenced by hostile Snipers. The wires being doubled in one case shelled in two others. The buried or ditched lines stood the air. Headquarters Battalion Group moved up to Z's sta. gun position H27 d 11.3.	

Army Form C. 2118.

WAR DIARY
or
INTELLIGENCE SUMMARY

(Erase heading not required.)

Instructions regarding War Diaries and Intelligence Summaries are contained in F.S. Regs., Part II. and the Staff Manual respectively. Title pages will be prepared in manuscript.

Hour, Date, Place	Summary of Events and Information	Remarks and references to Appendices
8ᵗʰ	No firing by Bulten grp. Hanging & laying wires to observation stations continues. I ordered to fire A.B. OS for the grp. 8'Battery is sending a Liason officer at H.Q. of right attack. Two telephone wires are being laid (north, wire) Khim – Gul 709 – Liason offices. Have an alternate method of communication by helio or electric signalling lamps. 2t. J. L. Taylor posted F.O.O. Btc R.H.A. Arm.Col.	
9ᵗʰ	No firing by Bulten grp.	
10	'O' fired 12 rds in conjunction with Canadian train in Somme de la MARLAQUE at 11 pm. B/93 fired a few rounds at a sniper house – wire laying changing continued.	
11ᵗʰ	H.Q. Bulten Group moved back to H.20.C central. Z Battery left 2 officers and 15 men with ten guns at H.35 b. The remainder of the detachments being withdrawn to support lines and all gunpositions. No firing by Bulten grp.	
12	8/93 fired 2 rounds at a working party.	
13	5.5 a.m. Germans exploded a mine under our parapet in 3 P. and shelled entrenches 20 S.R. sent out SOS 2 S-BR. Bulten Group received the messages S.R. an & opened fire. 'O' Battery fired 36 rounds and 93 B.L. R.F.A fired 23 rounds. The Germans did not attack.	

WAR DIARY or INTELLIGENCE SUMMARY

Army Form C. 2118.

(Erase heading not required.)

Hour, Date, Place	Summary of Events and Information	Remarks and references to Appendices
14th	"O" fired 143 rounds experimental H.E. at German trenches.	
15th	93rd Bde fired a few rounds - "O" did not fire - The 5th Bde R.H.A. are collecting material and making preparation for wire. It is hoped shields overhead cover for horses &c. installed	
16th	Positions reconnoitred for two new forward guns in front trenches. "O" Bty and 93rd Bde fired a few rounds.	
17th	B/93 + C/93 fired as support of Infantry. Lt Taylor from 5th Bde Am. Col. attached to "O" for duty.	
18th	A/93 registered hit at N.5.d.4.2. "O" fired a few rounds.	
19th	B/93 fired 3 rounds at German working party.	
20th	9.45 am - "O" Battery heavily shelled. Two direct hits on two guns and a third slightly damaged. No casualties. Over 100 shells - 5"9 howitzers. There appeared to be at least 2 Batteries firing. Farm building used as a billet was also hit. "Z" Battery moved guns again at 4.35p.m. full detachments. No firing by Battery. Groups moved to "Z" old position at H.33.G.0.8.	

WAR DIARY
or
INTELLIGENCE SUMMARY

Army Form C. 2118.

(Erase heading not required.)

Hour, Date, Place	Summary of Events and Information	Remarks and references to Appendices
21st	B.W. happened monthly b-0 and A/93 fired early 30 mins. Afore during the day at German line - "O" fought hits infront of NH a 3.6 - MH a 7.6 - M16 9.2 - 4. N16 B.4 -	
	A/93 fired on line & photographs at N5 d 4.2	
	B/93 fired 2 rounds shrapnel & air checking up & taken a form tacke	
	The enemy did not reply much. Two hostile aeroplanes over during afternoon	
8 p.m. to 12 midnight	A/93 fired 32 rounds S. support trenches from N5d 6.0 to N16 2.8.	
	C/93 ———— 32 ————	N6c 4.1 to N16 7.6
	B/93 ———— 32 ————	
	T/93 ———— 32 ————	
22nd		
9 am to 11 am	"O" RHA and A/93 rectified 30 rds per gun on German line as on 21st.	N5d 6.0 to N16 2.8
12 noon to 2 pm		N6c 4.1 to N16 7.6
8 pm to 12 mn	Trentalations of 93rd Bde fire as for 21st.	
	Lt A.B. Chadwick from Base attached to this Bde and joined Z. for duty	

Army Form C. 2118.

WAR DIARY
or
INTELLIGENCE SUMMARY
(Erase heading not required.)

Instructions regarding War Diaries and Intelligence Summaries are contained in F.S. Regs, Part II. and the Staff Manual respectively. Title pages will be prepared in manuscript.

Hour, Date, Place	Summary of Events and Information	Remarks and references to Appendices
23rd	12 mn to 8am. Two inch trench 93rd Bde fired on on 22nd. The enemy did not reply much "yesterday"	
	8 am to 10 am } During these hours 'O' and A/93 each fired a strong bomb a gun as	
	12 mn to 2pm } German wire opp. 21st Sept. No HE fired since beginning of bombardment	
	3pm to 4pm	
	4.25pm to 4.35pm. 'O' and each Bty 7/93rd Bde fired 10 rounds a gun at hostile parapet opposite our front	
	During the afternoon C/93 fired 20 rounds HE and 40 rounds shrapnel at Connaught Ross, Grer in N6a	
	Very little reply from the enemy during the day.	
	8.2.pm each Battery fired 1 round gun fire at hostile parapet opposite our front.	
	2/Lt. T.J. Craig from 23rd Bn. attached B/O for duty.	
	8.30pm to 12 mn. Two each gun Btys 93rd Bde fired 10 rounds shrapnel any known or suspected enemy	
	Wind salient N5d 4.2 and support trench N11b 85.65 B/N6c 4.1	

Army Form C. 2118.

WAR DIARY
or
INTELLIGENCE SUMMARY

(Erase heading not required.)

Instructions regarding War Diaries and Intelligence Summaries are contained in F. S. Regs., Part II. and the Staff Manual respectively. Title pages will be prepared in manuscript.

Hour, Date, Place	Summary of Events and Information	Remarks and references to Appendices
25th 4pm	12 mn to 4 am. one Btty. 93" Bde fired 4 rds. shrapnel every ½ hour N11 85.65 & N11 6c 4.1	NNSD 4.2 steam Battery
	4.25 am to 4.32 am. all Batteries at Potter fired front fired 8 rounds shrapnel. 4/93 on N6c 7.5 sweeping to extreme side. Total of Antoine Barrage about Courant du Rossig. NOZ between trenches and N6a 7.1.	40 4/93 in N25 positions
	1.5 pm to 6 pm "O" Bty, 1 pm A/93 and 1 pm – 8/93 undertaken during night 2.3"/94" 1.26 positive in front parapet at N6b 1.1. N5d 9.8. N5d 3.8 - Bore has been kept rain 8 pm 572 mm and the mud was very bad.	
	6 & 8 pm, 93" Bde during the day reached COURANT du ROSSIG NOZ in square N6Z firing total 40 rds shrapnel + 20 HE.	
	10. am. 2 men wounded in "O" Bty, trenches.	
	8 am to 10. am. } "O" Bty, catmine about N11 A.1.5.	
	12 noon to 2 pm } A/93 -- near N5 d 4.2 - Total 30 rds frepm shrapnel 3 p.m to 4 pm } were fired.	Each battery.
11. a.m.	D/93 fired 12 rds shrapnel at Target #4 (N24 a 5.9) where flashes were seen.	

Army Form C. 2118.

WAR DIARY or INTELLIGENCE SUMMARY

(Erase heading not required.)

Hour, Date, Place	Summary of Events and Information	Remarks and references to Appendices
24th cont.		
7 p.m. to 12 midnight	Two batteries 93rd Bde. fired each 8 rds. shrapnel every ½ hour; one at support trench behind N.5.a.4.2 the other at support trench N.11.b.8.2. 6.2 to N.6.c.4.1 D/93 Battery comes under orders of Col. Loring for Counter Battery work, remaining under British front for experience	
25th Midnight to 4 a.m.	Two batteries 93rd Bde. fired each 8 rds. shrapnel every ½ hour as above.	
	The infantry will attack at 4.30 a.m. The German trenches from opposite WELL FARM SALIENT to the LE BRIDOUX ROAD. Capt T.T. Wallace O'RHA is the Liaison Officer with R.A. in the attack. Double telephone line laid. Thin wire from Group headquarters - this line is entrusted also to forward par of 'O' Battery. Spareditzian kite lines from T.O.O. D/93 and C/93 and D/93 - RHA back Office batteries (all double). There are double lines from T.O.O. B/93 and 'O'RHA one buried, one air direct to group headquarters. One of the latter lines is connected forward guns of A/93 and B/93. An alternative method of communication by lamp or helio has been arranged from 'O' and B/93 forward observation stations to group headquarters.	
4.25 a.m. to 4.30 a.m.	Butler front. One Battery 9/93 fired on N.6.c.7.5. Coming apart of 20m² by sweeping 100° on each side of this front - firing 5 rounds per gun in 'preparation'. HE & shrapnel. Right A/93. B/93 and 'O' Battery [Barrage]. Beginning with trenches from The Circus an Posen G.no being reached young Eaten limit. Barrage extending from support trench to reach N.6.c.7.1 - 5 rounds per gun, shrapnel only.	
	One gun A/93 under Lt Elliott fired a machine-gun apparatus on front parapet N.5.d.4.2 R.N.5.d.7.0 first 10 rounds rapidly, then fire pre 30 sec. for 30 minutes. Fire was out of action for some minute, shortly after 4.30 a.m. as parapet fell on it.	

WAR DIARY or INTELLIGENCE SUMMARY

Army Form C. 2118.

(Erase heading not required.)

Hour, Date, Place	Summary of Events and Information	Remarks and references to Appendices
4.25 am to 4.30 am (Contd.)	One gun "O" Bty under Lt Fryburgh in foreground opened fire at 4.25 am rapidly as possible for 5 min. After that any opportunity of again is coming in the taken. Lt Fryburgh + Frew, his detachment were wounded by shellfire about midday. One gun B/93 under Lt Woodward fired on target at N6c4.4. The first 10 rounds as rapidly as possible then gunfire 30 secs. Rate kept up for 30 min. Opportunity of again firing for the watched for.	at CORNER FORT
4.31 to 4.40	C/93 — fired as for 4.25 am to 4.30 am. 10 rds per gun shrapnel only. A/93, B/93 and O RHA fire as for 4.25 am to 4.30 am — ten gun shrapnel only.	HE in proportion 3 to 1. Right barrage — 10 rounds
	A/93 forward gun (No.1) fired as for 4.25 to 4.30 am. morning. No casualties. Ceasedfire at 4.25 am B/93 forward gun (No 2) fired as for 4.25 to 4.30 am. No casualties. during the morning.	No.1 gun fired total of 51 HE during bt No.2 forward gun fired total of 70 rds HE

Army Form C. 2118.

WAR DIARY
or
INTELLIGENCE SUMMARY

(Erase heading not required.)

Instructions regarding War Diaries and Intelligence Summaries are contained in F. S. Regs., Part II. and the Staff Manual respectively. Title pages will be prepared in manuscript.

Hour, Date, Place	Summary of Events and Information	Remarks and references to Appendices
4.31 am to 4.40 am	6 B.5 forward guns (No 3) ceasefire when Infantry advanced at 4.30 am. Total misfires by no 3. Battery morning 29 H.E.	
4.30 am	Capt Wallace hit. H.Q. night strose, reports bombardment appears very effective - very little reply from enemy - little rifle fire.	
4.4 to 5. am	C/93 a.f. 4.25 am to 4.30 am. 20 rounds a gun	
	A/93. B/93 and 'O' RHA = Right Barrage after 4.25 am to 4.30 am. 20 rounds a gun	
4.30 am	approximately	Right barrage
	A/93. B/93 and 'O' RHA continue a/f 4.25 to 4.30 am	
5.7 am	Order received from 8th Bn. Att for C/93. A/93. B/93 and 'O' RHA to lift having rate of fire.	
5.40 am	Message received from Capt Wallace since 5.2 am Right attack apparently gained footing in Germantrench. AAA enemy bombers active tree directly on our arrival	
5.45 am	Capt Wallace confirmed that right attack had taken first line Germantrench	

1247 W 9299 200,000 (E) 8/14 J.B.C. & A. Forms/C. 2118/11.

Army Form C. 2118.

WAR DIARY
or
INTELLIGENCE SUMMARY

(Erase heading not required.)

Instructions regarding War Diaries and Intelligence Summaries are contained in F.S. Regs., Part II. and the Staff Manual respectively. Title pages will be prepared in manuscript.

Hour, Date, Place	Summary of Events and Information	Remarks and references to Appendices
6.5 am.	Message recd from Capt Wallace. Right attack is in German 2nd line trench. Keeps attack - no rifle fire very little shell fire.	Rodgers/Dunlop
6.32. am.	Verbal message from Capt Wallace. Right attack have 2 Companies in German 2nd line trench. Right attack not yet joined Centre attack so left of right attack is held up.	
6.40 am.	A/93. B/93. C/93 and "O" Rifle need troops in same direction. Lists again where enemy fire by half. 9 rounds per gun per minute.	
8. am.	Fire still being kept up as above.	
8.10 am	Capt Wallace reports "Right attack upon having been bombed out of 2nd line trench."	
8.40 am	Verbal orders received from Brigadier 8th Div Arty that C/93 Battery is to move at once to NOUVEAU MONDE Church to come under orders of 20th Bde 2.	
9.30. am	Capt Wallace reports - Rifle fire enfilading German trenches from Corner Fort before Rue Cross Current du Bois is at N.62.c.7 - The Germans are trick on the right	

WAR DIARY or INTELLIGENCE SUMMARY

Army Form C. 2118.

(Erase heading not required.)

Instructions regarding War Diaries and Intelligence Summaries are contained in F. S. Regs., Part II. and the Staff Manual respectively. Title pages will be prepared in manuscript.

Hour, Date, Place	Summary of Events and Information	Remarks and references to Appendices
10 am	B/93 went forward onto 67 fuze. – Capt. Baker reports right edge of LOZENGE.	Centre attack is appears
10.8 am	"O" Bty onward 8 cause fuze. A/93 and B/93 left on right Barrage observing fire 1 minute.	
12.20 pm	Right attacks having started for Schilling sector A/93 is turned onto N6d 2.6 switch fire 1 min.	
12.30 pm	B/93 fires onto front trench & support trench near A/93 is turned onto N6d 4.7 – "O" Bty on Couvent du Rossignol just in rear. Batteries being informed right, right attack does not start beyond Couvent Fort. Ack. battns. at action file 1 minute.	
12.55 pm	"O" Battery and A & B/93 continue firing on Registered Fire – observers state front trench & support trench have been taken & stopping at 1.8 and	
1.2 pm	Right attack reported. Rus bombardment on their right sea sufficient. Batteries ordered to keep firing at 1.8 and 1.10 pm	
1.40 pm	Right attack reports all quiet on their right slope.	
2.20 pm	A/93 switch fire 100° Klonw fine new front trenches and outflg trenches Woody Common front to trench heads to Couvent du Rossignol – Burst fire 1 min.	

WAR DIARY or INTELLIGENCE SUMMARY

Army Form C. 2118.

(Erase heading not required.)

Instructions regarding War Diaries and Intelligence Summaries are contained in F. S. Regs, Part II. and the Staff Manual respectively. Title pages will be prepared in manuscript.

Hour, Date, Place	Summary of Events and Information	Remarks and references to Appendices
4 p.m.	Capt Wallace reports Rifle Bde unable to withdraw owing gradually along enemy attempts rate of fire increased. A/93 and B/93 on Rossignol Section fire 30 sec.	Comment on Rossignol - fire 30 sec.
4.5 p.m.	"O" Ak, asked to cover retirement of Rifle Bde. See fire 30 sec.	
4.10 p.m.	1 Red rocket sent up + S.O.S. Left flank Rifle Bde. received. B/93 were Rifle Bde picked on barrage as for this morning.	B/93 were Rifle Bde picked on
4.35 p.m.	Capt Lodge reports Rifle Bde now back – Battn hqrs Cens firing & repel march to F Bn Con Wallace Kuidage Officer hit – right attack sent in constant and valuable information during the day. Artillery. All telephone comn. broken except with Bt hqrs of gun after he was wounded, very good all day. B/93 Battery left Bulloo Farm and marched 07.15pm 20 = B.	
7.30 p.m.	found from 7 A/93 area B/93 withdrawn to Battery position during night. "O" Cmd not get kens out owing to very bad ground being rain.	"O" Cmd not
Night 25th/26th	Night firing during night 25/26. A/93 fired on Sapping trench N6C 4.1 . B/93 on a.a. N6 c 5.5 .	
	Casualties, firing two rounds shrapnel every ½ hour from 7.30pm to 4.30 am. Same time haw + half hour on the selected.	
	Total Ammn – fired during 25th by Bullet fring. 8pm 24, fd 6.5pm 25th = D.A's, 713 shrapnel 68 HE = A/93, 974 sh. shrapnel (exclusive moon/gun) B/93, 581 shrapnel (ex moon/gun) B/93. 263 shrapnel. C/93 not known. Total Casualties. 1 Officer 6 men wounded. all in "O" Bty Rifle Bde. or when carrying forward gun.	
26th 12.15 p.m.	A/93 and B/93 fired on N5d 4.2 and on N6c 4.4 respectively for 5 min 5. shrapnel per gun. ½ HE and ½ shrapnel.	

WAR DIARY or INTELLIGENCE SUMMARY

Army Form C. 2118.

Hour, Date, Place	Summary of Events and Information	Remarks and references to Appendices
26th (contd)	2.45 pm. aaaa900. "D" Bty. fired 1 section on N6C 4.4 and one on N5 d 4.2 for five minutes each section. Fire 20 rounds executive lag H.E. and half shrapnel.	
12.30 pm	Verbal orders received for remainder of 93rd Bde to move off by single vehicle at 10 min interval to Rendez-vous about M3 d 8.0, leaving British group rejoining 20 Div. "Z" Bty. marched back to old position near CROIX BLANCHE by section during day, which has been used by "D" Bty since 20th. "O" moved back to old position just W. of CROIX BLANCHE by sections.	
8 pm	32nd Bty. moved into position at H28.C.1.2 and N12 Z and "O" became BUTLERS group.	
	During night 26/27th "O" Bty. fired 10.30 pm to 1.30 am. 30 rounds as communication trenches N12 a 6.8 and N6 d 8.6. "Z" fired 20 rounds advantage targets from 7.30 pm to 10.30 pm.	
27th	3.55 am. 27th order received "No more firing except in case of urgent necessity".	
	4 pm 5th Battery R.F.A. comes into British group. Lieut. Craig att. "O" Bty. from 23rd Bty. rejoined his own unit.	

Army Form C. 2118.

WAR DIARY
or
INTELLIGENCE SUMMARY

(Erase heading not required.)

Instructions regarding War Diaries and Intelligence Summaries are contained in F.S. Regs, Part II. and the Staff Manual respectively. Title pages will be prepared in manuscript.

Hour, Date, Place	Summary of Events and Information	Remarks and references to Appendices
28th	No firing by 'O' n'Z' – Lt R.O. Lyons and 1 Gunner 'Z' Battery having applied for service with Armoured Motor Cars. 6 p.m. Cell attached Batterie left Batteries (except 'O' & 'Z' remaining as in original Times). 3" Coy Gunners inspected One Officer and 10 other ranks for at G.O.d. and advanced base in the operation of 25th Sept.	Batrs 6,23",B=
29th	No firing by 'O' or 'Z' –	
30th	No firing by 'O' or 'Z' –	
'Z' Battery wire cutting 2nd–Oct 4th.	The following is short account of 'Z' Battery's doings from 21st to 26th Sept. Bombardment Sept 21, 22, 23. x. 'Z' Battery (under Graham fires) out hostile wire from a front of 200 yards the East of the West edge of CORNER FORT. Range about 1400*. 300 rounds per day allowed. Reduction fire fairly actions every afternoon. Reports of the Battery has been directed, and the wire reported there excellent. Communications. On air line now front trenches of any use at all – wire much like buried in Comm trenches or fogged wh' hostile lst had one shafter ___	Driving to pieces in any out hostile wire Reported by of Capt Adj, 5t Bd, R.H.A.

1247 W 3209 200,000 (E) 8/14 J.B.C. & A. Forms/C. 2118/11.

8th, Division.

5th, Bde. R. H. A.

October, 1915.

121/74449

8th Hussars
5th Bde. R.H.A.

Oct -15

Vol XI

Army Form C. 2118.

WAR DIARY
or
INTELLIGENCE SUMMARY 5th BURMA

(Erase heading not required.)

Instructions regarding War Diaries and Intelligence Summaries are contained in F. S. Regs., Part II. and the Staff Manual respectively. Title pages will be prepared in manuscript.

Hour, Date, Place	Summary of Events and Information	Remarks and references to Appendices
October 1st	Amm Colmn moved from H.8 to G.20 at 11.a.m. New Rev Battery fred.	
2nd	'Z' Battery fired one round at Test S.O.S. No other firing by the Brigade.	
	'O' Battery reconnoitred new position at H.26 d 6.5	
3rd	'Z' fired 4 rounds at various times when Test S.O.S. signals sended by 23rd Inf. Bde.	
	'O' " 1 " " do do	
4th	2nd Lt E.A.W. Rogers from the Am Col attached the Brigade as at F.O.	
5th	Each Battery fired 3 rounds at Test S.O.S. early 23rd Inf Bde.	
6th	Neither Battery fired.	
	Nither Battery fired. Road to being called from Town of Nieppe. Into standings nowhere. Cover hut positions and billets fast in order. Some wooden canvas huts are being issued.	
7th	No firing by the Brigade - 'O' moved one section at night to new position as H.26 d 6.5.	
8th	1 Section of 'O' registered from new position - Position 4 from March here at night.	

WAR DIARY or INTELLIGENCE SUMMARY

Army Form C. 2118.

5th Bde R.H.A.

(Erase heading not required.)

Hour, Date, Place	Summary of Events and Information	Remarks and references to Appendices

9th — 'Z' did not fire. 'O' fired 32 rounds at trenches about N5d3.2.
3" Bty, 32nd Bty, 57th Bty and 'O' under command of O.C. 5th Bde RHA. John Turpin ac
the C.O. did duty to annoy the German trenches about N5d 4.2.

10th — O. 3" 32nd & 57th Bty,s rapid fired 10 rounds at salient N5d 4.2 between 2pm & 4.30pm.
'Z' did not fire.

11th — 'O' 32nd & 57th Btys fired at salient Ns d 4.2 at 7.10 p.m. 7.35pm and 8.20pm 12 rds a Battery.
'O' fired 11 rounds about 11 am at repairing party of Infantry in what takes be German shelled
our trenches heavily at N41 —
4.30pm German aeroplane fell near O & Z waggon lines. Got pilot who was being captured.
The plane had been forced to descend by one gun flames. Aircraft on fire
fired 11.20 am to 72 Square and at 3.10pm at
'Z' did not fire. N5d 4.2. Total 12 rds per Battery.
trenches near

12th —

13th — 5 am — 'O' — 3" — 32nd — & 57th Btys each fired 12 rds at trenches near N5 d 4.2.
3 pm — F.O.C. RA went to wagon line 'O' & 'Z' to see trials of slabbing & harness for Cooking.
2.45pm — 3.15pm — German 5.9 registered 'Z' W line position and 6" gun cleanly strike –
9.55pm SOS T31/3 sent out by Infantry over the wagon lines. Fired 9 rds — S excellent
Aeroplane fujisette over the Infantry, but it was a false alarm.

Army Form C. 2118.

WAR DIARY
or
INTELLIGENCE SUMMARY   5th Bde RHA

(Erase heading not required.)

Hour, Date, Place	Summary of Events and Information	Remarks and references to Appendices
14th	Z did not fire - "O"- 3rd- 39th - & 57th Batteries fired little or no rounds near NSd 4.2, half the rounds between 11, and 11.15am and half between 3. and 3.15pm	
15th	"O"- 3rd- 32nd- & 57th Batteries fired at trenches near NSd 4.2. 3 rounds per Battery at 11.30 am. 6 rounds per Battery, at 1.10 pm and again at 3.10 pm	
	Z did not fire.	
16th	"O"- 3rd- 32nd- & 57th by Australian fired each 10 rounds at trenches near NSd 4.2 at 5.am	
17th	Z did not fire.	
	Neither Battery fired	
18th	Inniskilling Battery Field. Lt. J (H.D. Ross from 8th Div Am Col attached) to Brigade - attached to Z Battery.	
19th	Neither Battery fired.-	
20th	Neither Battery fired.-	

Army Form C. 2118.

WAR DIARY
or
INTELLIGENCE SUMMARY 5th Bde RHA

(Erase heading not required.)

Hour, Date, Place	Summary of Events and Information	Remarks and references to Appendices
21st October	Neither Battery fired.	
22nd	Z fired 3 rounds at party of enemy in road N.18.C.2.8 - "O" did not fire.	
23rd	A party of munition workers from England visited "O" Bty at midday. "O" fired 6 rounds of shrapnel while they were in the Battery.	
24th	Z fired 9 ths shrapnel at report of Infantry during the day, at P.S. Myburgh Turnder 25th Sept. struck nr Hd Qtrs of the Brigade.	
25th	Neither Battery fired. not cold all day	
26th	Neither Battery fired.	
27th	Section Z Battery fired 6 rounds at German working party. "O" did not fire.	
28th	Z fired 6 rounds at German working party. "O" did not fire	
29th	Neither Battery fired.	

WAR DIARY
or
INTELLIGENCE SUMMARY 5th Bde R.H.A.

(Erase heading not required.)

Army Form C. 2118.

Hour, Date, Place	Summary of Events and Information	Remarks and references to Appendices
30th October	"O" fired 5 Rounds Retaliation at request of Infantry. "Z" fired 32 Rounds checking Registration. And six rounds while party of Infantry broken from Hyland where being shown round the Battery.	
31st —	Neither Battery fired. Lt. C.F.T. Lindsay posted from "Z" Battery to "F" Battery 5th Bde R.H.A.	
		M Orme Capt Adj. 5th Bde R.H.A

8th, Division.

5th, Bde. R. H. A.

November, 1915.

8th Division

5th Bde R.H.A.

No V.
Vol XII

12/76944

WAR DIARY
or
INTELLIGENCE SUMMARY

5th Bde R.F.A.

Army Form C. 2118.

(Erase heading not required.)

Hour, Date, Place	Summary of Events and Information	Remarks and references to Appendices
November 1st	Neither "O" nor "Z" fired. Wet all day.	
2nd	Neither Battery fired.	
3rd	do ""	
4th	do ""	
5th	"O" Bty. did not fire. "Z" Bty. fired 6 rds shrap. byorder. Fine sunny day. Stars rising. Neither "O" nor "Z" Bty fired. Major Shirley O.C. "O" Bty left the Brigade for the 2/y S. Brigade R.F.A. 4th Division. Captain Dirks transferred from Adjutant this Brigade to Command temporarily. "O" Battery.	
6th	"Z" Bty fired 11 Shrapnel. "O" Bty did not fire. 2nd Lieut Lauger joined Brigade H.Q. as orderly officer.	
7th	"Z" Bty fired 6 shrapnel. "O" Bty did not fire.	
8th	"Z" Bty fired 6 shrapnel. "O" Bty did not fire.	
9th	"O" Bty fired 8 shrap (Instructional shoot) "Z" Bty fired 10 shrap. 14 rounds "rivers for brigade.	doits latest known to aim at snipers
10th	"O" Bty did not fire. "Z" Bty fired 10 shrap.	
11th	"O" Bty did not fire. "Z" Bty fired 6 shrap. Enemy Guly in action near Petit Rue located by Reuter tomike — angle from H. 33b 29 — 152°30' R. of Heudrie Church	
12th	"O" Bty did not fire. "Z" Bty fired 6 shrap as ordered.	
13th	do do	
14th	"O" Bty fired 6 shrap (Instructional shoot) "Z" Bty fired 6 shrap.	
15th	"O" Bty did not fire "Z" fired 20 shrap aut 4 H.E.	

Army Form C. 2118.

WAR DIARY
or
INTELLIGENCE SUMMARY

5th Brigade R.H.A

(Erase heading not required.)

Instructions regarding War Diaries and Intelligence Summaries are contained in F. S. Regs., Part II. and the Staff Manual respectively. Title pages will be prepared in manuscript.

Hour, Date, Place	Summary of Events and Information	Remarks and references to Appendices
November 16th	"O" fired 6 bombs (8) Instructional Shoot "Z" fired 6 (8) as usual.	
17th	"O" did not fire. "Z" fired 10 (5) and 2 H.E. Observation Station lightly shelled.	
18th	"O" fired 11 shrap (Instructional) "Z" fired 6 shrap as usual.	
19th	"O" fired 4 shrap. Nothing further below 10. "Z" fired 6 shrap as usual.	
20th	"O" did not fire. "Z" fired 6 shrap.	
21st	"O" fired 4 shrapnel at T.O.P. "Z" fired 6 shrap 1 S.H.E at M.G. Emplacement.	
22nd	"O" did not fire. "Z" fired 6 Shrapnel.	
23rd	"O" did not fire. "Z" fired 6 Shrapnel 3 armour.	
24th	"O" did not fire. "Z" fired 6 Shrap usl. at two bait	
25th	"O" did not fire. "Z" fires re Shrap in retaliation. one section Sect of "O" + "Z" batteries relieved by a section of A.R.B. Batteries of the 90th Brigade.	
26th	"O" did not fire. "Z" fired 9 shrap. 10 H.E. Remaining sections of "O" + "Z" relieved by Major "J" Brie marched to Lynde into Army by means of School of A.H.B. 190. Recrd	
27th	Brigade H.Q & Ammunition Column marched to Lynde. Very short halt.	
28th	Units rested. Food abundant today. Brigade H.Q established in Lynde. Units in montebello.	
29th	All units started training. Could not do much owing to state of ground. Thourset in.	
30th	Units continued with same run. Units drilling & training.	

1247 W 8290 200,000 (E) 8/14 J.B.C.&A. Forms/C. 2118/11.

8th, Division.

5th, Bde. R. H. A.

December, 1915.

5th Base Rhtra.

Dec / Vol XIII

Army Form C. 2118.

WAR DIARY or INTELLIGENCE SUMMARY

5th Brigade R.H.A.

(Erase heading not required.)

Instructions regarding War Diaries and Intelligence Summaries are contained in F. S. Regs., Part II. and the Staff Manual respectively. Title pages will be prepared in manuscript.

Hour, Date, Place	Summary of Events and Information	Remarks and references to Appendices
December 1st to December 19th	All units drilling & training. 2nd Lt. J.M. Cowper (O.O) left Brig.H.Q. to attend course of Javelin duration at 3rd Corps School of Signalling - Racquinghem. Major A.O. Boyd joined Brigade from 20th Division on 3-12-15 and was posted to O/149.	
20th	Marched out as a Division to Manœuvres - Billets in Clarques for night.	
21st	Manœuvres - Billets between CAYEUX and DENNEBROEC HQ at PETIGNY S of R.HS.	
22nd	Do.	
23rd	Marched back into 23rd Inf. Brigade to Reserve Billets near LYNDE.	
to 31st	All units drilling & training. 2nd Lt. Cowper returned to Brig HQ on 29th inst:	

W. Onslow Donough
Lt R.F.A.
Adjt 5th Brigade R.H.A.

8th, Division.

5th, Bde, R. H. A.

January, 1916.

8th Dec. 5 Bde R.H.A.
Jan
Vol XIV

WAR DIARY
or
INTELLIGENCE SUMMARY

5th Brigade R.F.A.   January 1916.

Army Form C. 2118.

Hour, Date, Place	Summary of Events and Information	Remarks and references to Appendices
January 1st to 10th	Divisional Training in Army Reserve	
11th	One Section of both "O" and "L" Btys marched to relief of 20th Div Arty - halting half way for the night	
12th	Advance Sections marched up to positions vacated by Sections of 20th Div Arty. Remaining Sections marched from Reserve area - halting halfway for night	
13th	Advance Sections registered "O" Bty firing 16 H.E. + 3 Shrap. Remaining Sections marched in to positions	"L" Bty firing 25 Shrap. Completing relief.
14th	Brigade H.Q. and Brigade Am. Col. marched up through + 1 H.E. "O" Bty fired 26 Shrap. Checking Zero line. Hornillebra also in registration also in registration Scheme - Left front. "L" Bty " 4 Shrap " in registration 22 H.E. in retaliation at regist of Infantry.	"L" Bty fired 40 Shrap registration.
15th	"O" Bty 3 shrap at time in retaliation	
16th	"O" Bty did not fire	"L" Bty fired 12 H.E. and 8 Shrap at various targets.
17th	"O" Bty fired 25 H.E. and 5 Shrap in retaliation Brigade Scheme for left front also 18 Shrap registering Sat trade gun in front trench - "L" fired 1 H.E. on M.G. emplacement at request of Infantry.	
18th	"O" Bty fired 8 Shrap - hit flank gun firing 8 Shrap also	"L" Bty fired 28 Shrap + 1 H.E. registration
+ 19th	"O" Bty " " +4 H.E. firing Corrector re also 12 Shrap in front bombardment of Hostile Bty at N.23.A.0.5. "L" Bty " 30 Shrap at time about N.10.b.7.3.	
20th	"O" Bty fired 4 Shrap +4 H.E. finding Corrector re 18 Shrap in retaliation + 6 Shrap 8".O.A Relocation Scheme Case I.	"L" Bty fired 7 Shrap + 8 H.E. finding Corrector from time for registration - first to "O" Bty

+ Capt: Doroty'ke T/Hewler Territorials attached from home for instruction

WAR DIARY or INTELLIGENCE SUMMARY

Army Form C. 2118.

5th Bde RFA   January 1916

Hour, Date, Place	Summary of Events and Information	Remarks and references to Appendices
January 21st	"O" Bty fired 4 shrap + 6 H.E. at O.P - 5 shrap + 16 H.E. at Sept last + 10 shrap + 5 H.E. at trenches. "Z" Bty fired 14 shrap + 6 H.E. at house believed to be O.P. + 13 shrap at parapet.	
22nd	"O" Bty fired 20 shrap + 14 H.E. at various targets in retaliation. "Z" Bty " 36 shrap " " at W. Party trenches. There was considerable shelling by the enemy throughout day. "O" had 2 layers sent hurt by 2 guns	
23rd	Off one of the guns to a farm who set on fire close to "O" Bty fired 10 rounds shrap + from Infantry gun retaliation. "Z" Bty fired 29 shrap at various targets.	
24th	"Z" Bty fired 5 shrapnel at working party with good effect. "O" Bty did not fire	
25th	"O" Bty fired 70 shrapnel and 78 H.E. mostly at trenches. "Z" Bty fired 120 shrap + 10 H.E. from Inf. flank gun in accordance with scheme + 10 shrap + 6 H.E. from Bty position	
26th	"O" Bty fired 9 shrap at various targets + 4 shrap at N.57 on S.O.S. "Z" fired 30 shrap and 2 H.E. at various targets. Took in O.P. started by R.E.s	
27th	"O" Bty fired 14 shrap + 14 H.E. at various targets in retaliation "Z" " " 2 shrap + 3 H.E. at house registering.	
28th	"O" Bty " 14 shrap + 4 H.E. at various targets. "Z" fired 9 shrap + 24 H.E.	
29th	"O" " 16 shrap - "Z" Bty fired 4 shrap + 19 H.E. 179 shrap on various other targets from infantry gun retaliation, also 33 H.E.	
30th	"O" " "Z" Bty fired " at W. Park - Gun replaced successful respectively –	
31st	Neither "O" nor "Z" Bty fired – Trench raid see App. trench raid but more or less normal day – Capt. Inclyk, London Territorials returned to England. Very quiet	

W Averell Bowroughs Lt R.A.

8th, Division.

5th, Bde. R. H. A.

February, 1916.

WAR DIARY
or
INTELLIGENCE SUMMARY

Army Form C. 2118.

5th Bde R.H.A.   February 1916.

Hour, Date, Place	Summary of Events and Information	Remarks and references to Appendices
February 1st	"O" Bty fired 18 H.E. and 3 shrap at various tgts. Instructional Shoot – "Z" Bty. Air up tgt. Capt. Buchan of the Brigade Arm. Col. left on posting to the 45th Brigade R.F.A. being relieved by Capt. Sherlock. Observing posts to the Brigade & Arm. Col. with effect from this day. 2/Lieut Headley was attached to "Z" Bty from the D.A.C. for instruction 2/Lieut Ross of "Z" Bty being attached to the D.A.C. in his place.	
2nd	"O" Bty fired 12 shrap. "Z" Bty fired 29 H.E. at various houses attempting many direct hits.	
3rd	"O" fired 15 H.E. & 3 shrap at various houses in retaliation – "Z" fired 20 H.E. at various houses and 3 shrap & 3 H.E. at Road J. Shooting very accurate. Very cold & misty. Two performances by R.A. Band at J – Y X roads.	
4th	"O" fired 8 shrap accly to left rout programme – also 13 H.E. and 7 shrap at roads & various. "Z" " 9 H.E. and 3 shrap at trench roads.	2/Lieut Taylor left on Signalling Course at Hinges.
5th	"O" fired 11 shrap & 42 H.E. in Scheme Retaliation "Z" fired 6 shrap & 6 H.E. at Roads A & J.	
6th	"O" 8 shrap & 3 H.E. at various targets – "Z" fired 10 H.E. & 6 shrap at various targets & 15 H.E. at a 77 mm Battery – firing from map.	2/Lieut Bell returned from Arty Course at Lillers.
7th	"O" fired 5 H.E. Enfilement of infantry. "Z" fired 12 shrap & 12 H.E. at W. Ind. Front E.	
8th	"O" fired 12 H.E. and 8 shrap. at roads 4 and 4 ordered by O.C. left group. "Z" fired 12 H.E. and 12 shrap at Roads Sandis. 6 H.E. coder A. 11 H.E. dispersing working party.	
9th	"O" fired 6 H.E. and 4 shrap at Road 3 and 3 shrap at B. house (flank gun). "Z" fired 11 shrap at working party Art. Course at Lillers left. McBacon	
10th	"O" fired 25 shrap & 8 H.E. at house and 8 H.E. at request of inf. in retaliation. "Z" fired 4 shrap and 16 H.E. at house enflade gun. 3 H.E. and 2 Shrap in retaliation. Main Batte replaced him.	Lieut. Col. A.T. Butler left to take tempy Command of Div Arty.
11th	H.E. at request of infantry. "Z" fired 47 H.E. in retaliation.	2 H.E. listing for destruction of flash from O.P.
12th	"O" fired nil. "Z" fired 18 H.E. and 22 shrap. in Retaliation. "O" Bty did not fire "Z" fired 16 Shrap and 3 H.E. at various targets 12 Shrap on Road 3.	

Army Form C. 2118.

WAR DIARY
or
INTELLIGENCE SUMMARY

(Erase heading not required.)

5th Brigade R.H.A.   February 1916 (cont)

Hour, Date, Place	Summary of Events and Information	Remarks and references to Appendices
February 14th	"O" Bty fired 4 shrapnel and 6 HE at various targets "Z" Bty fired 6 shrapnel at various targets	
15th	"O" Bty did not fire. "Z" Bty fired 3 HE and 2 shrapnel at a house and 6 HE in conjunction with trench mortars.	
16th	"O" Bty fired 6 HE and 3 Shrap. at various targets "Z" Bty fired 22 shrap registration and 8 shrap in conjunction with trench mortars.	
17th	"O" Bty did not fire. "Z" Bty 18 Shrap and 10 HE at various targets and 15 HE in retaliation	
18th	Neither battery fired.	
19th	Z did not fire	
20th	Z Bty registered from their reserve position. Fired about 30 rounds chiefly in retaliation for enemy shelling	
21st	Quiet day dull	
22nd	Frost and slight fall of snow	
23rd	Slight snow. Y/ C.N. Salvolin posted to Ia Bde.	
24th	Both batteries fired a few rounds.	
25th	No firing	
26th	A little firing. Thaw set in.	
27th	No firing	
28th	"Z" battery fired 1 round at intervals during the night at gap in enemy wire.	
29th	Very little firing. Moved the Bde H.Q to old 45th Bde H.Q	

W Everett Bonnef
Lt Col R.H.A.
Adjt 5th Brigade R.H.A.
1-3-16

8th, Division.

5th, Bde, R. H. A.

March, 1916.

5 Bde R.H.A
Vol XVI

Army Form C. 2118.

WAR DIARY
or
INTELLIGENCE SUMMARY
(Erase heading not required.)

5th Bde RHA   March. 1916

Hour, Date, Place	Summary of Events and Information	Remarks and references to Appendices
March 1st	"O" Bty fired a few rounds in registration from their new position. "Z" Bty fired on a bombardment communication trench.	
2nd	"O" and "Z" Bty registration with forward gun.	
3rd	"O" Bty did not fire. Z fired 12 rounds at various targets. "O" Bty did not fire. "Z" fired 5 rounds at targets, also 3 rounds for the purpose of photographing flashes, which was satisfactorily done.	
4th	Neither battery fired during the day.	
5th	The enfilading guns assisted in a bombardment of the Sugar Loaf by the heavy artillery. Z fired at various targets in retaliation 41 rounds	
6th	"O" Battery did not fire.	
7th	"O" Bty did not fire. "Z" Bty fired with advanced gun at various points. Enemy retaliated near gun.	
8th	"O" Bty did not fire. "Z" Bty fires 2 rounds at request of infantry.	
9th	"O" Bty fires 2 rounds at Sugar Loaf at request of infantry. "Z" Bty fires 22 rds at various targets in retaliation for hostile shelling.	
10th	"O" Bty fired 34 rounds at trench targets at request of infantry "Z" Bty fires at various targets in retaliation to enemy shelling.	
11th	"O" Bty fires one round at request of infantry. Z Bty fires on communication trench on relief were reported. Capt Sherlock left this Brigade on being to command 54th Bty.	
12th	"O" Bty fires 4 rounds at request of infantry. Z Bty fires 26 rounds at various targets. Aand B Btys of 179th Bde Jones their guns for instruction	
13th	"O" Bty fires 4 rounds. "Z" Bty did not fire. D/186 Howitzer Bty joins for instruction.	
14th	Neither Bty fires	
15	"O" Bty fires 9 rounds at working party. Z fires 18 rounds at various targets. Z Bty forward gun heavily shelled	

WAR DIARY
INTELLIGENCE SUMMARY

5th Bde R.H.A.   March. 1916

Hour, Date, Place	Summary of Events and Information	Remarks and references to Appendices
March 1st	"O" Bty fired a few rounds in registration from their new position. "Z" Bty fired on a prominent communication trench and registration with forward gun.	
2nd	"O" Bty did not fire. "Z" fired 12 rounds at various targets.	
3rd	"O" Bty did not fire. "Y" fired 5 rounds at targets, also 3 rounds for the purpose of photographing flashes, which was satisfactorily done for the hostile batteries' guns during the day.	
4th	The exploding guns assisted in a bombardment of the SUGAR LOAF by the heavy artillery. Z fired at various targets in retaliation 4 rounds.	
5th		
6th	"O" Battery did not fire.	
7th	"O" Bty did not fire. "Z" Bty fired with advanced gun at various points. Enemy retaliates near gun.	
8th	"O" Bty did not fire. "Y" Bty fired 2 rounds at request of infantry.	
9th	"O" Bty fired 2 rounds at SUGAR LOAF at request of infantry. "Z" Bty fired 22 rds at various targets.	
10th	"O" Bty fired 34 rounds at trench targets at request of infantry "Z" Bty fired at various targets in retaliation for enemy shelling.	
11th	"O" Bty fired one round at request of infantry. "Y" Bty fired on communication trench on which was reported Capt Shorter left this Brigade on being posted to command 59th Bty.	
12th	"O" Bty fired 4 rounds at request of infantry. Z Bty fired 26 rounds at various targets. A and B Bty joins this group for instruction.	
13th	"O" Bty fired 4 rounds. "Z" Bty did not fire. D/186. Howitzer Bty joins for instruction.	
14th	Neither Bty fired.	
15th	"O" Bty fired 9 rounds at working party. Z fired 14 rounds at various targets. ZBty forward gun heavily shelled.	

WAR DIARY or INTELLIGENCE SUMMARY

Army Form C. 2118.

5th Bde R.H.A. *(Erase heading not required.)*

March 1916.

Hour, Date, Place	Summary of Events and Information	Remarks and references to Appendices
March 16th	"O" Bty fired 8 rounds at station in which a train was reported. "Z" Bty fired 20 rounds at various targets.	
17th	"O" Bty did not fire. "Z" Bty fired 24 rds registration of new forward position.	
18th	"O" Bty fired 14 rds at various targets. "Z" Bty fired 9 rounds in retaliation.	
19th	"O" Bty fired 9 rounds at various targets and "Z" Bty 8 at various.	
20th	"O" Bty fired 4 rounds at targets. "Z" Bty 2 rounds.	
21st	"O" Bty did not fire. "Z" fired 12 rounds.	
22nd	"O" Bty fired 3 rounds and "Z" Bty 6 rounds.	
23rd	"O" Bty fired 2 rounds and "Z" Bty fired 60 rounds on enemy batteries for instruction of officers & attacks on Sgt Du Attaches P.O/p. left.	
24th	Neither the enemy or ourselves fired during day. "Z" fired 10 rounds in conjunct. with mine blown up by 157th Bde 35th Divn. Arrived.	
25th 26th	Neither battery fired Advanced party of 157th Bde 35th Divn arrived.	
27th	"O" Battery fired nil. "Z" 17 rounds checking registrations to be handed over.	
28th	Neither unit fired. Relieved by 159. Bde RFA 35th Division. The relief took place at 7.0 pm when Lt Col. Bedford RFA took over the defence of the line. At 10.0 pm Bde HQ. and "O" Bty marched arriving at MERVILLE soon afternmidnight.	
29th	"O" Bty and HQ. commenced to entrain at about 2.30am and Completed the entrainment about 5.0am. The train left at 6.15am. "Z" Bty left their wagon line at 2.0am and arrived at MERVILLE shortly after 5.0am.	

Army Form C. 2118.

WAR DIARY
or
INTELLIGENCE SUMMARY
(Erase heading not required.)

5th Bde R.H.A.   March 1916.

Hour, Date, Place	Summary of Events and Information	Remarks and references to Appendices
March 16th	"O" Bty fired 8 rounds at station in which a train was reported. "Z" Bty fired 20 rounds at various targets.	
17th	"O" Bty did not fire. "Z" Bty fired 24 rds registration of new forward position.	
18th	"O" Bty fired 19 rds at various targets. "Z" Bty fired 9 rounds in retaliation.	
19th	"O" Bty fired 9 rounds at various targets and "Z" Bty 8 rds at Jarvin.	
20th	"O" Bty fired 4 rounds at targets. "Z" Bty 12 rounds.	
21st	"O" Bty did not fire. "Z" fired 12 rounds.	
22nd	"O" Bty fired 3 rounds and "Z" Bty 6 rounds.	
23rd	"O" Bty fired 2 rounds and "Z" Bty fired 60 rounds on enemy forming up for a heavy Trench Mortar attack on B'lp left. Attackers blown up by fire of Sgt Div. Attackers blown up by fire of 10 rounds.	
24th	Neither the enemy or ourselves fired their mine was in conjunction with.	
25th	Neither battery fired. Advanced party of 157th Bde 35th Div. arrived.	
26th	"O" Battery fired rd "Z" 17 rounds checking registrations to be handed over.	
27th & 28th	Neither unit fired. 159th Bde R.F.A 35th Division. The relief took place at 7.0 pm when Relieved by the Lt Col Bedford R.F.A took over the defence of the line. At 10.0 pm Bde Hq and "O" Bty marched arriving at MERVILLE soon after midnight.	
29th	"O" Bty and HQ commenced to entrain at about 2.30am and completed the entrainment about 5.0 am. "Z" Bty left their huts at 2.0 am and arrived at MERVILLE shortly after 5.0 am.	

Army Form C. 2118.

WAR DIARY
or
INTELLIGENCE SUMMARY

5th Brigade RHA (Erase heading not required.) March 1916

Hour, Date, Place	Summary of Events and Information	Remarks and references to Appendices
29th (Cont).	Their entrainment was accomplished satisfactorily and 8.15 a.m. There was no halt for watering and feeding the journey through DOULLENS and AMIENS to LONGEAU. The 1st train containing "D" Bty and H.Q. arrived. They then marched via AMIENS, ST. SAUVEUR, and LA CHAUSSÉE to billets in BELLOY.	The train left at during the horses where the brigade detrained at about 2:30 p.m. to billets
30th -	The Ammunition Column who entrained at LESTREM and about 8 p.m. They arrived in their billets soon after midnight. The remainder of the Brigade settled themselves in their new wagon lines.	arrived at LONGEAU
31st	Thereafter was glorious. Having first settled and stalled forms its parade. 6th day.	

B. Wentworth
Lt. RHA
Adjt. 5th Brigade RHA

WAR DIARY
or
INTELLIGENCE SUMMARY

5th Brigade R.H.A.   March 1916

Army Form C. 2118.

Hour, Date, Place	Summary of Events and Information	Remarks and references to Appendices
29th (Cont).	Their entrainment was accomplished satisfactorily and the train left at 8.15 am. There was no halt for watering and feeding the horses during the journey through DOULLENS and AMIENS to LONGEAU where the brigade detrained. The 1st train containing "O" Bty and H.Q. arrived at about 2.30 pm. They then marched via AMIENS, ST. SAUVEUR, and LA CHAUSSÉE to billets in BELLOY.	
30th	The Ammunition Column train entrained at LESTREM and arrived at LONGEAU about 8 pm. They arrived in their billets soon after midnight. The remainder of the Brigade settled themselves in their new wagon lines.	
31st	Thereafter was spent settling and stables forres the remainder of the day.	

BrockBonney
C.P.O.3.A
Adjt 5th Brigade R.H.A

8th, Division.

5th, Bde, R. H. A.

April, 1916.

Army Form C. 2118.

WAR DIARY
or
INTELLIGENCE SUMMARY.
(Erase heading not required.)

5th Brigade R.H.A.   April. 1916.

Place	Date	Hour	Summary of Events and Information	Remarks and references to Appendices
	April 1st		Lt. Col. A.T. Butler left to take temporary Command of the Divisional Artillery. Major Boyd commanding "O" Bty took Command of the Brigade	
	2nd		Two packs took place. Lt. C.G.G. Nicholson R.F.A. left "Z" Bty to take up his appointment as A.D.C. to H.C.R.A. 8th Division.	
	3rd		The usual routine of Battery Parades.	
	4th		Some rain. No usual Parade.	
	5th		Advanced section marched to BEHENCOURT rest Here tonight.	
	6th		Advanced Section and HQ came into the line. The remaining sections marched to BEHENCOURT	
	7th		Remaining sections came into the line and at 7.0 pm took over the defence of the line from 32nd Div Arty.	
	8th		Group under the Command of Lt Col A.T. Butler C.M.G. consisting of the 45th Bde R.F.A and "Z" Bty R.H.A covers the Left Section of the 8th Div line.	
	9th		Very little firing.	
	10th		Working parties locating and firing on working parties, trenches and fires on	
	11th		Two large working parties south of LA BOISELLE being heavily shelled. Bombardment took place an trench south of LA BOISELLE being heavily shelled	

Army Form C. 2118.

WAR DIARY
or
INTELLIGENCE SUMMARY
(Erase heading not required.)

5th Brigade RHA April (Cont) '16

Hour, Date, Place	Summary of Events and Information	Remarks and references to Appendices
April 12th	"Z" Bty did not fire. Quiet day.	
13th	"Z" " fired a few rounds at a large working party.	
14th	"X" " dispersed with their fire a large party seen working behind enemy lines.	
15th	"Z" Bty did not fire, quiet day.	
16th	"Z" Bty did not fire. HQ 5th Bde moved to the outskirts of ALBERT.	
17th	"X" Bty did not fire	
18th	"X" Bty did not fire. Quiet day	
19th	"X" Bty fired at various targets rather more activity	
20th	"X" Bty fired at checking zero lines.	
21st	"Z" Bty fired at various targets. Very little enemy artillery	
	Read P.S. My through rejoined the Brigade.	
22nd	"X" Bty fired and dispersed a working party. Aeroplanes active. "Z" Bty did not fire	
23rd	"Z" Bty fired on a hostile O.P.	
24th	"Z" Bty didn't fire	
25th	"Z" Bty fired at various targets	
26th	"Z" Bty fired at various targets chiefly in retaliation for hostile fire	
27th	"X" Bty fired a few rounds.	
28th	"Z" Bty fired at suspected German observation station.	
29th	Aeroplanes reported for two of the batteries of the group	
30th	Early in the morning the Germans bombarded heavily south of BOISSELLE the bombardment was repeated between 7.pm and 8.pm	

8th, Division.

5th, Bde. R. H. A.

May, 1916.

Army Form C. 2118.

WAR DIARY
or
INTELLIGENCE SUMMARY.
(Erase heading not required.)

Instructions regarding War Diaries and Intelligence Summaries are contained in F.S. Regs., Part II. and the Staff Manual respectively. Title pages will be prepared in manuscript.

Place	Date	Hour	Summary of Events and Information	Remarks and references to Appendices
May	1st		Some acknt'd with part of hostile artillery chiefly against trenches. "Z" Bty registered with aeroplane observation.	V. 15/8
	2nd		Quiet day, enemy artillery quiet, "Z" Battery fired at various targets.	
	3rd		Hostile artillery inactive.	
	4th		Major B.L. Duke the late "Z" Battery to take up his appointment as Brigade Major 25th Div.	
	5th		32nd Div on our left made a raid, we cooperated with artillery fire.	
	6th		Hostile artillery active against the left section of 8th Div line.	
	7th		Enemy bombard a portion of the front & retaliated successfully and there was no hostile raid on our front	
	8th		Hostile artillery quiet on trenches in front of Authuile Wood and communication trenches in the vicinity, were fired on, our fire was chiefly retaliation.	
	9th		Very quiet all day except that our trenches opposite LA BOISSELLE were bombarded, so shell falling there. Batteries all checked their zero lines and made necessary registration with a view to forth coming operations.	
	10th		Quiet during the day, arranged bombardment was carried out during the night	
	11th		At 4.0 p.m. the Right Group took over defence of the line, left Group leaving one section per battery in new positions.	
	12th			
	13th		Very little firing on either side.	

Army Form C. 2118.

WAR DIARY
or
INTELLIGENCE SUMMARY.

5th Brigade R.H.A. May 1916

(Erase heading not required.)

Instructions regarding War Diaries and Intelligence Summaries are contained in F. S. Regs. Part II. and the Staff Manual respectively. Title pages will be prepared in manuscript.

Place	Date	Hour	Summary of Events and Information	Remarks and references to Appendices
	14th		Lt. Col. A.T. Butler CMG took over temporary command of the Divisional Artillery, vice Lt. Col.	
	15th		Barker of the 19th. Quiet on the whole Divisional front.	
	16th		Quiet day.	
	17th		Brigade Ammunition Column merged into Divisional Ammunition Column v/Mr Ellis and Schuster posted to Divisional Column.	
	18th		The 128th Bde. 4.5" howitzers merged into 5th 45th and 33rd Btys. one from gun battery to each	
	19th		Quiet day. Capt C.F.T. Hudson proceeded to 8th Div Artillery School on a course	
	20th		Enemy shelled our trenches in front of AUTUILLE wood rather heavily	
	21st		Right Group did a practice barrage otherwise quiet day.	
	22nd		Quiet day.	
	23rd		Capt C.F.T. Lindsay returned from gas course.	
	24th		Very little firing on front covered by group.	
	25th		2nd Lt Packman joined a Trench Mortar Battery	
	26th		5th Bde took over command of the group	
	27th		Lt. Col. A.T. Butler CMG returned from temporary command of Divisional Artillery.	
	28th		Quiet day	
	29th		Mr A.B. Chadwick was posted to K 57th Battery R.F.A.	
	30th		The enemy were active with trench mortars against I.e.TM3.	
	31st		Very little shelling on either side, trench mortars fired intermittently during the day.	

Colonel H.Downay Lt. Col. R.H.A.
A.A. 5th Brigade R.H.A.

8th, Division.

5th, Bde. R. H. A.

June, 1915.

Army Form C. 2118.

WAR DIARY or INTELLIGENCE SUMMARY.

5th Brigade R.H.A.

JUNE 1916

(Erase heading not required.)

Place	Date	Hour	Summary of Events and Information	Remarks and references to Appendices
June	1st		Brigade H.Q. moved to dugouts in AVELUY wood, the joint HQ of 5th and 45th Bde RHA	45th Bde RHA
	2nd		Trenches in OVILLERS Sector were heavily shelled	
	3rd to 4th		Quiet day.	
	5th		More aerial activity than usual. Several hostile machines being engaged by our aviators.	
	6th		Quiet on the whole trench mortars active during the night.	
	7th		The 45th Brigade and 2 Battery marched to BEHENCOURT to take part in a practise camp.	
	8th		The Div. on our right carried out a successful raid on the enemy's trenches South of ALBERT	
	9th		BURY AVENUE and CHEQUERBENT STREET were shelled during the afternoon.	
	10th		The 45th Bde HQ moved to the dugouts in AVELUY WOOD	
	11th		Quiet on the whole. 6th Div front. The 32nd Div Arty active against THIEPVAL	
	12th		Trench mortars and oil cans were fired at our trenches opposite OVILLERS	
	13th		The 45th and 2 Battery returned from Practise Camp at BEHENCOURT	
	14th		On the nights of 13–14 and 14–15 the Batteries of the Left Group brought all their guns into action, two guns being previously in her valley. On 13th a memorial Service was held in	
	15th		Quiet day. ALBERT to the late Field Marshall Earl Kitchener of Khartoum. The Bde was addressed by the Colonel and	
	16th-17th		The rain and mist which obscured all the back line on both sides made shooting impossible. a party of N.C.O's and Men.	
	18th		Heavy guns fired on enemy works in rear, this caused a certain amount of retaliation.	
	19th		The usual intermittent firing by both sides.	
	20th		Great aerial activity, a Squadron of 81(?)ofile planes(?) being attacked, two were forced(?) dow(n) behind their lines D15 Bde the Howitzer battery of the Bde (were) effectively with aeroplane obsevation.	

Army Form C. 2118.

WAR DIARY
or
INTELLIGENCE SUMMARY

(Erase heading not required.)

5th Brigade RHA   June (Cont^d).

Place	Date	Hour	Summary of Events and Information	Remarks and references to Appendices
June	21st		Quiet day.	
	22nd		L Battery carried out certain registration	
	23rd		Registration completed, quiet day.	
	24th		Bombardments and wire cutting started between 4 a.m. and 5 a.m. 18pdrs cut wire on the various hostile lines during the greater part of the day. Very little hostile retaliation was provoked although several hundred rounds were fired in wire cutting during the day. During the night 18pdrs and machine guns fired with intensity where wire had been cut. Heavy guns were active against FLERS. Brigade fired O.940 Z.929 D.15. 872 rsm.	
	25th		Wire cutting went on with intervals throughout the day. From 10 a.m. to 10.30 a.m. Heavy artillery co-operating with 18pdrs which fired only Shrapnel opened a heavy bombardment of POZIERES which was effective. The heavies then fired on CONTALMAISON and BAZENTIN LE PETIT. Barrages to be employed during the infantry assault were practised. It was intended to liberate gas during the fortnight which was to be followed by a raid. The gas programme was however cancelled but the raid was carried out by the 2nd Battⁿ. Rifle Bde. The batteries of this group fired for 20 minutes prior to the raid being made. The hostile trenches were heavily held and our raiding party were heavily engaged but managed to return with one prisoner after losing 4 killed and 7 wounds. All fronts wore brought in. The brigade fired O.1869 1223 4pdr 1872 and D.1854 286 rounds.	

Army Form C. 2118.

WAR DIARY or INTELLIGENCE SUMMARY.

5th Bde R.H.A. June (Cont'd).

(Erase heading not required.)

Place	Date	Hour	Summary of Events and Information	Remarks and references to Appendices
June	26th.		Wire cutting continued satisfactorily, the rain however spoiling the light for certain periods during the day. For an hour during the morning the 18 pdrs tried a practice barrage. Smoke was discharged towards the enemy at this barrage. The smoke was very successful, heavy machine gun fire was opened by the enemy and hostile guns of all calibres were turned on to our trenches and communication trenches. The retaliation lasted about 20 minutes and was very heavy. Heavy guns bombarded all hostile villages back to the line FIERS — LE SARS. 18 pdrs and machine guns fired throughout the night intermittently on lines whenever usual. The Brigade fired 0 Bty 1837 Z Bty 2061 and D Bty 360 rounds the greater part of "O" and "X" Bty's ammunition being employed in cutting wire.	
	27th.		A practice artillery barrage was fired at 4:30 am which lasted till 5:50 am. Gas was liberated at 5:30 am and with it smoke, the wind was very favorable and the gas was gently wafted to the enemy the lines with the smoke. To cover the liberation of the gas intense rifle and machine gun fire was opened. There were two other special bombardments during the day at 6:30 pm and 7:30 pm. Both these bombardments were practice	

Army Form C. 2118.

WAR DIARY
or
INTELLIGENCE SUMMARY.
(Erase heading not required.)

5th Bde RHA June 1916 (cont).

Place	Date	Hour	Summary of Events and Information	Remarks and references to Appendices
June	27th (cont)		Barrage. The remainder of the day wire cutting was carried out. The light was rather spoiled on the evening on account of rain. Brigade fired O/Bty 2401, Y/Bty 2268 and D/Bty 678 rounds.	
	28th		Y Battery had a good deal of trouble with their guns, at one time there was only one gun in action. The remainder having trouble with the buffer cylinder, mainly springs. Heavy rain and mist spoiling observation, late in the day O/Bty had three guns out of action with defective inner spring cases. Wire cutting still continued. The Brigade fired O/Bty 1471, Y/Bty 1672 and D/Bty 660 rounds.	
	29th		Weather cleared and wire cutting was carried out on front system, throughout to day. At 4.30 pm a practice barrage was carried out. Y Bty still had only two guns in action. O has four. The Bde fired O/Bty 903, Y/Bty 969 and D/Bty 512 rounds. heavy night firing was carried on our patrols went out to inspect hostile wire.	

Army Form C. 2118.

WAR DIARY
or
INTELLIGENCE SUMMARY.
(Erase heading not required.)

5th Bde RHA.   June (cont.)

Place	Date	Hour	Summary of Events and Information	Remarks and references to Appendices
June	30th		Wire cutting and Special bombardments continued, two practice barrages being fired. Wire cutting was carried out slowing up remaining wire. 12" gun bombarded BAPAUME. Fire was kept up during the night on roads and approaches and on wire which had been cut. Patrols went out to examine enemy wire, found openings cut on their line. During the day F/Bde fired "O" Bty 1109, Y Bty 1084, and D Bty. 517. The Brigade fired all together during preliminary bombardments 2346t rounds.	

Broukbound
DSO.A
Ad, 5th Brigade RHA

8th Div.
I. Corps.

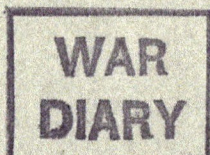

Headquarters,

5th BRIGADE, R.H.A.

JULY

1916

WAR DIARY
or
INTELLIGENCE SUMMARY.

Army Form C. 2118.

(Erase heading not required.)

No. 20

Instructions regarding War Diaries and Intelligence Summaries are contained in F.S. Regs., Part II. and the Staff Manual respectively. Title pages will be prepared in manuscript.

Title pages 5. Bde. R.H.a.

July 1916

Place	Date	Hour	Summary of Events and Information	Remarks and references to Appendices
	1st July 1916	6·25 A.M.	Bombardment commenced. Little or no retaliation up to 7·30 A.M. Zero time – Infantry advance – order of battle. 8th Division 23rd, 25th, 70th Inf. Brigades – 8th Div. only in support. This (Rfle) Group directly supporting 70th Inf. Brigade. On Right flank 34th Division on left flank 32nd Division. Lt. Colonel A.T. Butler, 5th Bde R.H.A. in command of Rifle Group. Forward Officers Lt. Colonel Hill H.S. Bty R.H.A. at 70th Inf. Brigade H.Q. Lieut. Wenham 1st R.H.A. at Left Battalion and Kieut Dixon 3rd Bty R.H.A. at Right Battalion H.Q.	
		7·38 A.M.	First wave reported over and 3rd Div. in front line trench at R.31.C.	
		7·50 A.M.	Col. Hill reported H.Q. of K.O.Y.L.I. moving forward or left flank of 25th Inf. Brigade going well. Kiser line to Ramberbridge St Burken.	
		8·00 A.M.	Rifle fire increased	
		8·12 A.M.	97th Brigade (32nd Div.) report that they are held up by rifle fire about X1a 3·8	
		8·20 A.M.	Report from Capt Magrath 59th Bty R.H.A. that according to where enemy are shelling infantry should have taken front 3 lines. Report by Colonel Hill no troops can be seen moving at present from 76th Inf. Brigade left O.P. Enemy barraging in "No mans land" opposite J X1/1 and X1/2 with 15cm (5.9 Bty) Heavy	
		8·25 A.M.	Dixon reported C.O. K.O.Y.L.I. a casualty.	
		8·30 A.M.	Wenham reported as having gone forward.	
		8·45 A.M.	Hear from 8th Yorks. Regt. reports he was wounded in 3rd line – advance progressing – 25th Inf. Brigade going well.	
		8·35 A.M.	Lt Stanley Capt H.S. Brigade R.H.A. from French Tree O.P. reported advance on R of 32nd Div. and our left successful so far.	
		9·00 A.M.	Col Hill reports that our Inf. are in the 3rd line & are held up.	
			Several times reported that our own infantry returning to our own lines opposite X7/10. One Battn reported seen to re-organize & go on again. German 1st line opposite X7/10 quiet – not known whether wounded men or attack failed at that point.	
		9·15 A.M.	Reported that Sherwoods – 2nd wave in support of K.O.Y.L.I. one going forward	
		9·30 A.M.	Major Shanlack 59th Bty R.H.A. at tree O.P. left & right to bad for observation.	
		10·00 A.M.	Colonel Hill reports 32nd Div. held up about R31 D1·3. Rest of situation uncertain.	
		10·05 A.M.	1st wave Sherwoods gone over. M.G's troublesome on left flank – Genl Gordon doesn't want any action taken – 32nd Div. has reached 3rd line and are attacking up valley but held up by M.G's in X.2.0.	
		10·15 A.M.	Shelling of NAB and to the right reported by 1st Bty.	
		10·18 A.M.	Col Butler reports barrage may be brought back to BROWN.	
		10·30 A.M.	Orders from 8th Div Arty to Kaber rate of fire & await orders. Queen reports enemy M.G's active, that 3rd Div is endeavouring to advance to 2·20.	

Wt. W2544/1454 790,000 5/15 D.D.&L. A.B.S.S./Forms/C.2118.
2353

Army Form C. 2118.

Instructions regarding War Diaries and Intelligence Summaries are contained in F. S. Regs., Part II. and the Staff Manual respectively. Title pages will be prepared in manuscript.

WAR DIARY
or
INTELLIGENCE SUMMARY.

(Erase heading not required.)

5th Bde R.H.A.   July 1916

Place	Date	Hour	Summary of Events and Information	Remarks and references to Appendices
1st July	1916	10.46 AM	"Z" Battery reports gun vickets form X2CII. German barrage is very near their front line at this point.	
		10.47 AM	Dixon reports enemy barrage in "No man's land" heaviest.	
		10.53 AM	Situation at 10.30 A.M. from 32nd Divn via Col Hill: 97th Brigade have reached line X1a 6.9 - R31 c6.8 OR 8 pr Battery is barraging German front line & trying to bomb along.	
			BROWN Barrage ordered at slow rate of fire. Special flank barrage by 1st Bty as for 0.18 - 0.28 at 1 round per gun per minute at request of General Gordon.	
		11-10 AM	Col Hill requested heaves for special barrage – also to halve rate of fire on BROWN Barrage.	
		11-14 AM	Rate of fire halved, 4 on special barrage rate of fire doubled for 10 minutes	
		11-30 AM	Col Hill considered that more heavier than 2.6" guns should be turned on to the portion being specially barraged by the 1st Bty as the valley is stiff with M.Gs. & they are holding up the advance of the 32nd Divn. Requests that more guns be turned on & Col Hill spoke to General Ringett.	
		11-53 A.M	Brigade Major reported 4.5 Hows had been put on points 291 - 219 - 289 - 3281 - 3233.	
		11-59 A.M	Col Wills requests PINK Barrage.	
		12.25	'Z' Bty reports one gun out of action.	
		12-45 AM	Rate of fire on BROWN Line halved again.	
		12-56 AM	97th Bty ordered to fire on points 3130 - 159 - 139 - 3162.	
		1-00 PM	Rate of fire on BROWN barrage halved.	
			57th Bty switched off above points on to 3181 - 3182, 3184 - 3215.	
		1-40 PM	PINK Barrage ordered. Rate of fire. Special barrage by 1st Bty 60 rounds per Bty per hour remainder occasional rounds	
		1-45 PM	Enemy heavy artillery ceased firing on our front.	
		1-53 PM	General impression that 70th Inf Brigade attack was broken up by M.Gs. in valley left of line of advance a little resistance in the attack at the commencement troops penetrated as far as can be ascertained up to 3rd line. In event of a bombardment a fair amount of heavy artillery might be allotted to the flank barrage with advantage. (Report by Col. Hele)	
		2-15 PM	Rate of fire 1st Bty 30 rds per hour. Hours 20 rds per hour.	
		2-45 PM	8th Divn reports bombing in front line. Between points 224 - 221. Enemy artillery less active. Only occasional rounds on front line. M.Gs. still active at times from left.	
		2-50 PM	Front Div Arty. 32nd Divn are going to assault info the valley. Take guns off barrage gg. K.O.Y.L.I. & Y & L.	
		3-50 PM	Dixon reports no movement visible in enemy's trenches. No information reference front line from X 8a 83 to X 2a 56.	
		4-15 PM	8th D.A. order slow bombardment on Blue line.	
		4-24 PM	5th Bty O.P reports 77 mm gun shelling XT/10 + vicinity of the NAB.	
		4-28 PM	General Gordon asks for slow bombardment on PINK line instead of BLUE.	

WAR DIARY or INTELLIGENCE SUMMARY

Army Form C. 2118.

5th Bde R.F.A.   July 1916.

Place	Date	Hour	Summary of Events and Information	Remarks and references to Appendices
	1916			
	1st July	4.29pm	Order from Div Arty to fire on PINK line instead of BLUE. 2 rds per battery per minute 18 pdrs - 1 round 4.5" hows.	
		4.55pm	Hustinskuns quiet Col. Wale reports no shelling of front line, Germans probably in entire possession of his front line trenches. No movement of any sort seen. Manhaesting have taken LEIPZIG SALIENT in R.31C & HINDENBURG TRENCH in R.31A.	
		5.24pm	Attack north of NAB has been stopped.	
			Enemy have opened a slow rate of fire in vicinity of Quarry Brae St with 10 Cm How & 77 mm.	
		5.40pm	3rd Rfly. report shelling as above ceased.	
		6.15pm	No movement visible in enemy trenches, no information re 8th R.W.L.I. Y&L.	
		6.40pm	Col. Hill reports that a wounded officer of Sherwoods has just crawled back from the German ft line. also reports that Parrage be put back to BROWN.	
		6.45pm	Left from PINK to BROWN one rd per Bty per minute 18 pdrs and one round per Bty per 2 minutes for Hows.	
		7.0pm	Aeroplane message reports enemy bringing up ammunition along all tracks and roads. Wagons actually seen galloping at X.3.C.8.9 and X.4.a.5.8.	
		7.10 p.m.	Reported by Div Arty that ammunition being brought up by these - 3rd Bty ordered to take on X.3.c.6.9 and 2 Bty X.4.a.5.8. One salvo and then 6 rounds every 5 minutes.	
		7.30pm	Batteries ordered to start their ordinary night shooting at ordinary rate of fire. No close shooting not close short of BROWN line. NAB & vicinity are being heavily shelled by 77 MM Battery about 12 rounds a minute.	
		8.30pm	Report from Major Rill to the effect that attack went straight across instead of half left & that 3 M.G.s were brought into action from behind our wave had gone on- orders received from 8th Div Arty with regard to holding the line & reliefs of infantry - 112th Divisional Arty to relieve 8th Divisional of infantry orders issued to units from this H.Q. with regard to defence of the line.	
		11.30pm	Colonel Hill returned from 90th Infy Bde H.Q. Report from 90th Infy Brigade that Lt Wenham just passed on way to hospital with broken arm, this tel. phoned killed. Diarn 2584 "Y" Bty 2307 and D Battery 1057. During the day the Brigade fired "O" Bty 2584 "Y" Bty 2307 and D Battery 1057. Casualties nil.	

WAR DIARY or INTELLIGENCE SUMMARY

Army Form C. 2118.

5th Bde R.H.A.   July 1916

*5 BRIGADE * ROYAL HORSE ARTILLERY * AUG 1916*

Place	Date	Hour	Summary of Events and Information	Remarks and references to Appendices
	1916 2nd July	8.30AM	Night firing on roads & approaches stopped by order of Div: Orly:	
		10.15AM	Div: Orty ordered fire on approaches between GREEN Line & line R.33.C.4.3. - X.3 central - X.9.G.4.8. 60 rounds per Bty per hour 18 pdrs & 45 rounds per Bty per hour 4.5" Hows.	
		1.40 pm	Div: Orty requested fire on point X.3.a.50.7 head to eastward as aeroplane reports enemy dumping on tramline. Put the 5th Bty + Z Bty on to them.	
		3.10 pm	19 Div: to attack LA BOISELLE at 4 p.m. Left Group to fire on front line 3.30 - 3.50 p.m. + to rake backwards & forwards between front & GREEN Lines from 3.50 - 4.30 p.m. Rate 2 rounds per minute. Smoke will be discharged 3.50 - 4.30 p.m.	
		6.20 pm	Major Rud reported that between X.20.2.2 + X.20.2.9 there are German sentries posted every 200 yards looking over German front line.	
		7.40 pm	Rate of fire halved until 9 p.m.	
		9.00 pm	Ordinary rate of fire resumed. During the day the Brigade fired :- "C" Bty 971 - Z Bty 1187 - D Bty 716. Casualties Nil.	
	3rd July	12.10 AM	Orders received from Div Arty for attack on OVILLERS LA BOISELLE by 19th Div.	
		1.15 AM	Left Group orders for firing sent to Batteries. Left Group imagine left of attack.	
		2.45 AM	Div Arty ordered 60% HE to be fired during bombardment.	
		3.45 AM	Batteries firing 1 round per gun per minute.	
		4.25 AM	F.O.O. with battalion of 36th Bde at QUARRY POST reports that left of attack went over well. Rest of rifle fire (t Colliers) with battalion of 36th Bde at QUARRY POST reports that left of attack went over well. Rest of rifle fire has practically ceased but bombing can be distinctly heard. On them being reported to Div Arty, R.M. states that left of attack is held up.	
		4.35 AM	Lt Collins says that men are still in the German front line but are being heavily bombed.	
		4.40 AM	Div Arty order to halve rate of fire received.	
		4.45 AM	OC 151/161 Bty says he has been asked to support 12th Div attack in R.3.a.c. + states his intention to keep the enemy engaged in X.2.a.	
		4.53 AM	Lt Collins reports that Germans have left front line for support line.	
		5.35 AM	Capt Magrath of 3rd Bty reports that enemy appear to be pulling up a smoke barrage from point 216 enemy still firing at a slow rate. Loss of AUTHUILE WOOD	

WAR DIARY or INTELLIGENCE SUMMARY

(Erase heading not required.)

Army Form C. 2118.

5 BRIGADE ROYAL HORSE ARTILLERY — AUG 1916

5th Bde RHA   July (Cont.)

Place	Date	Hour	Summary of Events and Information	Remarks and references to Appendices
3rd		5.42 AM	Div Arty order barrage on 273-285-271-888-895. Z Battery put on.	
		5.45 AM	Lt. Collins reports that from information received our troops reached the front line with practically no opposition, surprising the enemy.	
		6.0 AM	Div Arty ordered whole group to fire on barrage as above. I round per gun per 2 minutes. Y to barrage 888-895 3rd 271-888 1st Bty 285-271.	
		6.30 AM	Fire reduced to 2 rounds per battery per minute.	
		6.20 AM	News from Right Group that we got into 3rd line but were bombed out and are now holding 1st line being held up by machine guns	
		6.32 AM	Div Arty order rate of fire 2 rounds per battery per minute.	
		6.55 AM	Lt Collins reports that owing to Counter attack we are gradually retiring.	
		6.56 AM	Staff Capt asks how much ammunition we have on hand. Reply 1st Bty 2000 rds Z Bty 2000 rds 3rd Bty 2000 rds Z Bty 2450 rds 57th Bty 1800.	
		7.10 AM	Div Arty reduce rate of fire to 1 rd per battery per 2 minutes	
		7.16 AM	Howz. K. decrease rate of fire to 1 rd per battery 3 minutes.	
		8.10 AM	Rate of fire doubled	
		8.30 AM	Lt. Collins reports that we no longer hold hostile front line. a. Left attack Left Group 15 barrage X Ba 17 - X 2a 5.6 1 round per 2 minutes. 1st Bty 256-280 3rd Bty 280-273 Z-273-847	
		9.4 AM	Infantry back in our trenches	
		9.30 AM	Barrage X Ba 2.0 - 52 - 95 - 16 - 24 1 rd per Bty per minute. 3rd Bty 820-895. Z Bty 895-846-824. Howz (57th) 897	
		10.0 AM	3rd Bty cannot barrage as unable to clear trees. Z Bty ordered double barrage rate of fire 4 rds per battery per minute.	
		10.30 AM	Enemy heavily barraging W18C and Shelling X7C.	
		10.42 AM	Div Arty order rate of fire on Z Bty's barrage to be halved in 15 minutes.	
		10.58 AM	Div Arty order barrage on 820-892 only rate 2 rds a minute	
		11.35 AM	Infantry still in X12. 1st Bty R.P.inc 50 rds on hostile front line opposite.	
		P.30 PM	Barrage 229-271 1 rd per Bty per min. 1st Bty 229-280 3 Bty 280-271	
		1.55 PM	Z Bty to halve rate of fire.	
		5.00 PM	Order from Div. Arty to put ourselves at disposal of MX3a Pt. Batteries ordered to take up their night firing stations not made – 57-Bty put on parade 350-304-399.	
		7.10 PM	Rate of fire halved till 9 PM. To resume usual rate after that hour.	
			Orders from Div. Arty for relief – One section tonight by 12 Div Arty. 8th Div Arty to go back to Bétencourt. Michiécourt area	
		9.00 PM	Section relieved and moved to Havrincourt Wood.	

WAR DIARY
or
INTELLIGENCE SUMMARY.

5th Bde. R.H.A. July 1916.

Place	Date	Hour	Summary of Events and Information	Remarks and references to Appendices
July 4th	Midnight to 7.30 A.M.		Quiet, normal rate of fire on roads and approaches	
		7.30 AM	Rate of fire increased and approaches widened to roads for Bty to have fire 13 pdrs and occasional use of Howr.	
		10.15 AM	Enemy heavily shelling point South of the NAB - 1st and 3rd Batteries ordered to retaliate with 50 HE	
	Night of 4/5th		On German trench opposite.	
	5th		Relieved by 65th Brigade RFA 12th Divn. under the command of Lt Col Ault. Batteries marched to BÉTHENCOURT	
	6th		Brigade marched from BÉTHENCOURT to LE MESGE	
			Orders issued to entrain for 1st Army.	
	7th		Brigade marches of at 3.30 am H.Q. and D Bty, leaving X following at 3 hrs interval and B Bty shown later. Entrained at SAULEUX after this journey detrained at BÉRAS in 1st Army Area and marched to LAPUGNOY where the brigade was billeted, the last batteries arriving about 6 am on the 8th.	
	8th		New orders to 1st Corps 1st Army, complete rest for the men.	
	9th		Commanding Officer and battery Commanders paid a visit to reconnoitre the front and battery positions of the left division.	
	10th		Guns overhauled and inspected by I.O.M.	
	11th		Brigade inspected mounted by Sir Charles Monro.	
	12th		Work continued on guns.	
	13th		Brigade inspected by G.O.C. division. Maj General Hudson dismounted	

WAR DIARY
or
INTELLIGENCE SUMMARY.

5th Bde RHA   July 1916

Place	Date	Hour	Summary of Events and Information	Remarks and references to Appendices
	14th July		At 4 a.m. orders received to march. Batteries marched at 7 a.m. to FOSSE then to await guides. Guides taken on to LAVENTIE area. HQ Bde in LAVENTIE. Bde attached to 308th Bde of 61st Div Arty, Lt. Col FURSE Commanding. Batteries did not fire most of the day spent in strengthening their positions.	
	15th			
	16th		Batteries commenced wire cutting. O Bty very heavily shelled and compelled to cease firing, one man killed and two wounded later in the day. They started firing again, but were immediately heavily shelled. They were then ordered to cease fire for the day and endeavour (which was then position. X Bty fired about 400 rounds. Casualties 6 men killed, 2 wounded.	
	17th		Zero hour originally ordered for 4 a.m. altered to 8 a.m. and later to 11 a.m. then finally postponed altogether. Batteries did not fire spending the day strengthening their positions.	
	18th		Batteries orders to continue wire cutting. "D" Battery not firing. Artillery of the Left Group ordered to cut them wire. Major Boyd to arrange this. Batteries shewing the OPs were heavily shelled and	

WAR DIARY
or
INTELLIGENCE SUMMARY.
(Erase heading not required.)

Army Form C. 2118.

5th Bde RHA July 1916 (Cont'd)

Place	Date	Hour	Summary of Events and Information	Remarks and references to Appendices
	18th July		Capt. M.H.D. Parsons was killed and Major A.O. Boyle wounded while attempting to dig out some officers and men who were buried in a collapsed dugout at the Bentley.	
	19th	11.0 am	Rear Run.	
		11.3 am	O.C. C/305 reported battery on his right shooting short passed to O.C. B/305	
		11.45 am	Left Battalion report PICANTIN being shelled with Reserve passed to Reserves to deal with and Left Battalion reported all troops in position	
		12.15 pm	Reported that H.E. falling short opposite N14/1	
		12.30 pm	Reported again that enemy shelling PICANTIN + also our own H.E. bursting short near N14/1	
		12.35 pm	Message sent to C/305 to check laying	
		1.00 pm	Laying of C/305 checked and report O.K.	
		1.30 pm	B/305 report whole of the O.B. on Rue TILLELOY on Rue TILLELOY are being subjected to a furious bombardment 5.9 or heavier shells.	
		2.0 pm	Riflemans Trench being shelled by 5.9s forwarded B/305 report to Reserves.	
		2.2? pm	Enemy seen retreating to support Trench opposite N14/1	
		1.58 pm	Our F.O.O. reports that an aeroplane with British markings identical in pattern with that which was observed flying over our Battery on the 13th is flying up Riflemans trench from SE to NW at a low altitude.	
		2.2 pm	Report by Left Group of 1st Div. Arty. Enemy firing few shrapnel on front line – Stopped shelling support lines. A few shells 77mm on BOND ST – nothing on BURLINGTON ARCADE. Enemy seems to have very few batteries + to be searching wide with them.	
		2.35 pm	B/305 being heavily shelled direct hit on one gunpit remainder carrying on. Report from F.O.O. reports that O.P. in TILLELOY still being bombarded steadily. Guns out of question to use them. Trying to collect less O.P. impossible make any statement on condition of hostile wire on account of dense smoke – RIFLEMANSTRENCH Still being heavily shelled	
		3.01 pm	8/316 commenced firing on targets in phase C.	
			Capt. Wallace "O" Sty R.H.A. reports wire on his front does not appear to offer serious obstacle except patch of 20 yds near N14 C 2.6 and 20 yds near N14 C 2.9	
		3.40 pm	6 and 7 Batteries ordered to open fire on to support line.	
		4.00 pm	Battery D.D. & E. opened on enemy wire during with view of widening gaps – Remainder of wire practically clear	

WAR DIARY or INTELLIGENCE SUMMARY

Place	Date	Hour	Summary of Events and Information	Remarks and references to Appendices
	July 19th	4.05pm	Report on wire cutting to Bgde H.Q. as follows:- X9.10.11.12.13 clear X13 to 14 long grass impossible to say definitely cut but of rounds look into it X14-15 clear to X15-16 clear except for patches or apparent obstacle to Infantry advance X16-17 20 gap now widened X18-X19 no report.	
		4.15pm	Batteries cutting from 12-16 have turned on to wire in front of support lines.	
			3.51 for also Barrage are lifted Germans did not mount their fire but kept up a steady rate on our support and communication trenches. Wire getting very thin German parapet badly damaged and breached in places. Message from C/306.	
		4.40pm	Shelling by heavy gun at a slow rate not sufficient to constitute a barrage. Message from A/306	
		5.00pm	Report from C/306 that enemy front line parapet from N14.c.16 - N14.a.84 and support line from N14.c.5.7 - N14.a.8.1 have been badly damaged & damage is still spreading on our lifting enemy fired slow rate of fire in his mans land not sufficient to form a barrage.	
		5.30pm	Infantry report lot of shell fire in his mans land.	
		5.40pm	Ordered "O" "Z" and D/15 to send officers to TEA HOUSE, FARM HOUSE and SNOWDEN respectively for night purposes	
			A/15 Bty. report firing appears effective observation difficult owing to smoke. Hostile retaliation at intervals along	
	6.00 Time of Assault		TILLELOY with ''y'' mm 10.5 cm 4 15 cm.	
			C/306 report enemy parapet in their sector is a mass of ruins.	
			Capt Wallace reported our shells bursting well on hostile trenches.	
		6.24pm	B/305 reports red rocket observed over our lines at 5-53 pm and a white rocket at 5-55 pm.	
		6.35pm	"O" Bty reports Germans shelling their own front line.	
			"Z" Bty report Germans seen firing rifles from West.	
		6.45pm	Infantry seen going over parapet at N14.C.3.1.?.	
			Capt Rushworth of 16 Bty. R.W.a. reports particularly heavy hostile barrage machine gun and rifle fire + no infantry movement opposite front N13/ his hostile shelling on Snow front.	
		7pm	Message from B.O. Major 61st Div Duty to effect that some battery shelling Tich will must be stopped immediately.	
		7-10pm	61st Battalion report that their attack failed being driven back by machine gun fire, with heavy casualties the Battn on his left + right	
		7-30pm	Slight shelling of LAVENTIE reported. enemy trenches.	
		7-45pm	"O" Bty reported ammunition in dump down to 50 rds a gun another drawing up fresh 100 rounds a gun.	

Slight Shelling of LAVENTIE reported.
Wt. W2544(1454) 700,000 5/15 D.D.&L. A.D.S.S./Forms/C. 2118.
2353

WAR DIARY or INTELLIGENCE SUMMARY

Army Form C. 2118.

Place	Date	Hour	Summary of Events and Information	Remarks and references to Appendices
	19/5		B/15 Bty 10 rounds a gun area target established. A/306 reports hostile shelling between N14.c.1.6 - N14.c.3.4. Rate of fire halved for all Batteries 18prs. 1 round per gun for 4 minutes. "B" and "Z" Batteries ordered to turn on to front line parapet between WICK and N13 d 9.6 also sections of A/306 and C/306. "Z" Battery reports that he has seen nothing of our infantry and can see Germans in their front line.	
		8.00pm	B/15 Battery report rather more hostile fire during last hour - practically no machine gun or rifle fire.	
		8.10pm	A/306 reported nothing seen of infantry advance very little hostile shelling except in rear of hostile trenches.	
		8.30pm	Infantry resumed their infantry attack except for a party in the German trenches about N14.C.2/4 all other assaulting Infantry back in our trenches. Contemplated further attack cancelled. Orders issued to Batteries as follows:- "G" Bty or N13 d 9.6 - N14.c 2½.2½ at 1 round per gun per 4 minutes. A/306 and C/306 1 Section each N14.c 2½.2½ - N14.c 8.6 at 1 round per gun per 4 minutes. B/305 on N14.c 5.9½ - N14.c 8.6 at 1 round per gun per 4 minutes. The following at 1 round per gun per 10 minutes.	
			Z Bty. N13 d 9.6 - WICK	
			A/306 (1 Sec) N13 d 9.6 - WICK	
			C/306 (1 Sec) N13 d 9.6 - WICK	
			B/305 N14.c.5.9½ - N14.07.3½	
			9/15 Support line from N14.c 5½.9½ - N14.c 7.9½	
			B/306 ...-...-... N14.c 7.9½ - N14.a 9.15	
			Especially C.T. at Leton point	

WAR DIARY
or
INTELLIGENCE SUMMARY.

5. Bde. R.H.A.   July.

Place	Date	Hour	Summary of Events and Information	Remarks and references to Appendices
	20th		Intermittent shooting throughout the day to keep open the hostile wire. DAC take up a portion of dump at guns.	
	21st		Defence of the line taken over by 61st DA. Batteries withdraw their telephone wire and prepare to move. Move at 9.30pm marching to BEUVRY.	
	22nd		Arrived at BEUVRY about dawn and then went into billets. Parties visited the position of line to be taken over. Sections moved into action.	
	23rd		Remainder of batteries came into action taking over from batteries of the 40th and 15th Divisions. Col. A.T. Butler took over command of the left group consisting of Z/D75 and the 45th Bde. relieving Lt. Chester of the 15th Dn.	
	24th		Batteries employed registering their new front and calibrating the guns.	
	25th		Very little hostile shelling. RIDGE MASON O.P. was fired on and some damage done.	
	26th		Very little shooting; registration, and retaliation at the request of infantry who are much troubled by trench mortars and rifle grenades	

Army Form C. 2118.

WAR DIARY
or
INTELLIGENCE SUMMARY.

(Erase heading not required.)

Instructions regarding War Diaries and Intelligence Summaries are contained in F.S. Regs. Part II. and the Staff Manual respectively. Title pages will be prepared in manuscript.

5th Bde R.H.A.   July 1915

Place	Date	Hour	Summary of Events and Information	Remarks and references to Appendices
	27th		Quiet day.	
	28th		Very little firing by either side. The 3rd Battery put 1 gun in an enfilade position to enfilade their own zone.	
	29th		Quiet day. The A.S. Howitzers co-operated with the heavies in a successful shoot on a trench mortar emplacement (in the DUMP) which was annoying the infantry.	
	30th		About 11 p.m. the enemy commenced a heavy barrage and under cover of this belted our trenches from which he was driven out. At another point he attempted to raid but was driven off before reaching our wire.	
	31st		Quiet day.	

HBrereton Bonney
Lieut. & Adjt.
for O.C. 5th Brigade R.H.A.

8th, Division.

5th, Bde. R. H. A.

August, 1916.

C O N F I D E N T I A L.

8th DIVISIONAL ARTILLERY.

W A R   D I A R Y

O F

5th Brigade RFA

From 1-8-16 To 31-8-16

(VOLUME 21)

With APPENDICES Nos. None

Army Form C. 2118.

WAR DIARY
or
INTELLIGENCE SUMMARY.
(Erase heading not required.)

M.B.W.M.A.   August 1916.

Instructions regarding War Diaries and Intelligence Summaries are contained in F.S. Regs., Part II. and the Staff Manual respectively. Title pages will be prepared in manuscript.

Place	Date	Hour	Summary of Events and Information	Remarks and references to Appendices
CUINCHY	1st		Brigade in CUINCHY Sector.	JAL
"	2nd		Generally quiet day.	JAL
"	3rd		Few rounds fired at working parties and in retaliation for hostile shelling.	JAL
"	4th		D/s on completion of relief marches to begin the	JAL
NOYELLES	5th		Left Group under Lt. Col. A.T. Butler moves its headquarters to NOYELLES Chateau and became Right Group. 2 Battery remains in position at ANNEQUIN under 43rd H.A. Group. Jr Counter Battery work. O Battery remains under Left Group. 1 Sect. Y. subsec. bot(?) at CUINCHY D/s Battery (How) moves one Gun into position near VERMELLES.	JAL
"	6th		Second Gun of D/s moves into position.	JAL
"	7th		Registration of new Zone (QUARRY SECTOR).	JAL
"	8th		D/s the 3rd Gun brought into action.	JAL
"	9th		took on all positions continues.	JAL
"	10th		Quiet throughout	JAL
"	11th		Very little firing during the day.	JAL
"	12th		Little firing except in retaliation for hostile fire.	JAL
"	13th			JAL

Army Form C. 2118.

WAR DIARY
or
INTELLIGENCE SUMMARY.

(Erase heading not required.)

5th Brigade R.H.A. Aug. 1916. (Cont^d.)

Place	Date	Hour	Summary of Events and Information	Remarks and references to Appendices
BETHUNE	Aug 14th		5th Brigade R.H.A moved to Rest billets in BETHUNE Lt. Col. A.T. Butler handing over command of Right Group to Lt. Col. H.W. Hill.	JM
"	15th to 22nd		Brigade Commander received orders to supervise the wagon lines. During this period he visited all battery wagon lines and reinforcing gun positions.	JM
"	23rd		L Battery moved to G15d7.7 in support of a raid to be carried out by the 2nd Battn Rifle Brigade on the both trenches on either side of HULLUCH road. Raid did not take place due to sight of Enemy at the S.E. corner of HULLUCH with effect the raid returned to position at ANNEQUIN	JM
"	24th		O Battery was detailed to cut wire as a feint to the raid. projected position of the raid.	JM
"	25th		Raid took place at 12-midnight 24th/25th. "O" and D/c fired L Bty fired 880 rounds returning to ANNEQUIN position on completion of raid.	JM

Army Form C. 2118.

WAR DIARY
or
INTELLIGENCE SUMMARY.
(Erase heading not required.)

5th Brigade R.H.A.   Aug. 1916 (cont^d)

Place	Date	Hour	Summary of Events and Information	Remarks and references to Appendices
BETHUNE	25th		"Z" Battery was transferred from 43rd H.A. Group to the Left Group 8th Div.	JM
"	26th		Lt. Col. Butler CMG RHA received orders to take command of a Composite division of Artillery to cover the 3rd Division in the HULLUCH and 14 BIS Sectors.	JM
"	27th		Brigade Commander went round to HULLUCH and 14 Bis Groups.	JM
NOEUX LES MINES	28th		Lt. Col. Butler with Major Sir T.P. Larcom RHA as Brigade Major and Lt. W.E. Bonnar as Staff Captain and staff moved to NOEUX LES MINES to the H.Q. vacated by the 16th Div Arty.	JM
"	29th		The 3rd Div Infantry arrived.	JM
"	30th		Lt. Col. Butler went round the battery positions of the Composite Divisional Artillery, under his command viz HULLUCH GROUP Lt. Col. Alcard. 14 Bis Group Bt. Col. Craven.	JM

Army Form C. 2118.

WAR DIARY
or
INTELLIGENCE SUMMARY.

5th Brigade R.H.A. Aug 1916 (contd)

Place	Date	Hour	Summary of Events and Information	Remarks and references to Appendices
NOEUX LES MINES	31st		33rd Div S/g took over from 32nd Div S/g in HULLUCH sector & Command of the HULLUCH Group R.A. passing from 8th D.A. to Col. Butler. "L" Battery came into position under 15th Command & 1st OC. HULLUCH Group.	ill.

G. T. Parker

31. 8. 16.

Lieut. Colonel, R.H.A.
Commanding 5th Brigade, R.H.A.

8th, Division.

5th, Bde. R. H. A.

September, 1916.

C O N F I D E N T I A L.

8th DIVISIONAL ARTILLERY.

WAR DIARY

OF

5th Brigade R.F.A.

From 1-9-16 To 30-9-16.

(VOLUME XXIII)

With APPENDICES Nos. None.

Army Form C. 2118.

WAR DIARY
or
INTELLIGENCE SUMMARY.

(Erase heading not required.)

5th Brigade R.H.A.   September . 1916

Instructions regarding War Diaries and Intelligence Summaries are contained in F. S. Regs., Part II. and the Staff Manual respectively. Title pages will be prepared in manuscript.

Place	Date	Hour	Summary of Events and Information	Remarks and references to Appendices
NOEUX LES MINES	1st		Z Battery RHA moved from position at ANNEQUIN to a new position in VERMELLES coming under the HULLUCH Group of the 3rd Composite Divisional Artillery. Lieut Col A.T. BUTLER DMG RHA took over the Artillery defence of 3rd Div line. O Battery RHA took part in a bombardment in support of our TMs. 2nd Lieut SILVESTER went to 1st Army School of Medium TMs.	Jal.
	2nd		'O' and D/S Batteries still in their positions near ANNEQUIN and VERMELLES under the Left Group 8th Div. Q. Balfour Shell fell near and in 'O' Batteries gun position.	Jal.
	3rd		D/S Howitzer Battery engaged several targets, one being a train in HAISNES Stn. 'Z' Battery continued to register their new zone.	Jal.
	4th		2nd Lieut DEAN joined 'O' Battery, attached for duty from 16th Div.	Jal.
	5th		Very little activity on either side.	Jal.
	6th		Trench mortars on either side active little or no artillery fire.	Jal.
	7th		D/s drew new howitzer from 1 am to replace one condemned, put in action.	Jal.
	8th		Bombardment to cover the firing of one 2" Trench mortars.	Jal.
	9th		'O' Battery and a section of 'Z' Battery, which did not move until leaving to VERMELLES assisted in a bombardment in support of the 2nd East Lancashire Bgd. who raided at 2.20 am. Lieut T.A. PACKMAN 'O' Battery was killed while doing duty with 2" TMs opposite HOHENZOLLERN.	Jal.
	10th		'O' Battery fired in cooperation with the 32nd D.A. to cover a raid by a battalion of the 32nd Div.	Jal.
	11th		Lieut PACKMAN was buried at VERMELLES Plot 5 Row B Grave 18. 2nd Lieut Silvester rejoined from TM school. With the exception of a bombardment in conjunction with 2" TMs there was little firing. 2nd Lieut DEAN left to rejoin 16th Div.	Jal.
	12th		Ammunition allotment cut down. 2nd Lt. HUNTER and 2nd Lt. WILKINSON joined the brigade from the 63rd Division.	Jal.

Army Form C. 2118.

WAR DIARY
or
INTELLIGENCE SUMMARY.
(Erase heading not required)

5th Brigade R.H.A. September 1916.

Place	Date	Hour	Summary of Events and Information	Remarks and references to Appendices
NOEUX LES MINES	13th		No event. Quiet day. 2/Lieut DEAN rejoined 16th Bde Div.	JW
	14th		Quiet day.	JW
	15th		2nd Lt. SILVESTER attached to Trench Mortars from O Battery. 2/Lt. BACON rejoined O Battery from Trench Mortars. One Section of "L" Battery relieves by section of 45th Battery 3rd Division moved back to rejoin 8th Div; going into position at ANNEQUIN.	JW
BETHUNE	16th		Lt. Col. A.T. Butler returned to 1st Brigade, Lt Composite Div. Arty 3rd Div. being relieved by the 3rd D.A. Remaining sect. of "L" Battery returned to position at ANNEQUIN.	JW JW JW
	17th		Very little activity on either side.	JW
	18th		Quiet.	JW
	19th		Night of 15th/20th "L" Battery fires in support of raid by 2nd Lincolns.	JW
	20th		Batteries took part in a concentrated bombardment. Major Larcom "L" Bty	JW
	21st		Quiet.	hospital JW
	22nd		Hostile artillery active. Our retaliation effective. Lt. J.G. Taylor rejoined from hospital "O" Bty	JW
	23rd		Artillery on both sides active. Lieut Rogers "O" Bty & 2/Lieut Collins "L" Bty went on leave	JW

Army Form C. 2118.

WAR DIARY
or
INTELLIGENCE SUMMARY. September 1916

(Erase heading not required.)

5th Bde R.H.A.

Place	Date	Hour	Summary of Events and Information	Remarks and references to Appendices
BETHUNE	Sept	24th	Lieut. Col. A.T. BUTLER took Temporary Command of the Bde. Arty in the absence of the General on leave. Hostile T.M.s very active also artillery. Many rounds were fired in retaliation for T.M fire. Raid supported by "O" T.M.s still active against our trenches. "I" Bty covered raid by 2nd Batt. R. Berks.	
		25th		
		26th	Hostile T.M.s again very active during considerable damage. Retaliation by D/5 Bty on T.M.s near DUMP. D/5 took over forward 15 pr gun from 54th Bty.	
		27th	Considerable T.M activity on the part of the enemy before 8 am after them quiet day	
		28th	Quiet day	
		29th	- do -	
		30th	- do - Major Foreman Z Bty returned from leave to U.K.	

W. Everett Bourne_ Capt.
for O.C. 5th Brigade R.H.A
1/10/16.

8th, Division.

5th, Bde. R. H. A.

October, 1916.

C O N F I D E N T I A L.

8th DIVISIONAL ARTILLERY.

W A R   D I A R Y

O F

5th Brigade R.F.A.

From 1-10-16 To 31-10-16.

(VOLUME XXIV)

With APPENDICES Nos. nil.

Vol 23

Army Form C. 2118.

WAR DIARY
or
INTELLIGENCE SUMMARY.

(Erase heading not required.)

5th Bde R.H.A.   October 1916.

Instructions regarding War Diaries and Intelligence Summaries are contained in F.S. Regs., Part II and the Staff Manual respectively. Title pages will be prepared in manuscript.

Place	Date	Hour	Summary of Events and Information	Remarks and references to Appendices
BETHUNE	Oct 1st		Quiet day.	N/A
	2nd		Enemy H.T.M.s near the DUMP active against our trenches, they stopped however on a few rounds being fired by D/5.	¥d
NOYELLES	3rd		5th Bde. HQ. moved to NOYELLES CHATEAU to take over the Command of Left Group from 335 Bde R.F.A. Left Group temporarily under Command of Lt. Col. A.T. Butler Cmg RHA at HQ 8th D.A.	¥d
PHILOSOPHE	4.		Orders received for 5th Bde R.H.A. mkt 1st Battery R.F.A. attached to take over the relieve of the HULLUCH sector from the 161st Bde. "D" "L" and 1st moved into position night 4/5th. D/5 did not move but took over the howitzers in the Chalk Pit (H5 central) handing over one of their howrs in its place.	¥d
"	5.		Batteries registered their new zone covering the 23rd Inf. Bde. Gas attack was carried out in HULLUCH sector also in 14 Bde and QUARRIES sectors batteries fired in accordance with scheme	¥d
"	6.		at 2.7 am. Carried out a raid with artillery support but failed to penetrate German lines, losing many killed and wounded. Remainder of the day quiet.	¥d
"	7th		Quiet day. a good deal of movement seen behind the enemy line.	¥d
"	8th		Quiet day. Major C.B. Rich R.F.A. took over Command of HULLUCH Group in the absence of Lt. Col. A.T. Butler Cmg RHA on leave.	¥d
"	9th		Quiet day.	¥d
"	10th		2 sections of "Z" Battery moved back to ANNEQUIN position.	¥d
"	11th		Remaining section of "Z" Battery moved to enfilade position at CUINCHY relieved by sect. 40th Dn. D/5 moved back to its old position in Right Group (QUARRIES sector). 5th Bde HQ to over the Command of the Left Group (HOHENZOLLERN) under Major Paul composition @ X 35d 36d and 55th (How.) Batteries.	¥d
NOYELLES	12th		"D" Battery rejoined Left Group moving from CORONS de RUTOIRE to old position in ANNEQUIN.	¥d
	13th		"O" Battery's new OP. The Rizted shelled otherwise quiet.	¥d

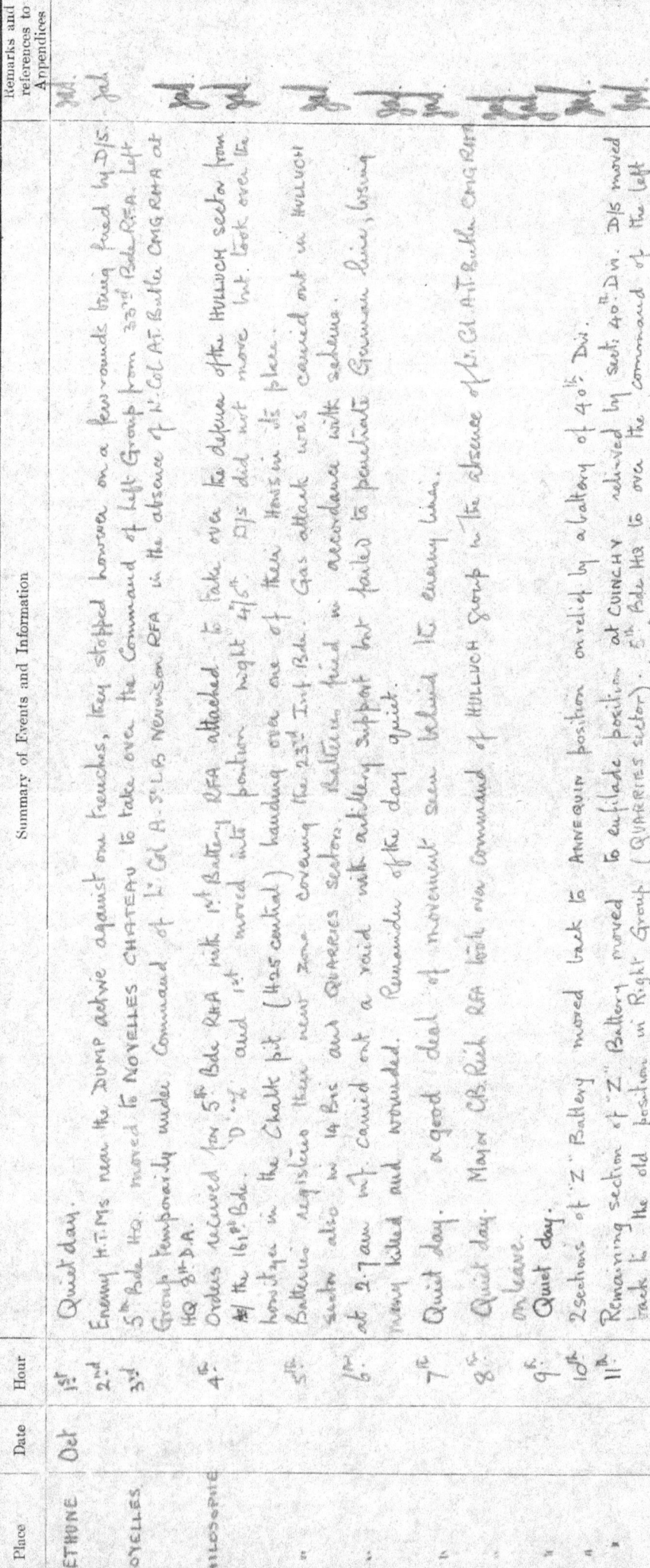

Army Form C. 2118.

WAR DIARY
or
INTELLIGENCE SUMMARY.
(Erase heading not required.)

5th Bde RHA   October 1916.

Place	Date	Hour	Summary of Events and Information	Remarks and references to Appendices
NOVELLES	Oct	14	Some trench mortar activity.	yd
"		15	Batterys registered their zone of CAMBRIN sector. A 6.0pm Batteries took over their new zone. D/5 passed from Right to Left Group to cover Quarries front.	yd
CAMBRIN		16	5th Bde HQ under Major Sir T.P. Larcom Bt RHA took over CAMBRIN sector from Left group 2nd Divn. Composition "O"-12. 36th (How) and 532nd (How) Batteries.	yd
"		17	Quiet day. Trench mortars fired against our front and support lines. We fired group salvoes on FRANK's and RYAN's traps.	yd
"		18	Advanced parties of 21st Divl Arty arrived.	yd
"		19	Quiet day.	yd
"		20	Battery Commanders of 21st Divl Arty visited positions.	yd
"		21	Lt. Col A.T. Butler returned from leave and took over CAMBRIN group. 1 sec. of each Battery moved to LAPUGNOY.	yd
~~LILLERS~~ LAPUGNOY		22	CAMBRIN group passed to 21st Divl Arty. 5th Bde marched to LAPUGNOY to billets.	yd
BERGUENEUSE	"	23	5th Bde continued its march to BERGUENEUSE billeting there.	yd
WAMIN AMPLIER	"	24	Bde continued its march to WAMIN and OPPY billeting there.	yd
~~Beauvais~~		25	Bde continued march to ~~Beauvais~~ AMPLIER billeting there.	yd
MIRVAUX		26	Bde continued march to MIRVAUX billeting there.	yd
DAOURS		27th	Bde continued march to DAOURS billeting there.	yd
CITADEL Camp		28th	Bde continued march to CITADEL Camp near FRICOURT, one officer pr battery left to be attached to the Bdes of 51st DA unit to be relieved by 5th Bde.	yd

Army Form C. 2118.

WAR DIARY
or
INTELLIGENCE SUMMARY.

5th Bde R.H.A.   Oct. 1916.

Place	Date	Hour	Summary of Events and Information	Remarks and references to Appendices
CITADEL	Oct	29th	Bde and Battery Commanders went up to look at their portion of the line.	
"	"	30	1 sect. per battery relieves 1 sect. per battery 56th D.A.	
"	"	31	Remaining sections of batteries moved into position on relief of 56th D.A. Covering the 33rd Div. immediately on the left of the French. Bde HQ established near GINCHY.	

3rd Nov.

A.T. Butler
Lieut. Col. R.H.A.
Comdg. 5th Bde R.H.A.

8th, Division.

5th, Bde. R. H. A.
December, 1916.

CONFIDENTIAL.

6th. DIVISIONAL ARTILLERY

WAR DIARY

OF

5. Brigade B.T.A.

From 1-11-16   To. 30-11-16

(VOLUME XXV)

With Appendices Nos.

Army Form C. 2118.

WAR DIARY or INTELLIGENCE SUMMARY.

5th Bde. R.H.A.   November 1916.

Place	Date	Hour	Summary of Events and Information	Remarks and references to Appendices
GINCHY	Nov. 1st		Batteries ordered to support attack made by 100th Infy. Bde. against the Western portion of HAZY and BORITSKA trenches in conjunction with French attack on BORITSKA and MIRAGE trenches. Zero hour 3.30 pm. "Z" Bty to find a Liason officer with Right (attacking) Batt. Lt. J.W. Pearse detailed. GLASGOW HIGHLANDERS attacking Batt. failed to reach their objective. French captured BORITSKA and MIRAGE Trenches to the South of the International Boundary pushing their left up to N3bc.6.0. 2 Casualties reported. 1,540 18 pr. DAS, 1 DAS, E. Nose barrage to cover French left. Carried out all right. Ammunition Expended 492 Shrap. 298 HE 18 pr. 4.5" HE. Robot received static French front captured to CONTE Trench. Parties of prisoners taken by E. French passed through. Ordinary day firing Enfilade Barrage to support French left put on all night. NO Casualties. Amm. Expended 1176 Shrap. 952 HE. 590 4.5" HE	Jul.
	2nd			Jul.
	3rd		Orders received for the Batteries to fire in support of attack by 175th Infy. Bde. against Blue Line from junction of HAZY and BORITSKA trenches to about T5 b.9.4. to form the French left. Zero hour 4.0 pm. Barrages commenced at 3.5 pm. Enemy barrage got heavier during the afternoon. 4.9 pm the infantry were reported to have gone over. Situation uncertain. Our barrage ceased at 6.45pm. Warning order received for NW cutting preparations for attack on LE TRANSLOY. Night firing as usual. Barrage to cover French left. Z Bty 3 Casualties 1 killed. Right firing as usual. Barrage. 413 ME 40 4.5" HE	Jul.
	4th		Order received 990 Shrap. Cutting for TRANSLOY attack. "O" Bty with 2 offrs. Batteries ordered to cut wire in front of TRANSLOY as a Bluff to mislead enemy in direction of French proposed attack on 5th. Lt. FLETCHER M.D/5 wounded Night firing as usual. D/C. 1 man wounded Amm. Expended Shrap. 1654 HE 444 4.5" HE 263.	Jul.
	5th		Orders received for a General attack by 4th and 5th British armies and 6th French Army. Bde Corard 100th Infantry Bde. Attacked commenced at 11.0 am. 100th Bde were reported in BORITSKA early in the afternoon and afterwards gained their final objective MIRAGE Trench. French attack succeeded in BUKOVINA gaining only portions of the South. Enemy aero plane shooting is reported in the 4.5 HE was very excellent. O. and Z1 wounded	Jul.

*353 Wt. W2544/1454 200,000 5/15 D.D.&L. A.D.S.S./Forms/C. 2118.

WAR DIARY
or
INTELLIGENCE SUMMARY

Army Form C. 2118.

5. Bde R.F.A. Nov. 1916.

Place	Date	Hour	Summary of Events and Information	Remarks and references to Appendices
GINCHY	6th		No organized bombardment. 100th Bde and 19th Bde now held from 300 yards NE of MIRAGE in a N.W. direction to top yards NE of SUMMER Trench. Night firing roads and approaches to LE TRANSLOY. Ammunition Expended 1288 Shrap 458 HE 335 SLEET Trench during the day. O Bty fired from 9 am Orders received to fire occasional bursts into SLEET trench. Amm. Expd. 57 HE 202 4.5" HE	Jul
	7th	6.10 pm	Z Bty from item till dusk. Night firing target SLEET trench.	Jul
	8th		Practically no day firing. 2/Lt THOMAS joined the Bde. Night firing occasional rounds on SLEET Trench. Z Bty 1 Killed and 5 wounded. Amm. Exp. 731 Shrapnel 384 HE 20 4.5" HE	Jul
	9th		Batteries fired in conjunction with Siege Artillery in morning, and took part in an organised bombardment of LE TRANSLOY at 7.30 pm the howitzers firing gas shell. Night firing as usual. Ammunition expended 335 Shrapnel 156 HE 32 4.5" HE.	Jul
	10th		Bright day large numbers of Enemy balloons and aeroplanes up. Batteries fired several salvoes at various times on selected points. 8" fired heavily to the left of D/5 doing a great deal of damage to batteries of the 4.5". Bde. R.F.A. Night firing as usual no fire to 5.15 am on stunt of Right Art Bde. Amm. Exp. 525 Shrapnel 287 HE 232 4.5" HE Capt Lindsay Z' Bty wounded. Capt Lindsay Z' Bty relieved by Lieut offr with Right Art. Bde. Fired 200 rounds on Special Tasks. Moon Trench also 4.5" Hows. At about Misty day batteries	Jul
	11th	9.10 pm	The enemy commenced a heavy bombardment of the valley in the with gas shells firing at rate of 4 rds a min. This caused little damage. The opened again later firing at greater rate. Casualties nil. Amm Exp. 608 Shrapnel 177 HE 160 Bty 4.5" HE	Jul
	12th		Bombardment by enemy with gas shells still continued a large number falling around X Bty's position and a few round 'O'. X Bty lost 2 OR killed and B wounded and 'O' 1 OR Killed. Batteries fired 200 rounds at Special Tasks. Ammunition expended 628 Shrap. 245 HE 4.5" HE 126. 2/Lt I.W. Pearse evacuated as the result of slight gas poisoning.	Jul
	13th		Batteries fired during the day a specially allotted tasks and the ordinary night firing. 2/Lt M.G. Taylor evacuates suffering from gas Poison. Lieut W.H. Don posted to D/5 from D.A.C. Ammunition expended 1134 Shrapnel 493 HE Amm 393 4.5" HE.	Jul

Army Form C. 2118.

WAR DIARY or INTELLIGENCE SUMMARY

5th Bde. R.H.A.   November 1916.

Place	Date	Hour	Summary of Events and Information	Remarks and references to Appendices
GINCHY	14th		Batteries fired on Special Tasks, in the evening fire was concentrated on Moon trench by order of 8th D.A. Night firing as usual. Ammunition expended Shrapnel 546 HE 191 4.5" HE 80	JM
	15th		During the morning enemy artillery very active indeed all battery positions being heavily shelled especially D/s who suffered casualties 4 killed and 1 wounded, shelling continued during the afternoon. O Bty having a gun put out of action. Batteries fired on Special Tasks. At 3.30pm it was reported that our trenches were being heavily shelled and Batteries were ordered to open fire on Moon trench firing intense for 5 mins then dropping to slow for ten mins. At 4.0pm batteries were ordered to fire at slow rate on S.O.S lines. At 5.15pm this was stopped and night firing began. Ammunition expended 677 Shrapnel 218 HE 4.5" HE 74.	JM
	16th		Batteries fired on Special Tasks. Moon Trench being engaged by the Howitzers and one 18pdr Battery. Night firing as usual. Ammunition expended Shrapnel 744 HE 270 4.5" HE 75	JM
	17th		Batteries fired Special Tasks. Night firing as usual. Ammunition expended 508 Shrapnel 192 HE 4.5" HE 80.	JM
	18th		Batteries fired Special Tasks as for 17th. In addition all batteries fired in support of the attack on gun pits at N36c6.8 which was launched at 4.0pm. At 8.30pm a special bombardment of the exits from TRANSLOY took place in which all batteries took part the howitzers firing gas shell. Lieut E.A.W Rogers O Bty was slightly wounded but remained at duty. 2 O.R of 'O' Bty were wounded. Ammunition expended Shrapnel 1041 HE 332 4.5" HE 105 Gas shell 149.	JM
	19th		Batteries fired Special Tasks on SUNK Rod and MOON Trench. Hostile artillery quiet low usual. Night firing as usual. Ammunition expended 510 Shrapnel 184 HE 4.5" HE 75.	JM

Army Form C. 2118.

WAR DIARY
or
INTELLIGENCE SUMMARY.

(Erase heading not required.)

5th Bde. R.H.A.   November 1916.

Place	Date	Hour	Summary of Events and Information	Remarks and references to Appendices
GINCHY	20th		Battery fired Special tasks. 18pdr SLEET Fund and vicinity 4.5" Hows SUNK Road. Night firing as usual. Ammunition expended Shrapnel 686. HE 213. 4.5" HE 76.	J.L.
	21st		Special day tasks for 18pdrs. as for 20th. Hows. Gun Pits. Night firing as usual. Ammunition expended 532 Shrapnel 175 HE 4.5" HE 36.	J.L.
	22nd		Special task as for 21st. in addition 18pdrs registered a zone in French area for Support barrage. Night firing as usual. Ammunition expended 532 Shrapnel 196 HE 4.5" HE 49.	J.L.
	23rd		Special Tasks 18pdrs as for 20th. Hows SUNK Road. Night firing as usual. At 11.0 pm the enemy commenced an intense bombardment of trench front line with gas shell, lasting till 3.30 am 24th. Carnelhoe 20R Suffering from gas poisoning. Ammunition expended 354 Shrap. 196 HE 4.5" HE 90.	J.L.
	24th		Special tasks 18 pdrs fired on S.O.S. barrage line. tours on tracks. Night firing as usual. Ammunition expended. 80 Shrap. 126 HE 4.5" HE 110.	J.L.
	25th		Special tasks as for 24th. Night firing as usual. Ammunition expended 120 Shrap. 200 HE 4.5" HE 60.	J.L.
	26th		Special tasks as for 25th. 1 section of batteries relieved by sections of 81st Bde. RFA. Night Firing as usual. Ammunition expended 80 Shrap 240 HE. 4.5" HE 60.	J.L.
	27th		Remaining Sections relieved and marched to wagon lines. Amm. fired during month 7594 Shrap 3225 HE 4.5" HE 1514.	J.L.
	28th		Brigade remained at wagon lines, billeting party sent to rest area	J.L.
	29th		Brigade marched to DAOURS from wagon lines.	J.L.
	30th		Brigade continued the march to ARGOEUVRES billeting there.	J.L.

A. T. Pawle
Lieut Col Bde
Cmmg. 5th Bde RHA

8th, Division.

5th, Bde. R. H. A.

December, 1916.

CONFIDENTIAL.

6th. DIVISIONAL ARTILLERY

WAR DIARY

OF

5. Brigade RFA

From 1.12.16 To 31.12.16

(VOLUME XXVI)

With Appendices Nos.

5 Bde RFA Vol 25

Army Form C. 2118.

WAR DIARY
or
INTELLIGENCE SUMMARY.

(Erase heading not required.)

5. Bde R.H.A.   December 1916.

Instructions regarding War Diaries and Intelligence Summaries are contained in F.S. Regs., Part II. and the Staff Manual respectively. Title pages will be prepared in manuscript.

Place	Date	Hour	Summary of Events and Information	Remarks and references to Appendices
BOISRAULT	1st		Brigade continued the march from ARGOEUVRES to the rest area. HQ was billeted in BOISRAULT. "D" and "E" Batteries in BEZENCOURT. D/5 Bty in GUIBERMESNIL. Arrived in billets 4.0 p.m.	Nil.
	2nd		Quiet day.	Nil.
	3rd		Rest and harness cleaning and general clean up	Nil.
	4th		Brigade was inspected dismounted by Major Gen. Hudson Cmdg 8th Div.	Nil.
	5th		Batteries sent horses and small stores to 39th and 45th Bdes to complete them before the	Nil.
			moved into the line. Major Bir T.P. Lincorn to 8th Div Arty as a Brigade Major.	
	6th		Training began. Laying. Marching drill, rifle drill etc.	Nil.
	7th		Lt Col A.T. Butler CMG left on short leave to England.	Nil.
	8th		Training continued.	Nil.
	9th		Usual parade.	Nil.
	10th		Training	Nil.
	11th		Presentation of Military Medals to N.C.O's and men * and to Gnr de Guerre to Bdr R.H. O'Bry by	Nil.
			Brig. Gen G.H.W. Nicholson CMG. Div. Arty moved to HAILLENCOURT	
	12th		5th Bde HQ moved from BOISRAULT to BEZENCOURT	Nil.
	13th		Section gun-drill riding drill etc.	Nil.
	14th		Training	Nil.
	15th		Training	Nil.
	16th		Training half-day.	Nil.
	17th		Church parade. N.Cd. AT Butler CMG. returned from leave.	Nil.
	18th		Training	Nil.
	19th		Training	Nil.
	20th		N. Col Butler to 8. Div Arty. Acting CRA.	Nil.

* Sergt. Routledge · D Bty.
  Cpl Haynes · 5 Bde HQ
  a/Bdr Creasor · O Bty.
  Sergt Smith · O Bty.

Army Form C. 2118.

WAR DIARY
or
INTELLIGENCE SUMMARY.

5th Bde. R.H.A.

(Erase heading not required.)

December 1916.

Instructions regarding War Diaries and Intelligence Summaries are contained in F.S. Regs., Part II. and the Staff Manual respectively. Title pages will be prepared in manuscript.

Place	Date	Hour	Summary of Events and Information	Remarks and references to Appendices
BEZENCOURT	21st		Training.	
	22nd		Training.	
	23rd		Training. Batteries made up to strength in horses.	
	24th		Training and training remounts.	
	25th		Church Parades.	
	26th		Training Remounts.	
	27th		Getting ready for march into action.	
	28th		1st Group of half batteries of 4th, 8th, 33rd and 40th Divisions marched from training area to Saint Sauveur (billeting there).	
	29th		1st Group resumed the march to VAUX-SUR-SOMME. 2nd Group marched from training area to Saint Sauveur.	
	30th		1st Group resumed march to Camp 14. 2nd Group marching to VAUX-SUR-SOMME.	
	31st		2nd Group marched to Camp 14. Gun detachments of the 1st Group of half batteries relieved half batteries of 33rd Bde RFA "O" relieving 32nd Bty "Y" 33rd and B/c 55th.	

B. Monstown
for Lieut. Col. R.H.A.
Cmdg. 5th Bde. R.H.A.